DESIGN A
BETTER BUSINESS

DESIGN A BETTER BUSINESS

NEW TOOLS, SKILLS, AND MINDSET FOR STRATEGY AND INNOVATION

Written by Patrick van der Pijl, Justin Lokitz, and Lisa Kay Solomon

Designed by Maarten van Lieshout and Erik van der Pluijm

Cover and interior design by Erik van der Pluijm & Maarten van Lieshout

This book is printed on acid-free paper. ∞

Copyright © 2016 by John Wiley & Sons, Inc. All rights reserved.

Published by John Wiley & Sons, Inc., Hoboken, New Jersey.
Published simultaneously in Canada.

For general information about our other products and services, please contact our Customer Care Department within the United States at (800) 762-2974, outside the United States at (317) 572-3993, or fax (317) 572-4002.

Wiley publishes in a variety of print and electronic formats and by print-on-demand. Some material included with standard print versions of this book may not be included in e-books or in print-on-demand. If this book refers to media such as a CD or DVD that is not included in the version you purchased, you may download this material at http://booksupport.wiley.com. For more information about Wiley products, visit www.wiley.com.

ISBN 9781119272113 (pbk); ISBN 9781119272120 (ebk); ISBN 9781119272137 (ebk)

Printed in the United States of America

10 9 8 7 6 5 4

Does this page make you feel uncertain or freak you out? ☐ YES ☐ NO

HOW TO

CONTENTS

8 | CHAPTERS

48 | CASE STUDIES

20 | TOOLS

7 | CORE SKILLS

29 | DESIGNERS

36 | HACKS

>**150** | VISUALS

USE THIS BOOK

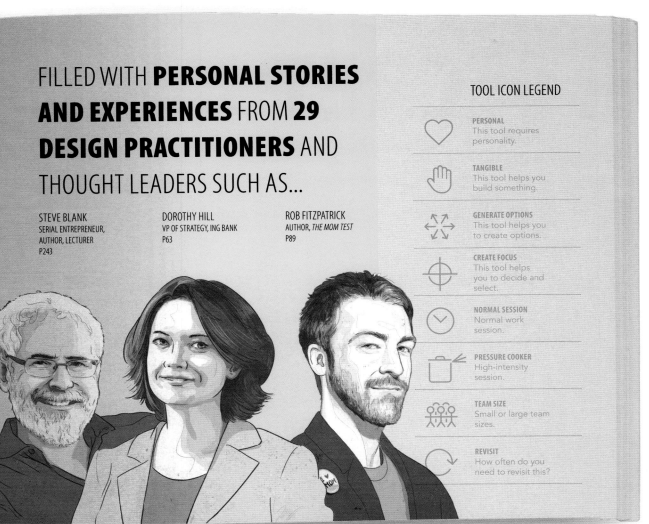

FILLED WITH **PERSONAL STORIES AND EXPERIENCES** FROM **29 DESIGN PRACTITIONERS** AND THOUGHT LEADERS SUCH AS...

STEVE BLANK
SERIAL ENTREPRENEUR,
AUTHOR, LECTURER
P243

DOROTHY HILL
VP OF STRATEGY, ING BANK
P63

ROB FITZPATRICK
AUTHOR, *THE MOM TEST*
P89

TOOL ICON LEGEND

PERSONAL
This tool requires personality.

TANGIBLE
This tool helps you build something.

GENERATE OPTIONS
This tool helps you to create options.

CREATE FOCUS
This tool helps you to decide and select.

NORMAL SESSION
Normal work session.

PRESSURE COOKER
High-intensity session.

TEAM SIZE
Small or large team sizes.

REVISIT
How often do you need to revisit this?

We've designed this book with you in mind! Unlike most books, this one can be read in several ways.

For one, you can read this cover to cover. The chapters build on each other. You can also scan for things that interest you, like new tools and skills. Additionally, we've included fast passes in this chapter (page 22) in case there is something specific you want to learn about right now.

START READING!

UNCERTAINTY: YOUR SECRET WEAPON

The world around you – and your business – is filled with uncertainty. But within that uncertainty exist innumerable opportunities to design (or redesign) game-changing businesses. These opportunities are there for the taking, if you know how to look for them.

The world has changed. Not only are consumer habits, technologies, and other trends uprooting once-thriving businesses, entire markets are shifting and emerging out of the uncertainty and unpredictable nature of today's network economy. Interestingly (and infuriatingly to some), many of the companies leading the charge – and the change – did not exist two decades ago. It's not that these new players are just lucky or employ smarter, more capable people. So, how is it that they've found gold in some of the most unlikely places? In a word: design.

Design is fundamentally about enhancing the way you look at the world. It's a learnable, repeatable, disciplined process that anyone can use to create unique and qualified value. Design is not about throwing away the processes and tools you have. In fact, quite the opposite is true. Just as design has enabled countless upstarts to create new business models and markets, design will also help you decide when to use what tools in order to learn something new, persuade others to take a different course, and at the end of the day, make better (business) decisions.

Most of all, design is about creating the conditions by which businesses thrive, grow, and evolve in the face of uncertainty and change. As such, better businesses are ones that approach problems in a new, systematic way, focusing more on doing rather than on planning and prediction. Better businesses marry design and strategy to harness opportunity in order to drive growth and change in a world that is uncertain and unpredictable.

This book will provide you with new tools, skills, and a mindset to harness opportunities born of uncertainty in order to design a better business. We've included tons of real-world examples of people who have mastered the fundamentals of design, as well as case studies of companies that have created change using design as the underlying foundation for decision making. And, just as design is a repeatable process, this book is meant not only to guide you on your design journey, but also to provide an ongoing reference to help you scale the design beyond one project or product to an entire company. ∎

YOU'VE GOT EVERYTHING TO GAIN

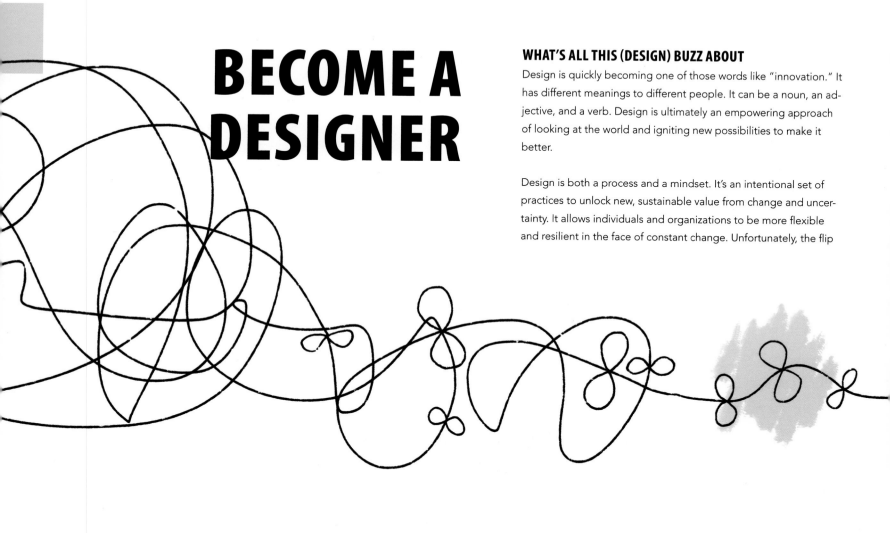

BECOME A DESIGNER

WHAT'S ALL THIS (DESIGN) BUZZ ABOUT

Design is quickly becoming one of those words like "innovation." It has different meanings to different people. It can be a noun, an adjective, and a verb. Design is ultimately an empowering approach of looking at the world and igniting new possibilities to make it better.

Design is both a process and a mindset. It's an intentional set of practices to unlock new, sustainable value from change and uncertainty. It allows individuals and organizations to be more flexible and resilient in the face of constant change. Unfortunately, the flip side of design is where we often find ourselves: scrambling when unforeseen change happens to us.

WITH GREAT POWER . . .

The good news is that you are already a designer, at least some of the time. Every time you intentionally develop strategy or make a decision based on insight, you are acting as a designer. The not-so-good news is that many of the tools that you have probably been using to help make those decisions are likely not as useful as they once were, at least not on their own. So, what do designers do and what tools do they use that help them make better decisions?

ITERATION

The key to design – and design tools – is that it is an iterative process by which designers, like you, start with a point of view, go out and observe the world to inform that point of view, create options that may address the opportunities you see, validate those options, and execute the ones that best address the opportunities. Most important, designers never focus on simply scaling the execution of the chosen option. Design is continuous and iterative; it's built to deal with ambiguity and change in a long-term way. ■

DESIGN IS A DISCIPLINED APPROACH TO SEARCHING, IDENTIFYING, AND CAPTURING VALUE.

DESIGNER: A REBEL WITH A CAUSE

THE 7 ESSENTIAL SKILLS

IT ALL STARTS WITH
THE CUSTOMER.

THINK AND WORK
VISUALLY!

DON'T FLY SOLO.
YOU ARE NOT
SMARTER THAN
EVERYONE ELSE.

TELL STORIES
AND SHARE THE
EXPERIENCE.

Observing customers to understand them will give you fresh insights into their needs. You must ask the right questions to get the answers you seek.

Working visually helps you to see the bigger picture, gain clarity on complex topics, create a visual anchor for your strategic conversations, and engage with your audience.

Gather different insights by working together. Connecting the brains in the room and in your market will enable you to uncover hidden opportunities.

Stories have a clear beginning and end, and most likely they have heroes your audience can connect with. Cool stories stick. Cool stories will be told by others. Cool stories spread.

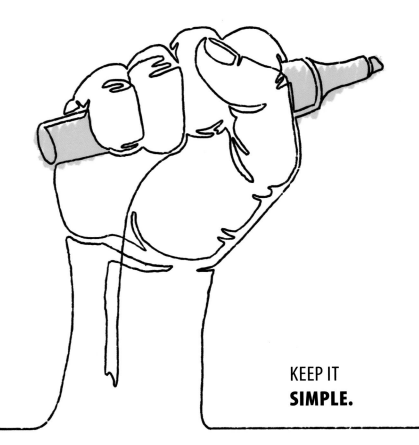

KEEP IT **SIMPLE.**

Just start. Don't try to build the final product. Don't add features that don't solve real problems.

SET UP SMALL EXPERIMENTS AND LEARN SHIT.

Every little iteration and trial will net tons of useful new insights – things you wouldn't have learned if you just started building. Reality is different than what you assume.

EMBRACE UNCERTAINTY. **IT'S CANDY FOR THE BRAIN.**

Except for change, there is no such thing as certainty in business. Accept this and harness opportunities from uncertainty.

DESIGN A BETTER

CONNECTING INNOVATION, BUSINESS, AND STRATEGY

So, now you're a designer who's been imbued with the goal of designing a better business. What does a better business look like? And, how would one go about designing a better business?

Many existing, established businesses, especially non-startup businesses, focus solely on getting products to market while reducing costs and increasing margins. In these businesses, strategy is executed in a linear way: prepare; execute. What's often missing in this story is the customer on the other side of the transaction, as well as the person designing and developing products and services to satisfy some need for the customer.

 POINT OF VIEW P46

Designers, on the other hand, are always thinking about the customer. They approach people and problems from a particular perspective, one informed by design-specific tools like ideation, prototyping, and validation. They use human-centered tools, skills, and a mindset to search for, design, and execute new value propositions and business models based on what they've learned. Designers do this continually, iterating constantly to uncover opportunities within the fog of uncertainty.

BUSINESS

In this book, you'll find the designer's journey represented in a new way. Your point of view is at the center of the design process, which is always influenced and informed through understanding, ideation, prototyping, and validation. This process is iterative and cyclical.

So, what's a better business? A better business is one that puts the person at the center and connects design tools, practices, and processes.

To do this you must employ a design rigor – using your new tools, skills, and mindset – to guide business decisions and outcomes rather than solely driving day-to-day (business as usual) execution.

In doing so, your options for the future will become much clearer; as a designer, you will unequivocally begin to see opportunities within the fog of uncertainty. >>

 **UNDERSTAND** P82 —  **IDEATE** P124 — **PROTOTYPE** P152 — **VALIDATE** P180 —

There's a continuous search for new customers, value propositions, and business models – with business execution and scale. As a designer, it's your job to make this connection. It's your job to consider and test new options for business sustainability and growth (by design). It's your job to consider the person you're designing for, which will inform your own unique point of view.

THE DOUBLE LOOP

A DESIGN JOURNEY

The double loop is founded on a simple observation: every project, product, company, change, or idea starts with a point of view. It might be based on fact. It might be based on assumptions. Whatever your point of view, using it to create lasting change requires work and a movement toward the goal line.

The double loop takes your point of view into account, while adding rigor and continuity to the design process. This means that your point of view is always informed by understanding and that that understanding will spark new ideas, further enhancing your point of view. These ideas are prototyped and validated to test and measure their effectiveness. This, in turn, further informs your point of view and enables you to execute your ideas successfully.

Every design journey also has a beginning and . . . a goal. In the case of this design journey, the beginning starts with preparation, at the left of the design loop. Preparing yourself, your team, your environment, and the tools you'll use is essential for your successful journey. At the right of the design loop is the goal: scale. In this book, scale refers to two things. First, we talk about scaling the execution of your idea or change; this begins with your point of view. Second, we talk about scaling the design process. This is, after all, a book about designing better businesses. Design is at the core. And it is design that is meant to scale. ■

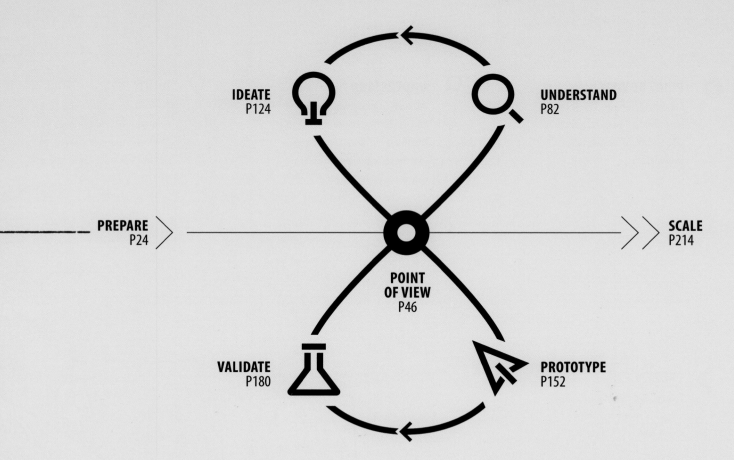

IDEATE
P124

UNDERSTAND
P82

PREPARE
P24

SCALE
P214

POINT
OF VIEW
P46

VALIDATE
P180

PROTOTYPE
P152

THE DOUBLE LOOP LANDSCAPE

POINT OF VIEW P46

Design is human. The journey you take will help to inform your point of view going forward.

UNDERSTAND P82

All design journeys start with the customer, context, and your business in mind. Understanding these is the key to designing something better.

IDEATE P124

There is no single right solution. Ideation will enable you and your team to unlock and build upon each other's ideas.

PREPARE P24

Design is a team sport that requires preparation to be done well.

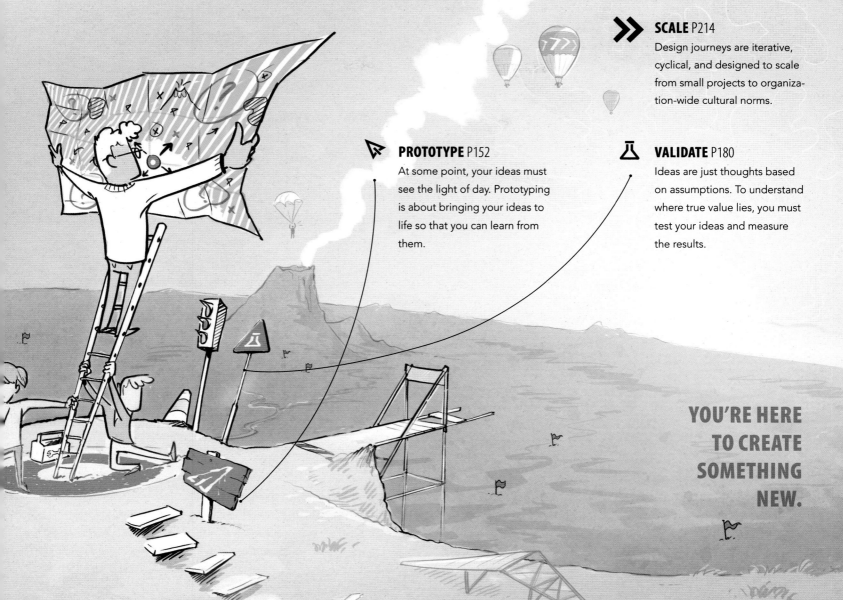

SCALE P214

Design journeys are iterative, cyclical, and designed to scale from small projects to organization-wide cultural norms.

PROTOTYPE P152

At some point, your ideas must see the light of day. Prototyping is about bringing your ideas to life so that you can learn from them.

VALIDATE P180

Ideas are just thoughts based on assumptions. To understand where true value lies, you must test your ideas and measure the results.

YOU'RE HERE TO CREATE SOMETHING NEW.

YOUR TOOLS

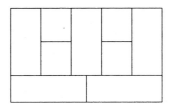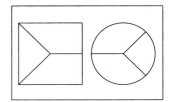

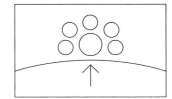

As a designer, your first mission is simply to step out of the box you're in and observe the world and your customers in their natural states. Don't come at this with preconceived notions about what your customers are trying to achieve or how the world is ordered. Just watch and listen.

The first tool comes from skills we already possess – observation. When was the last time you stepped back and just watched and listened to your customers? Try it. We're sure you'll learn something new.

CREATING IMPACT

As you're watching and listening, start to look for patterns as well as interesting, unexpected actions, events, or occurrences. These create fodder for anecdotes that you can use to draw your manager or other team members into the human stories behind your products. If you've never used actual customer anecdotes and stories in a presentation, we can tell you that you're in for a great surprise.

All people like stories and will be more interested and invested than they would if they were presented with only data. In fact, in the next chapter you'll find a tool specifically meant to help you design stories to deliver the impact you're looking for.

NOT OBSOLETE

As you become comfortable simply watching and listening to your customers, it's time to start using some new tools – design tools. Rest assured, you do not have to stop, nor should you stop using the tools that you're comfortable with. In fact, just as you cannot hope to change your company overnight, it's very unlikely you'll get everyone to believe your current tools are obsolete; and they're probably not. Instead, just as you might employ a new set of tools to work on a project at home, start to add a few new design tools to your belt (you wouldn't use a screwdriver to measure a wall, would you?!).

USEFUL DESIGN TOOLS

First, employ observational tools. These include tools that help you capture people's wants, needs, pains, and ambitions. You might also add to your belt tools for questioning and problem framing. After all, you can't expect to learn everything about your customers by simply watching them. Beyond observational tools, other design

 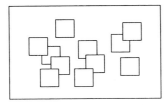

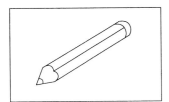 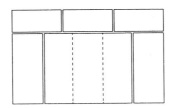

tools include ideation tools, prototyping, and validation tools, as well as decision-making tools. These concepts might be quite familiar to other people on your team who have been designing for a while. But, no matter. We've included a variety of incredibly useful tools in this book to help you take business design to the next level.

GROW COMFORTABLE

As you become more comfortable using some of these tools, you'll no doubt notice that your old tools are becoming auxiliary or backups. You might even couple your old tools with your new (designer) tools to complement each other. For instance, you can use market data to bolster the anecdotes you gather in the field. Imagine the possibilities! The key here is that you start small and slowly develop mastery of the new tools and practices that at first may feel uncomfortable to wield. Don't worry, after you've used your designer tools a few times, they will become easier and more comfortable to use. And, through your new design-colored glasses, we are confident that you will begin to see the world in a whole new light. ■

THERE IS NO **TOOL CULTURE** (YET)

Where accountants, doctors, and surgeons are trained to use tools, business people are well trained for operations. They think they can innovate, but they lack the right skills and tools to do so.

Whereas Apple and Amazon continuously reinvent their business models and are successful in doing so, other companies are helpless. Their traditional corporate structures conflict with design processes and innovation. It is in nobody's P&L so they just don't care. Sure, companies innovate their products. But they have a hard time going beyond product innovation and traditional R&D.

Nowadays an increasing number of business schools are teaching business model innovation as well as the tools for design and innovation. But we are still very much at the start.

I am excited to learn more about how others develop and use tools for design, innovation, and strategy as the new drivers of business.

Alexander Osterwalder
Co-founder Strategyzer, Lead Author of *Business Model Generation* and *Value Proposition Design*

FAST PASSES

WANT QUICK ANSWERS?

We have provided you with some fast tracks so you don't have to stand in line waiting for your future. These fast tracks will guide you to the relevant tools, skills, or case studies. Learn from the experience of others and apply it now.

I WANT TO DESIGN A STRATEGY

I need a plan of action to take my team to our desired future state.

STEPS: **PAGES:**

» Understand your current business model(s) and understand your customers by observing and asking questions — 86

» Develop a point of view by creating your 5 Bold Steps Vision® and transforming your vision into a story and seeing if it resonates — 58

» Ideate new business model options — 142

» Prototype new value propositions — 152

FLIGHT

DB BIZ8

TIME

05MAR

GATE

G13

SEAT

19B

I WANT TO DO BUSINESS PLANNING

I want to move beyond spreadsheets and explore business planning with my team.

STEPS: **PAGES:**

» Map the current context you operate in — 110

» Understand your current business model — 114

» Understand your (future) customers — 98

» Revisit your company's vision — 56

» Design future business model options — 142

» Propose ideas to prototype — 152

TIME **20:00** SCREEN **03** ROW **15** SEAT **21**

4.11

I WANT A STRONG & SHARABLE VISION

I want to develop a North Star with my team so we know where we are headed.

STEPS: **PAGES:**

>> Develop your point of view and make a
Cover Story vision® with your team   64
>> Validate your cover story in- and
outside your company   180

360 DEGREES 3D VISION
Cinematic View 3D VISION

TIME **20:00** SCREEN **03** ROW **15** SEAT **22**

4.1

I WANT TO CREATE A SWOT OF MY BUSINESS

What are the strengths, weaknesses, opportunities, and threats for my business?

STEPS: **PAGES:**

>> Understand the context of your business   110
>> Understand your business model(s)   86
>> Determine strengths and weaknesses   116

•UNIQUE OFFERING! -FAST PASS-•

I WANT TO INNOVATE /GROW MY BUSINESS

There are no shortcuts, but we do provide you with some fast tracks so you don't have to stand in line waiting for your future.

STEPS: **PAGES:**
>> Do the Double Loop   16

I WANT TO WORK AS A STARTUP

Here's how you can work lean and mean when you want to bring your idea to market. Learn from startups.

STEPS: **PAGES:**

>> Prepare your point of view   48
>> Understand: observe and ask
questions (!)
>> Ideate your business model options   86
>> Sketch a low- and high-fidelity prototype   142
                                               172
>> Validate, validate, validate   180
>> Tell stories during your journey   72

Class Economy
Ticket type Fast&Cheap
Price £9,90
Issue date 02AUG17

CHEAP AND FAST

GRAB **YOUR** PASS!

PLATINUM TRAVEL CARD
FAST PASS
8000 4563 98   3 476
8000
UNTIL 09/20
D B BUSINESS

USE A FAST PASS OR PREPARE FOR A FULL JOURNEY >>

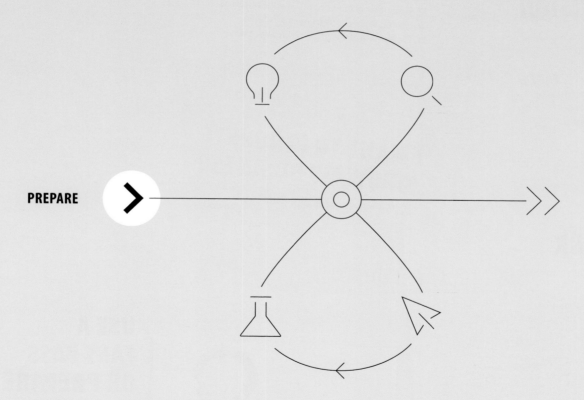

PREPARE

THE DESIGN JOURNEY **PREPARE**

PREPARE YOUR **TEAM**

PREPARE YOUR **ENVIRONMENT**

PREPARE **HOW YOU WORK**

EVERY JOURNEY STARTS WITH **PREPARATION**

Whether you're about to go on a journey of exploration to understand your customer or design new business models for your future, preparation is key. You wouldn't go into battle without preparing first. Likewise, you'll need to prepare before launching a design (or redesign) initiative.

DESIGN IS ABOUT PREPARATION

The design process requires preparation in order for it to run well. You must prepare to observe and understand your customers, business, and context. You must prepare to ideate, prototype, and validate. What this boils down to is that to set yourself and your team up for success, you must prepare your team for the journey ahead, prepare your environment for the work that will ensue, and prepare your tools so that you'll get the best results from everyone.

SET YOURSELF UP FOR SUCCESS

The design process may be different from many of the other processes you're used to. For one, it is not really linear; it's cyclical and iterative. It's about embracing uncertainty. Not everything can be planned or controlled. It is also a full-contact team sport. Teams that take the time to prepare often enjoy much better results and outcomes. Design also requires physical space to work in. And not just people hunched over computers. The people designing the better business will need space to ideate, prototype,

and validate. It also requires that you employ new tools, which also necessitate preparation in order to achieve the best results. Last but not least, design requires that you get used to a new way of working and a new project structure. It's not about planning. It's about maximizing the chance of a positive outcome and empowering others to make real change. There are things you can control and things you can't. Set yourself and your team up for success by controlling what you can; don't leave things up to chance.

PREPARE YOUR TEAM

Babe Ruth, the famous American baseball player, once said, "The way a team plays as a whole determines its success. You may have the greatest bunch of individual stars in the world, but if they don't play together, the club won't be worth a dime." The same can be said about designing great businesses: the best businesses are the products of great teams.

That said, not just any team will do. A team that will generate the most useful ideas from its key findings, and that will most

TIP! Not just any team will do. The people on your design team must want to be there. Otherwise, they'll push for business as usual.

thoroughly prototype and validate those ideas, is made up of a diverse group of unusual suspects (think the *A-Team*, not *Friends*). They will find diamonds in the rough where no one else has. They will challenge each other. And, by virtue of their diversity, they will bring with them a network of other people and resources that will come in handy when it's time to get down and dirty.

SEARCH FOR THE REBEL

When it comes to big hairy questions or initiatives, most of us are unwilling to take a leap and try something new to achieve the outcome we dream of. In order to do this, we need a rebel. A rebel is someone who is willing to stand up and announce that the time has come to take a new approach to solving a problem or answering a question. This person has the ability to carve out time and broker for resources for the design journey. The rebel is the one who will persist and ensure that you're able to try something new before going back to the old way of doing things.

PREPARE YOUR ENVIRONMENT, YOUR SPACE

By now you're aware that design is not linear. It is an iterative process in which you will constantly need to refer to artifacts that have been developed along the way. Carting these around the office and sticking them on different walls every other day not only is it a pain in the neck, but it also reduces the time you have to actually design. This reduces overall productivity. Having a "war room" where the team can get together and see progress will boost productivity and efficiency tremendously.

PREPARE HOW YOU WORK (TOGETHER)

Tools like the screenplay – introduced later in this chapter – will help you design your meetings (or design sprints) to maximize your time together. Visual artifacts like the customer journey and Business Model Canvas will help your team hold more focused strategic conversations. Taking the time to think through how you'll use these tools will help you maximize their value. It's not hard work – but it's essential. **>>**

SO, WHERE SHOULD YOU START?

Think big, but be willing to start small! Most people approach big projects and new processes by seeking commitment from the board or an executive committee. This is fine and may work in some cases. Design doesn't require a certain outcome. Instead, it's about the journey, the findings you obtain along the way, and the options you generate and validate. With that in mind, here are some ways others have started their design journeys.

WITH THAT IN MIND, HERE ARE SOME WAYS OTHERS HAVE STARTED THEIR DESIGN JOURNEYS.

Of course, you could also start big and go straight to the board. If you decide to take that route, ask for a budget to train your team in design thinking for strategy and innovation. Whether or not there is an appetite for design in your organization, your colleagues will certainly develop skills and take journeys that deliver better business results, however small or incremental.

1 FIND YOUR SPARK

Change starts with a spark. Something in the world shifts, and someone reacts to that shift. Whether it's for yourself or your company, to start your design journey, you'll need a reason to take the journey in the first place.

2 FIND AMBASSADORS

Business as usual doesn't leave much room for design process if you don't have ambassadors on your side. Socialize your idea with a few potential ambassadors. If you get them on board, your journey will be a whole lot smoother.

3 RECRUIT THE RIGHT TEAM

Design is not a journey to be taken alone. Success in design comes when a team of people are in it together and are collectively compelled to see the process through. You'll need varying points of view, skills, and a good network to tap into. Build your team with this in mind and you can't go wrong.

4 RAISE ALL BOATS

Organize a targeted (not generic) training course or bring in a thought leader to help ignite interest in business model innovation or strategy design.

Courses and master classes are great ways to learn new ways of working while becoming familiar with a new set of tools, skills, and mindsets. Oftentimes you'll learn about other organizations that have employed design successfully. Use this insight to evaluate where and how you might further introduce design into your organization.

5 DESIGN WORKSHOP

Organize a design workshop focused on business model innovation or strategy to immerse yourself in the design process and determine where the goal is for you and your team to co-create a concrete deliverable. This could be the design of a vision, a business model, or a value proposition for a new concept.

6 FIND THE STRAGGLERS

Pick one of your existing products or services that's struggling to generate revenue (or profit). Run a workshop with a diverse team to generate new business model ideas.

7 GET OUT OF THE BUILDING

Get out of the building and talk to customers to understand what matters to them. What do they say? What do they think? Present your findings to others in your organization. ∎

FIND YOUR **AMBASSADORS**

Preparing for a small team is one thing. Preparing for a large company is quite another.

So how do you best prepare for an innovation journey as an established company? We asked organizations like 3M, Lufthansa, SAP, ING Bank, MasterCard, GE, Philips, and Toyota how they have been nurturing and supporting cultures of innovation and design thinking. They shared their findings during a summit in New York, February 2015.

Their biggest takeaway: in order to prepare for innovation and design thinking, it is an absolute must that companies identify champion users of design tools, such as the Business Model Canvas, the vision canvas, and other human-centered tools. The champions, or ambassadors, must be proficient in the "lean" approach to design and development and carry with them a designer's mindset at all times. No problem is too big or too small for these ambassadors.

When your goal is to scale design throughout your organization, it's essential to find and train more than one ambassador. In fact, you'll need to create an army of ambassadors who are familiar with and passionate about the new ways of working. They need to adopt and help spread design approaches to business by doing more than they talk. ∎

PREPARE YOUR **TEAM**

You won't win a soccer match with 11 strikers or a football match with only quarterbacks. The same holds for business. Whether you're trying to win in sports or in business, it's crucial to employ players with varying skills (and superpowers) – the team needs to be multidisciplinary.

Don't forget to have fun together! Hey! Who brought the drone to the party?!

Unusual suspects: that new graduate you just hired; a high-energy up-and-comer; or someone young, with interesting ideas, that you think of as an idealist.

Sales and marketing gurus who know the customer.

BUILD A MULTIDISCIPLINARY TEAM

The ideal team will be able to cover a wide range of tasks. Need someone to write a proposal? Add that person to the team. How about someone to design a pitch deck? And maybe we need a coder . . . You get the picture.

The more viewpoints the team brings to the table, the more options that team will be able to generate. There is no one single right solution in any design, business or otherwise.

FIND THE UNUSUAL SUSPECTS

If every team member has the same exact life experiences, skills, knowledge, and viewpoints, the range of options they will zero in on is incredibly narrow. To avoid that, intentionally design your team to include people from different departments – and with different skills levels, backgrounds, cultures, and mindsets.

ROLES: IT'S NOT ON YOUR BUSINESS CARD

When you look at a business card, what do you see under the name of the person? Likely a title, and that title is very likely not that person's role.

Roles describe the responsibilities that someone takes on, either formally or informally, as part of the team. They play a central part in getting things done. Roles, not titles, are critical to your success. It is important that each team member take ownership

A strategist or product manager who always has the North Star in mind.

Kickass visual facilitators to drive the project forward, harnessing all of the energy.

Lateral thinkers, mavericks and rebels, hackers, developers, and designers.

An executive sponsor takes responsibility when things get tough.

Ambassadors and fans to increase engagement.

of the design, both while working on the design and when it comes to pitching ideas to other stakeholders. Designing the right roles helps team members understand how and where they can best contribute to the end result. The roles people play on your design team will vary from ambassadors to sales, and from visual thinkers to engineers.

Just as you'll intentionally design who's on the team, you also need to design the roles people play on that team. When your team doesn't know the plays, you can't score a touchdown.

WHEN TO ASSEMBLE A TEAM

When considering your design team, it's essential that you assemble the right people, with the right attitudes, at the right time. You'll need this team for design workshops, brainstorming, and fieldwork: when you need to get out of the office to understand what your customers want, need, and do. You'll need to assemble a team to design and produce prototypes.

Unlike in most corporate settings, do not assemble a team for a project or to simply join meetings or discussions. Do not assemble a team to engage in planning if that same team is not going to engage in the design process. Do not assemble a team for project communication; that's what the facilitator is for. Your design team's goal is to do and make and learn and deliver results. ■

PREPARE YOUR **ENVIRONMENT**

Design is not business as usual. The spaces your team designs in must be able to handle a new way of working.

A SPACE FOR PEOPLE

If design is a contact sport, then the environments you play in must be able to handle the frequent interactions of the team. Design isn't about meeting, sitting, talking, and leaving the meeting to go back to email. It's about standing, interacting, writing on sticky notes, going outside, crunching numbers together, and assembling to update each other before doing it again.

The best design environments take into account how people interact – not just while they're seated, but also while they're standing, evaluating a canvas on the wall. These environments leave space for working together and presenting concepts. The best design environments are dedicated for a specific project, so that all of the design artifacts can be left as is, enabling the team to quickly track its progress.

HOME BASE

However you prepare for your environment, your goal is to create a home base where your team can be creative, soak in the information, and have meaningful discussions about it. When-

A PLACE TO HUDDLE
There should be places to huddle in order to think through and discuss new ideas.

GET ENOUGH SPACE
Does the room have the capacity to hold your entire team comfortably while sitting as well as moving around?

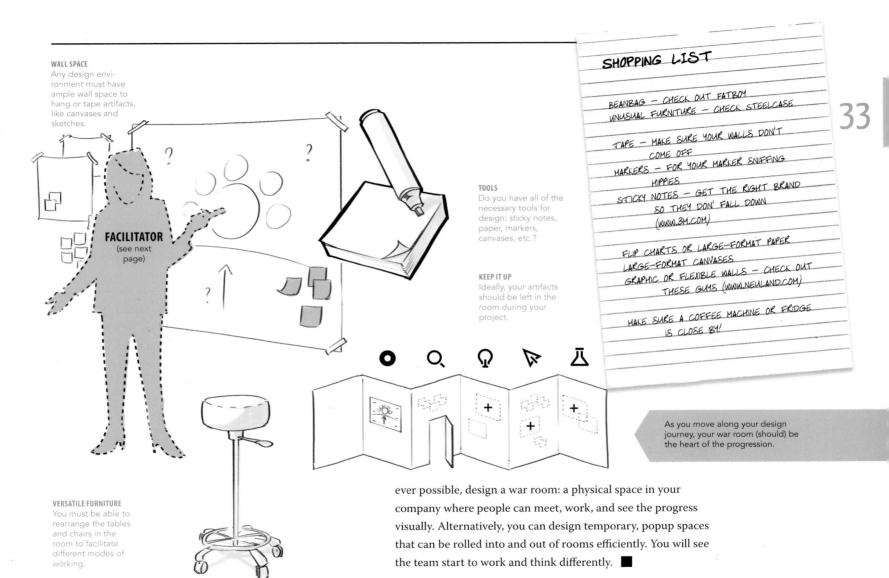

WALL SPACE
Any design environment must have ample wall space to hang or tape artifacts, like canvases and sketches.

FACILITATOR
(see next page)

TOOLS
Do you have all of the necessary tools for design: sticky notes, paper, markers, canvases, etc.?

KEEP IT UP
Ideally, your artifacts should be left in the room during your project.

VERSATILE FURNITURE
You must be able to rearrange the tables and chairs in the room to facilitate different modes of working.

SHOPPING LIST

BEANBAG — CHECK OUT FATBOY
UNUSUAL FURNITURE — CHECK STEELCASE

TAPE — MAKE SURE YOUR WALLS DON'T
       COME OFF
MARKERS — FOR YOUR MARKER SNIFFING
          HIPPIES
STICKY NOTES — GET THE RIGHT BRAND
               SO THEY DON' FALL DOWN
               (WWW.3M.COM)

FLIP CHARTS OR LARGE-FORMAT PAPER
LARGE-FORMAT CANVASES
GRAPHIC OR FLEXIBLE WALLS — CHECK OUT
              THESE GUYS (WWW.NEULAND.COM)

MAKE SURE A COFFEE MACHINE OR FRIDGE
         IS CLOSE BY!

33

As you move along your design journey, your war room (should) be the heart of the progression.

ever possible, design a war room: a physical space in your company where people can meet, work, and see the progress visually. Alternatively, you can design temporary, popup spaces that can be rolled into and out of rooms efficiently. You will see the team start to work and think differently. ■

MASTER **FACILITATION**

The design journey is all about preparation, and it's the facilitator's job to make that preparation and the journey ahead easy for everyone involved. A skilled facilitator is the master of ceremonies as well as the keeper of the light – the energy and intentionality in the room. It is up to the facilitator to help the team achieve the outcomes expected efficiently and effectively.

—Emmanuel Buttin Business Line CFO, BNP Paribas

MASTER OF CEREMONIES

A facilitator (you or someone else) must run meetings according to a screenplay while also providing space for the team to discuss and make decisions along the way, always being cognizant of the time (and need for frequent breaks, coffee, and food). The facilitator must also capture (or elect a scribe to capture) salient points of view, ideas, and decision points along the way.

Of course, there are many ways to do this. Using a whiteboard, chalkboard, or large flip charts, you can capture short bullet points about what's been said.

BECOMING A FACILITATOR

If you want to run a design process on strategy and innovation smoothly, engage with your team members, and develop leadership opportunities, you need facilitator skills. The more you know about how to design and run a good learning process, the more team members will feel empowered about their own ideas and participation. They will take on ownership and responsibility, resulting in better outcomes.

1 LEARN TO MANAGE ENERGY

Facilitation is first and foremost about managing energy. To maximize output, the team must feel energized. "Energy," in this case, describes how willing and able people are to contribute. "Good" energy helps the process. A discussion at the right time does just that. But hold a discussion at the wrong time, and exhaustion will quickly set in. The core skill of the facilitator is to manage the balance between going into the weeds and building energy.

2 IT'S MORE THAN JUST THE MEETING

Facilitation isn't about simply facilitating a discussion or a meeting; it's about facilitating the whole process. You'll need to become the mastermind of the operation. It's not about being right; it's about being effective in how you help teams by designing and managing the process. Facilitation is about the environment, information, the network, the team, and the energy. This includes communicating each step the team will take, as well as the promises made.

3 WEAR THE RIGHT HAT AT THE RIGHT TIME

There are times to be utterly optimistic and there are times to be critical. For instance, as ideation is about idea creation and expansion 90% of the time and evaluation and selection 10% of the time, it's vital that everyone on the team is wearing their optimistic hat at least 90% of the time, during idea creation.

But when it's time for evaluation and selection, it's okay for everyone to put on their critical hats. And in both cases, it's the job of the facilitator to ensure that optimism and criticality are employed at the right place and time in the journey.

4 VISUAL FACILITATION

The spoken word is intangible. What has been said five minutes ago only exists in memory. This prompts participants to repeat their argument over and over again.

David Sibbet, the pioneer of visual facilitation, found that by capturing the arguments on a big flip chart, big enough for all the participants to read, the need for repetition vanishes. Take a marker and write down what has been said, to allow the discussion to move on. ∎

DOING **THE DISHES**

In a meeting you have two types of people: the ones with "focused eyes" and the ones with "absent eyes"; business people versus designers. They play different roles in a meeting, but both are indispensible in a team.

The former are often misjudged to be shortsighted and judgmental, when they are actually taking things at face value (by nature). They give their opinions freely and have quick answers to everything. The latter's glazed-over looks are certainly not signs of disinterest. In their heads they are building on ideas and visualizing opportunities before speaking out.

From an outsider's perspective, it's hard to see how these people can work together effectively. In fact, you need both kinds of people on a team: fast movers and thinkers. It is my job to bridge those two worlds: Make them combine their brainpower and get them to share the same vision. When I see these situations arising, I offer a spark (or fire starter) to help steer them in the right direction. Then I step out to do the dishes while they perform miracles together.

Markus Auerbach
Director, Audi Innovation Research

MANAGING **ENERGY**

TIME MANAGEMENT

As with any process, the design process is deliberately designed with time in mind. When you're aiming for a goal, you're doing so with an eye on a specific date and time; you wouldn't ideate or validate forever. As a facilitator, it's your job to manage the timing of the process.

To keep everyone on the same page when you're working together, create an agenda using a flip chart and big permanent markers, and stick (or tape) it to the wall. Keep to the times and don't skip any breaks. You'll find that as people get more used to this structure, they'll deliver better results together.

DETAIL VS. OVERVIEW

While there are always big thinkers and strategic thinkers in groups, most often, the same people who think big and strategic thoughts are also stuck in the proverbial mud of the current operational execution engine. Of course, it's important to have people like this on board. But, this often becomes a challenge for the facilitator to steer the team forward into the expansive waters of strategic options.

This is especially true in big companies, where a constant balance exists between "let's move to action" and "let's make sure we are acting on the right things." This requires the facilitator

TIP! USE PUSH AND PULL TO MANAGE ENERGY

TIME MANAGEMENT
The best trick for time management is to put the participants in charge of keeping time. They'll start to work toward being efficient.

PUSH
Actions that push: moving into the group, putting words into people's mouths, making the group jump through formal hoops and structures, and arguing.

PULL
Actions that pull: taking a step back, not immediately having an answer, being silent, and asking honest, open questions.

HOLDING THE MARKER
Holding the marker means you have the power to frame the discussion and to move on – the arguments are recorded and need not be repeated.

and the participants to be able to bounce quickly between the big picture and the detail. This is one reason securing a core team, agreeing to a charter, and being transparent throughout the design process are so important. This is where the real facilitation takes place!

MAKE IT VISUAL

We humans are visual, spatial creatures. To really have an impact and sum up discussions and decision points so that they'll be remembered forever, do what David Sibbet says, and capture what's been said (at least some of it) visually.

The saying "a picture is worth a thousand words" was never truer than when you're trying to record and replay important context from a meeting or design sprint. An added bonus of holding the pen is that it will help you keep the center of attention on the whiteboard, flip chart or wall.

Furthermore, simply reviewing images allows you to replay entire conversations with nary a written word on the page. Whatever you decide, what's important here is that you capture the moments and decisions that lead to outcomes. ■

 For more information on visual facilitation, read:
Visual Meetings by David Sibbet

IT'S LIKE **JAZZ**

David Sibbet says visual facilitation is like jazz, playing within steady beats and formal structures that empower spontaneity and vitality.

Like live jazz, spoken words flow on. In meetings this often prompts repetition and hopes for real listening. Sibbet finds that capturing these words on large charts acknowledges the listening. The need to repeat diminishes. And a group memory is created. This frees the discussion to move to new levels.

Sibbet is one of the pioneers in visual facilitation, and practiced and taught in this space in the 1970s, when he started The Grove. Visual facilitation is a key to inspiring and engaging groups, supporting big-picture thinking, and the enacting what comes from having a group memory.

Some of his tools, such as the Cover Story Vision Graphic Guide® and the Context Map Graphic Guide®, are featured in this book.

David Sibbet
Author, Founder, and Chairman of
The Grove Consultants International

PREPARE **HOW YOU WORK** (TOGETHER)

You've put together a team and secured an environment to work together in. Now it's time to actually work together, efficiently and effectively. To achieve the best results as a team while continually staying on the same page, you'll need some design tools.

THE DESIGNER'S ESSENTIALS

There's a very good reason designers and creative types carry around sticky notes and big permanent markers. Sticky notes are expendable, additive, stick to anything, and have the added value of being constrained by size, while permanent markers are, well, permanent, and make what's represented on each sticky note more readable. Hand stacks of each of these tools to everyone and let the ideas fly. By the end of the day you should have a wall of ideas and a floor piled high with half-starts. You get bonus points for getting everyone to draw their points of view (visually) on sticky notes. For some simple sketching tips, check out the profile on Dan Roam, in the prototyping chapter.

More about sketching and visual thinking
PAGE 172

FRAME DISCUSSIONS USING A CANVAS

In just about every chapter of this book you'll find canvases, like the Business Model Canvas, Value Proposition Canvas, as well as others that can used for visioning, storytelling, validating, etc. These visual artifacts will help spark interesting conversations while framing the ensuing discussions.

These tools are not tools to be filled out and put away. As essential design tools, the canvases provided here are also living, breathing records that document your design journey. When you pair people, sticky notes, markers, and sketching, not only will the design process be faster and easier, you'll get much better results and learn to speak in a new shared language.

BETTER MEETINGS VIA SCREENPLAYS

Meetings have become a (bad) habit for most large organizations. In fact, this habit extends to the way we work: we sit behind our desk working independently from others. We send lots of email. We make a few phone calls. And when we're not sitting at our desks, we're in meetings.

Meetings are not necessarily bad, but more often than not, they are simply planned – not designed. In turn, nothing really happens at the meetings we show up to. There is no clear structure. What's the purpose of this meeting? Who is in the room? How do we make sure we get things done in this time slot? How do we know what is expected from us in this meeting? Those questions rarely get asked – and all the while, we have rooms full of people wasting time, resources, and energy.

> **TIP!** Have a walking meeting. When walking or standing up, not only is the body more mobile, but so is the mind. It is much harder to become entrenched in an argument when you are mobile.

What's more, using meetings to share information is also a waste of time. Meetings are more often social and political. We feel badly if we exclude colleagues when sending invites for a meeting. Instead of thinking about who are the right people to be in the room, we think about who we don't want to exclude. Not having the right people in the room – or having too many people in the room – leads to slow progress. This wastes everyone's time.

The key to good meetings – and even better workshops – is to create a screenplay. Not to be confused with an agenda, a screenplay details who will work on what when. Most notably, it will help you design a meeting based on the results you wish to achieve. ■

IMPROVISE LIKE A **CHAMP**

After I speak on stage or appear on television and radio shows, people often approach me and say, "You make it look so easy, as if you improvise on the spot! How do you do that?"

The answer is simple. It takes time. I invest a lot of time in my screenplay. Why? You are responsible for designing the flow of an event. When you go through it step by step, you feel where you need to give more energy, where you need to go slow or go fast, and where you can go in deeper.

Once you have a clear path and target in mind, you can take crossroads. In other words, once you get the basics right, you'll find places where you can improvise. A screenplay forces you to think about how you cut your message into digestible pieces and how you design for energy and interaction from the audience.

A message well sent is a message well received. Facilitate the receiver and work with a screenplay!

Rens de Jong
Moderator, Radio & TV Anchor,
Entrepreneur

TOOL **SCREENPLAYS**

Just like it does in movie-making, a screenplay provides an efficient and effective way to design a meeting. The more thorough the screenplay, the better the meeting.

THIS IS YOUR FACILITATION DESIGN TOOL

Screenplays help you to design a meeting or workshop and share this with the key stakeholders and facilitators. Well-designed screenplays enable you to gain clarity about what can be done during a workshop in order to make decisions about time, activities, and topics to be covered. Most important, a screenplay is a visual tool to help you design for results while managing all of the information in one simple document.

DESIGN FOR FLEXIBILITY

One misunderstanding is that the screenplay is fixed and therefore not flexible. That's not true. The screenplay should be co-created with the core team to help everyone design a results-driven meeting or workshop. In this way, a screenplay will actually help you to be flexible.

I LOVE IT WHEN A PLAN COMES TOGETHER.

// Hannibal, A-Team

Moreover, when you design your screenplays in blocks of time/ activities, it enables you to shift to new blocks should the expected-unexpected occur, like lateness due to traffic jams, etc.

BE EARLY
Make sure to arrive at least an hour before the start of the workshop to make sure everything works, that there is coffee and water available, and to test the wifi and the projector.

AGENDA, ROLES, RULES
Always start with agenda, roles, rules, and outcomes. Agree on these with the team.

TIME SLOTS
The minimum length to schedule is 15 minutes, but preferably work in 30-minute increments.

STRATEGIC VISION
You can design strategic vision. For more info look at the vision section in Point of View, page 58.

COFFEE BREAKS
Never skip coffee breaks. And yes, they really take 30 minutes. People need a break!

WRAP-UP
In the wrap-up, come back to the objectives and make sure everything is covered.

CALL SHEET

Who	Role
Marc McLaughlin	Host & Mc
Maarten van Lieshout	Visualizer
Eefje Jonker	Strategy de
Mr. Wolf	Facility mar
Josephine Green	Catering

SCREENPLAY Worksh

Location: Amsterdam
Time: 09:00 - 12:30

Time	Topic
09:00 15 min	**Setup and introduction**
09:15 90 min	**Team Exercise Strategic Visio** What is our long-term vision and a tion level? What impact does this on our business model? What are implications of our ambition level the business model?
10:45 30 min	**Break**
11:15 60 min	**Share your vision story!** Teams will present their visions t and get feedback
12:15 15 min	**Wrap-up**

p STRATEGIC Visioning for <Client> on <Date>

	Responsibility	Contact Details
	Inspire & guide throughout the day	<Phone> <Mail>
	Visual facilitation	<Phone> <Mail>
	Achieve best possible outco...	

ATEGIC Visioning for <Client> on <Date>

Activity	Who?
Short background – Why are we here? Agenda (drawing) Roles and rules Outcome of workshop	Workshop host
Explain exercise What is vision? (5 minutes) Explain strategic visioning map, 5 Bold Steps Vision® (10 minutes)	On screen by Strategy designer
Team exercise Divide into groups of 4–6 people Put sticky notes on vision, vision themes, and how this shows up (60 minutes) Determine the 5 bold steps (15 min)	Supported by facilitato...
Capture Collect flip charts and take pictures – mark cap- tured flip charts.	Strategy designer
Plenary presentations Plenary presentations by teams (30 min) Identify top 3 makers & breakers (15 min) Determine design criteria (15 min)	Teams present Strategy designer connects
Wrap-up Wrap-up of learning this morning. Next steps. End the workshop.	Strategy designe...

CALL SHEET
Make a call sheet with the most important people needed during the day. Take special care to be-come friends with the location's technical people – they can save your day.

LOCATION CHECK
Always check the location before you run a workshop there. Nasty surprises will ruin the outcome of your session.

LOCATION CHECKLIST

- [ ] LOTS OF WALL SPACE
- [ ] ABLE TO TAPE TEMPLATES TO THE WALL
- [ ] SPACE TO WALK AROUND
- [ ] DAYLIGHT AND FRESH AIR
- [ ] NO DISTRACTIONS
- [ ] REFRESHMENTS
- [ ] TABLES NOT AS CONFERENCE BUT TABLE GROUPS
- [ ] ABLE TO PLAY MUSIC DURING EXCERISES

DOWNLOAD
Download example screenplays and call sheets from
www.designabetterbusiness.com

41

CHECKLIST

- [ ] Check the lengths of the time slots and breaks.
- [ ] Clear actions per time slot.
- [ ] Call sheet.

NEXT STEP

> Run your workshop, meeting, or offsite.

TOOL **TEAM CHARTER**

PERSONAL

get to know your team

± **30** MIN

session

3—5

people per group

Now that you've put all of these unusual suspects and diverse characters together in one room, how will you agree on your goals, expectations, and values? And how will you deal with challenging situations? Design a team charter together!

SIGN THE CHARTER

You don't always get to decide with whom you work with. Even if you do, there's no guarantee that you'll be successful. Conflicts of interest and differing values or goals often get in the way of a team's progress.

A team charter will help you create a blueprint for the engine behind a project: a well-balanced team. As a co-created document, the team charter will help clarify the team's direction while establishing boundaries.

The team charter serves two purposes. Firstly, using the charter as an inward-facing document, team members can point out why the team was established in the first place, what the main focus is, and what direction the team will take to achieve its stated goals. Secondly, as an outward-facing document, the charter can help to educate managers and other organizational leaders about the focus and direction of the team.

GOOD TO KNOW WHO YOU'RE TRAVELING WITH!

TEAM VALUES

Together, you'll need to decide on the values your team upholds as part of its collaboration. These values will help form the foundation for a successful team, which will make it easier to reach the goal while reducing confusion about the team's objectives. What's more, the charter will provide clear guidelines about how team members will work together and what each person will contribute, which will help ensure the team moves forward and not backward.

Some of the things you'll want to include in your team charter are the following: team members; team goals, expectations, and the purpose for existing in the first place; team values; how the team handles trouble and obstacles; who the team leaders are. Don't be afraid to add things like "have fun!" and energy sources, like "team dinner once per week." These will go a long way in helping the team gel.

Whatever form your team charter takes, just make sure you're all on the same page. In the end you want to have a team of people who build off each other, not a group of people just doing a job.

TEAM CHARTER CANVAS

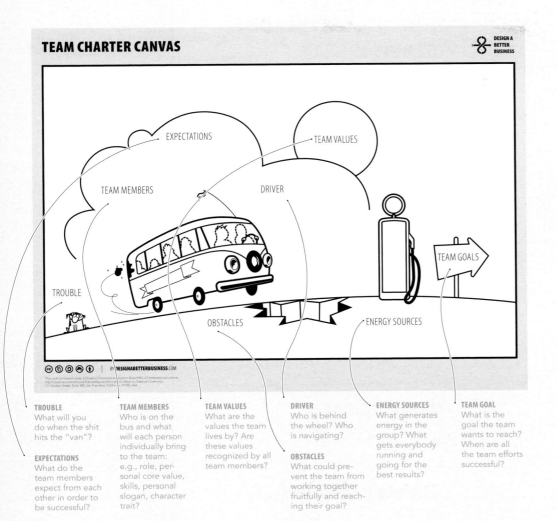

TROUBLE
What will you
do when the shit
hits the "van"?

EXPECTATIONS
What do the
team members
expect from each
other in order to
be successful?

TEAM MEMBERS
Who is on the
bus and what
will each person
individually bring
to the team:
e.g., role, per-
sonal core value,
skills, personal
slogan, character
trait?

TEAM VALUES
What are the
values the team
lives by? Are
these values
recognized by all
team members?

DRIVER
Who is behind
the wheel? Who
is navigating?

OBSTACLES
What could pre-
vent the team from
working together
fruitfully and reach-
ing their goal?

ENERGY SOURCES
What generates
energy in the
group? What
gets everybody
running and
going for the
best results?

TEAM GOAL
What is the
goal the team
wants to reach?
When are all
the team efforts
successful?

CHECKLIST

☐ You defined the team goal.

☐ You defined the driver, team
members, and values.

☐ You defined obstacles and
energy sources.

☐ You had everyone sign the
charter.

NEXT STEP

❯ Go get started with Point of
View!

YOU NOW HAVE . . .

> PREPARED **YOUR TEAM** — P30

> PREPARED **YOUR ENVIRONMENT** — P32

> BUILT **YOUR TEAM CHARTER** — P42

NEXT STEPS

> **DEVELOP A POINT OF VIEW** — P46
> It will help you decide how to approach your design journey.

> **DESIGN A VISION** — P58
> Fomulate an actionable vision with your team.

> **APPLY DESIGN CRITERIA** — P68
> What are the principles and the benchmarks of the change you're after?

RECAP

DON'T FLY SOLO. **THE LONE GENIUS IS DEAD.**

PREPARE. SET YOURSELF UP FOR **SUCCESS.**

BUILD A MULTI-DISCIPLINARY TEAM. DIVERSITY IS KEY.

FIND AN EXECUTIVE SPONSOR. CREATE AMBASSADORS.

WORK VISUALLY. YOUR BRAIN WIILL THANK YOU FOR IT.

MANAGE THE ENERGY.

45

NOW, LET'S GET STARTED!

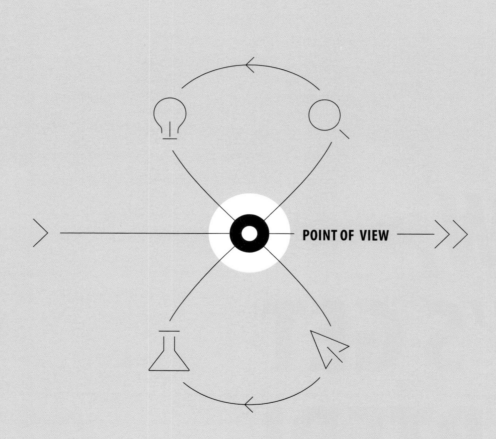

POINT OF VIEW

THE DESIGN JOURNEY **POINT OF VIEW**

BE A **REBEL**

DEVELOP **YOUR VISION**

DESIGN **YOUR STORY**

CREATE **DESIGN CRITERIA**

YOUR **POINT OF VIEW**

Every design journey starts somewhere. Perhaps that somewhere is a brand-new company searching for its sustainable (money-making) business model. Or maybe the journey is being taken by an existing business looking for new directions so it can stay competitive and grow. In every case, the journey you take will start with a point of view.

Whether it's about a market, or a customer, or a product or service, or even a competitor, we all have a point of view. Being at the center of the design journey, your point of view is your most valuable asset. It provides the litmus test for what's real and what's just a mirage. As a designer you are responsible for actively shaping your point of view based on what you learn along the way.

To create change, you must start with your point of view, even when the odds seemed stacked against you. Maybe you're thinking, "But it's just my point of view! What changes could I possibly make based on what I think?!" You wouldn't be wrong – or the first person – to think this. However, when you pair your point of view with specific tools, skills, and a mindset to match, you absolutely can create the change you're looking for.

THE FIRST STEP IS ALWAYS THE HARDEST

Developing new business ideas from scratch can seem like a daunting task. When you're a startup, you have hope in your heart that your company will become the next big thing. You work hard at developing and selling your product – but often, the harder you work, the further away your away dreams seem to be. When you're an established business, you've been driving the same executional strategy for many, many years. Your shareholders enjoy the fruits of your labor in the form of increasing share prices and dividends, and your board looks to past growth for future strategy. However, these past successes may become a burden as you try to steer your company into new waters.

BE A REBEL

If you're looking to influence someone, especially someone you need on your team to turn your point of view into a successful strategy, it may sound counterintuitive to say that you should be a rebel. But it's precisely the rebel, and the points of view that she brings with her, that will serve as the catalyst for change. Being a rebel does not mean you must go against everything that your company or leadership stand for. Rather, being a rebel is about coming to the table with a strong point of view toward the future. You do not need to buck the establishment – but you do need to question the establishment and bring to the table those big ideas that you feel in your gut are worth exploring.

For how to use a strong point of view to design a better business, read:
Zero to One by Peter Thiel

49

LET YOUR VISION BE YOUR ROADMAP

A strong point of view will serve as your catalyst for change. It is your vision for the future that will serve as the roadmap leading to the change you seek to make. People argue their points of view over beers. Visions set direction (maybe so that you can buy even more beer with the money you'll make in the future!).

Our definition of "vision" is different than what you'll find in other books or articles. It's not just a statement: it's a rallying cry. The concept of vision is all-encompassing; it includes the supporting factors that make the vision real, the steps you need to take to realize the vision, and the challenges and opportunities that you'll face on your way to achieving your vision. To make your vision tangible and useful, this chapter lays out co-creative tools that you can – and should – use with your team.

DESIGN YOUR STORY

When you enter that boardroom, or strategy meeting, or VC pitch, what are you going to say? How will you sway people to your point of view, or at least convince them to explore your vision with you? This is where stories make a big difference. Ever notice how the best speakers, whether giving a TED talk, presenting in a conference room, or holding court in a bar, use anecdotes and stories to convey the points they are making? Though naturally talented speakers may do this somewhat instinctively, anyone who does this well is deliberate about what stories they tell, how, when, and to whom: to make your mark and gain the buy-in you need, you'll need to explore your point of view. In other words, you'll need to design your story.

But don't let that worry you. Just as we are giving you new tools to create your vision, we are also sharing great tools to help you design your story.

DESIGN CRITERIA

Your vision points to a future state. Yet it's not just any future state. The changes you seek to make along your design journey likely must also meet a set of criteria about what you must, could, should, or absolutely won't do as you explore and evaluate options for the future. These are design criteria. They provide both a foundation and clear boundaries to help guide your decisions along the way. Your design criteria will be informed by the vision you create as well as the context surrounding your organization. Similarly, the options you explore will be informed by the same design criteria. ■

DARE TO **STEP UP**

Everybody has a point of view. Very few dare to step up. They believe they are not the right person to do that as it is not in their job description. It was not in mine either: I am the CFO. Yet I decided to step out of my comfort zone – the only way to make a difference.

WE WERE HUNGRY FOR VISION

Our organization had gone through some pretty rough times in the recent past. You could feel that in the energy of the organization. The financial crisis had taken a toll, and a merger between two companies (BNP Paribas and Fortis Bank) had created a cultural disconnect – and I realized that our discussions were too focused on what had happened in the past. People were questioning our company identity. I, of course, agreed with my co-workers, but even those conversations were very difficult and even disruptive.

TIP 1

STICK TO YOUR BELIEFS. IF YOU DON'T, HOW CAN YOU EVER TRUST OTHERS TO DO SO?

As a large ship sailing forward, we often don't think we have much time for self-reflection. But I felt we needed to take a step back, describe our situation, and then get over it and get going. This didn't mean sweeping our problems under the rug – we needed to talk about them and learn from them. And then we needed to move forward.

RESHUFFLE THE FOCUS TO THE FUTURE

With all of our fears, uncertainties, and doubts, I felt that it was time to reshuffle the focus and start looking forward. Although as the CFO it was not necessarily my role, I decided to step up and make it happen. In fact, I think that anyone and everyone in our organization should be able to step up and take new and broader sets of responsibilities than what they were hired for. But, as the CFO, I was a bit perplexed: how could I focus on the future and not just the forecasted future the numbers usually tell? What would the future look like? With changes happening rapidly in our world (the banking world), I knew one thing for sure: numbers would not tell the story we needed. Nor would numbers get people to believe in our future.

TIP 2

DARE TO BE YOURSELF: SHOW UP AT YOUR JOB THE SAME AS YOU WOULD SHOW UP IN YOUR PRIVATE LIFE.

To me, it became clear that our future is not as much about numbers as it is about our story. And to rebuild our story, I needed not just number-driven IQ, but also emotionally-driven EQ. I needed to get people to let go of their negative emotions and build our future based on positive ones. We needed to build on where we came from, what we had become, who we are, and what's in our DNA.

STEP FORWARD

I was the one who stepped forward. This was quite extraordinary when you consider that my role was the CFO – a numbers guy. This, in fact, was the first time in my career that I felt the need to do this. Sure, I'd held leadership positions for a long time. But this bank is in my DNA and I wanted to design a future that would last. **»**

I AM **MASTER OF MY FATE**

I never imagined myself being the host of our management offsite. But here I was, dressed in black, standing on a 360-degree stage and introducing my colleagues who presented their vision stories to an inspired audience. This was a vision designed and told by us. Not some boring strategic plan put together by consultants. We designed this experience in order to get 250 other colleagues to want to contribute as well. Our bank had never done this before. We empowered people to take one step toward the future. Music and scenes from the movie *Invictus* supported our vision, empowering people to be the masters of our fate and future.

It was an exciting journey and many people joined, exploring the unexplored. It was not easy. But the plan came together. I practiced what I preached. I am the master of my fate and future.

51

Emmanuel Buttin
Business Line CFO,
BNP Paribas

GO BEYOND YOURSELF EVERYDAY. ONLY THEN DO WE COMMIT OURSELVES TO GROWTH.

Inasmuch as I feel that people need to step out of their comfort zones and help steer the ship, I also believe you must feel somewhat comfortable stepping up and steering. That's not to say you won't be anxious the first time you step up. I know I was. But I believe being anxious enables you to be more open to new environments. You become sensitive to outside stimuli. And this is where you will find your vision. I did.

NO CLUE HOW TO DO IT

Being operationally minded, I did not know how to shift our focus to the near-term future. In fact, nobody on our team did. But I felt that if I made the first step forward, we would figure out how to make the next step together. At this moment, I realized that I was actually creating a movement. As people joined, they created the energy we needed to take more steps. Even more people were drawn to this energy and joined us. We had no clear path ahead of us as we took those first few steps, but it felt good to create our own optimistic path.

I also knew that most people in large organizations like ours would have a hard time joining movements like the one we started. It's not that they don't want to. It's just that most of the time, executing today's strategy using current information is the more comfortable path. That's what we all learn to do in school, after all. But using yesterday's information to execute yesterday's strategy is a terrible excuse for not moving forward. All of the information in the world will not guarantee success if it's based on yesterday. Sure, you can hire third parties to design your vision and strategy for you. But then you're not taking responsibility for making it a success.

DO IT TOGETHER

As I stepped forward, other people stepped up to help design our future together. As we all took those first steps together, I recognized that the most interesting ideas came from having people from different departments, with varying ideas, share with each other. We wanted to create something different from what we'd done in the past. We didn't want to simply write our ideas down on a piece of paper, only for them to be forgotten in a few days. We believed that in order to live the vision, we needed to co-create it together and not wait for the Executive Committee. We wanted people from all levels of the organization to explore the story and tell the story.

CREATING A VISION WITH 250 PEOPLE

With various people from the organization, all of whom had other daily responsibilities, we began to forge our path forward. We collected information, talked to customers, and synchronized our stories on a map. It felt to me that we had the beginnings of a strong vision.

We hosted a two-day "Management University" event later that year: an opportune time to share our collective stories with one another. This was not a small event. Management University brought together 250 people from all over the organization and all over the world to have conversations about the future of the bank. I thought it was the perfect time to share and validate the vision I and my (now) 35-person core team had been working on for the past year. We all stepped up to the raised bar.

Each person, as part of our movement, had to tell a part of our story to the other 250 people in the audience. And, to make it more inclusive, we decided not to use a regular stage. Instead, we opted for a 360-degree stage with the presenters standing right in the middle – at the heart of the conversation. To raise the stakes even more, we decided not to use slides at all. We would give TED-style keynotes that were meant to inspire our teams.

EXERCISE: WHO ARE WE AS A BANK?

Our vision story went over really well. But to get everyone involved – and not just the 35 people who co-created the foundations of the vision – we kicked off the day with a communal exercise focused on "who we are as a bank." Harkening back to our more creative days, we used scissors, pictures of car parts, markers, and tape to design the bank we felt we were in the present. Given how unusual this exercise must have sounded (and maybe even sounds to you now), we were surprised at

how readily people picked up their tools and designed a car together – it only took about 20 minutes. We had fun and shared stories about our company's DNA. Everyone felt proud that we had taken this step.

LASTING IMPACT FOR THE BANK

I can say without a doubt that the bank and the bank's leadership have learned a great deal. I feel that we made the first big step in embracing a new way of working together. This new way of working is about trusting others to help steer the ship. It's not about hiring consultants to draw you the map. We did it ourselves. We spotted new talent in our organization who stepped up and inspired others to do the same. And in the end, we now trust that we can think and work differently. ∎

53

An example of the template teams used to cut and paste their own interpretation of what the bank is using the car metaphor.

PIMP YOUR RIDE
THE BNP PARIBAS WORKSHOP

CHECK

Pritt

TANGIBLE STRATEGY

There was a Homer Simpson "duh" moment where we collectively realized one of the things we often did was completely over-engineer and over-design the next steps – so the 5 bold steps was a really easy way to record tangible next steps that were both audacious and compelling. Instead of an abstract strategy, we all were eager to take them!

// Vicky Seeley – COO – Sheppard Moscow LLC

Stay true to your vision – don't change to fit the agenda of others.

// Sue Black, University of Dundee

Siemens Healthcare, Turkey

As the Sales and Marketing Board of Siemens Healthcare, Turkey, we discussed our vision and business strategy during the aftermath of a recent restructuring and repositioning. All our discussions about our business model and context strongly related to our vision. The 5 Bold Steps Vision® Canvas became the source of most actions we agreed upon.

// Enis Sonemel – Siemens Healthcare, Turkey – Country Lead, Diagnostic Imaging

A Connected Vision

SallyAnn Kelly joined as CEO of Aberlour Childcare Trust with a clear mandate: to embed a clear strategy.
As she sought to achieve real lasting change, it became clear to her she would have to engage the whole organization.

JUNE 2014:
SALLYANN KELLY TAKES POST AS CEO AND FINDS AN ORGANIZATION IN NEED OF CLEAR DIRECTION.

JULY–AUG 2014:
SALLYANN TAKES AN INTERNAL SAFARI THROUGH THE ORGANIZATION TO CREATE A POINT OF VIEW.

DEC 2014:
5 BOLD STEPS VISION® AND STRATEGY WORK WITH SLT AND DIRECTORS.

JAN 2015:
CONNECTS 5 BOLD STEPS TO DRAFT STRATEGY AND PRESENTS TO THE BOARD.

JAN–FEB 2015:
CONSULTS WITH OVER 300 STAFF (13% OF ORG) FOR FEEDBACK, TO MAKE IT MORE PRACTICAL.

FEB 2015:
IMPLEMENTS REVISIONS IN FINAL DRAFT OF THE STRATEGY + CORPORATE BUSINESS PLAN FOR YEAR 1 OF 3-YEAR STRATEGY.

Mindpearl

At Mindpearl we needed to reshape the way we promote ourselves and talk about ourselves. Our language had become too complicated and distant. We defined a clear vision based on where we came from, who we are, and who we want to be. Our people are now able to reconnect with our global identity. We realigned our actions and narrative.

// Karin Dale, General Manager, Mindpearl

Now I can share my strategy on one page!

// Craig Mohan, Managing Director,
Market Technology and Data Services,
CME Group Chicago

BULLETPROOF VISION

While working on the cover story, one team from a producer of aramid fiber, the ballistics unit, came up with "Obama buys a bulletproof Dolce & Gabbana dress for his wife for Xmas." The entire team was laughing. Nobody really understood what it could mean at first. But then, as we came back down to earth, we realized it was about having fashionable bulletproof clothing. Not those ugly jackets and vests. There is absolutely a need for this, especially among rich and famous in certain countries.

55

A VISION PER DIVISION

Our departments of Orthopedics, Dermatology, Oncology, and Mother and Child took up the responsibility to map out a vision separately. We soon learned that it is more interesting/productive/better to use a co-creative design process. Vision is about alignment. It was crucial for us to create a vision with the customer in mind.

This was a huge step for our hospital; we previously had a perspective that prioritized expertise and excellent treatments, rather than a customer-centric perspective. After designing our new vision, we wanted to communicate both inside and outside the hospital. We used visuals and a move to create a clear story.

// Frits van Merode, Member, Executive Board Maastricht University Medical Center

WOULDN'T IT BE GREAT TO CREATE A MINI STRATEGY BOOKLET FOR EMPLOYEES?

MARCH 2015: PRESENTS STRATEGY TO THE BOARD.

APRIL–JULY 2015: WORKSHOP TO ENGAGE STAFF/EMPLOYEES WITH THE STRATEGY (WHAT DOES IT MEAN FOR YOU? WHAT ACTIONS WILL YOU TAKE?).

APRIL 2015: CREATES MINI VISUAL STRATEGY BOOKLETS AND SENDS A PERSONAL COPY + THANK YOU LETTER IN THE POST TO EACH EMPLOYEE.

MAY–DEC 2015: IMPLEMENTS YEAR 1 OF STRATEGY. NEW INITIATIVES LAUNCHED IN SUPPORT OF VISION ELEMENTS.

JAN 2016: STRATEGY REVIEW DAY. BUILD/MEASURE/LEARN LOOP PUT IN PLACE.

YOUR VISION OF THE FUTURE

The first thing most people do when they here the word "vision" in a business context is yawn. That's because most visions are vague, unclear, and, frankly, nothing to get excited about. Well-designed visions should be rallying cries for action, invention, and innovation.

VISION AS YOUR COMPASS

When you've formulated your point of view with an eye toward the future, it's the vision that will guide you and your team toward the North Star. A clear vision brings focus and provides an anchor point for making bold strategic choices. It drives the search for new business models. As a rallying cry, a clear and compelling vision provides direction in everything you and your colleagues do. Ask each other this question every day: Does this action, activity, experiment, project get us closer to realizing our vision? If the answer is no, then don't waste time, energy, and money on it. A vision is a compass that ensures your people and teams work on those things that matter to customers, clients, and other stakeholders. It will inspire, engage, and activate people so they are able to do a better job.

A VISION IS NOT A VISION STATEMENT

A vision statement is the headline to a much richer story about your future. It is an anchor for the bigger story. While a vision statement is an aspirational description of what your team (or organization) would like to achieve or accomplish in the mid- or long-term future, to be truly useful (and powerful), a vision statement must point out not only where you want to go and when, but also how you're going to get there.

A VISION BEYOND VISION STATEMENTS!

The first step in vision design is about going beyond the vision statement. Yes, the vision should address the vision statement, the underlying themes and the examples where vision shows up. However, if the vision is meant to be a rallying cry for the future, then it must be designed – or at least embodied – by the entire organization. The process of designing the vision must take into account the values your organization lives by as well your realistic mid- and long-term goals. The vision you create with your company (or team) must outline the key objectives as well as high-level tactics and the elements of your business and values that support them. This will enable the various teams in your company to develop strategies to achieve the goals stated in the vision. With a single unifying vision, employees will all be on the same page and marching to the same drummer. Your vision will become the North Star for the future.

THREE BUILDING BLOCKS OF A PRACTICAL VISION

A high-quality, practical, and inspiring vision for any organization should have three key characteristics: it needs to state where the company wants to be in the near future (2–5 years); it must contain a level of inspiration and excitement (the rallying cry); and it must detail the bold steps by which to achieve the vision.

WHERE SHALL WE START?

To craft a vision that becomes your rallying cry, bring together a team and empower them to design the future. This is about pairing energy, fun, creativity, and ambition. To get started, dream big. Don't worry about your daily job. Brainstorm with your team to visualize where you may see yourselves in the mid- and long-term future.

Ask yourself what problems your team (or organization) hopes to solve in the next few years. What do you hope to achieve? Who is your target customer base, and what do you want to do for them? What will your future business model look like?

WHAT SUPPORTS OUR VISION?

As you and your team begin to create the ideas of your future together, you'll also need to capture the aspects of your organization, your strategy, and the broader context that will help support your vision. The key to capturing the support for your vision is to ask yourself (and your team): "Why us? Why now?" What does your organization value or do that will support your vision? What parts of your organization's broader context – perhaps even trends – will further bolster your vision? ■

DON'T LOSE **SLEEP** OVER IT

Aart Roos, CEO of Auping, a Dutch-based bed design and production company, decided to approach his company's vision design in a very different way. Instead of formulating the vision in the Executive Suite, isolated from his customers, Aart turned to his customers to co-create Auping's vision with them and for them.

57

Customers stated, "Sleep is the most important thing for me to feel healthy and energetic, to be able to really live!"

Today, Auping's communication focuses less on the production of their beds and more on what their customers find important about their beds: an energetic day.
Their tagline: "Auping nights, better days."

Aart J. Roos
CEO, Auping

TOOL **5 BOLD STEPS VISION**®

Original created by David Sibbet, The Grove Consultants International

If you want to make positive, future-oriented change in your organization, you'll need to go beyond writing long-winded paper visions and come to a shared agreement about what you are going to fight for together and what steps you are going to take to get "there." The 5 Bold Steps Vision® Canvas is a perfect tool to align your teams in your organization.

THE STEPS TO TAKE

The vision canvas will help you co-design the vision as well as the 5 bold steps to achieve that vision. Additionally, using this tool, your team will be able to clarify what supports your vision, what challenges your vision, and what opportunities are created in working toward your vision. Best of all, the vision canvas will help you derive design criteria for your business model(s) and strategy.

COLLECTIVE STATEMENT

A vision statement is sometimes called a picture of your company in the future. But it's so much more than that. Your vision statement is your inspiration, the framework for all your strategic planning. When creating your initial vision statement you are essentially articulating your dreams for your business. This should stand as a reminder of what you're trying to accomplish together.

It may apply to your entire company or to a single division of the company. Whether for all or part of an organization, the vision statement answers the question "Where do we want to go?"

CONCRETE GUIDELINES

Probably the greatest aspect of the vision canvas is that your entire vision, including actions, supports, opportunities, and challenges, will be on one sheet of paper – not a book! It's simple to share and easy to translate into concrete guidelines that decision makers (and executors) need to get their jobs done. Even better, creating a visualization of the vision, based on this canvas, will help you spread the word.

READY, SET . . . GO!

Regardless of the approach you choose to compose your vision, you'll need to involve the right people. This includes the decision makers as well as everybody else! A vision without actions or ambassadors to carry the message forward is worth no more than the paper it's printed on, no matter how well crafted. ■

59

HOW IT SHOWS UP
How will the themes show up in our company? How will they make the vision themes concrete and how will they inspire others?

VISION STATEMENT
What is the future state of our company? How are we going to help our customers?

ESSENTIAL THEMES
What are the essential themes supporting our vision? Describe them in 1 or 2 single words.

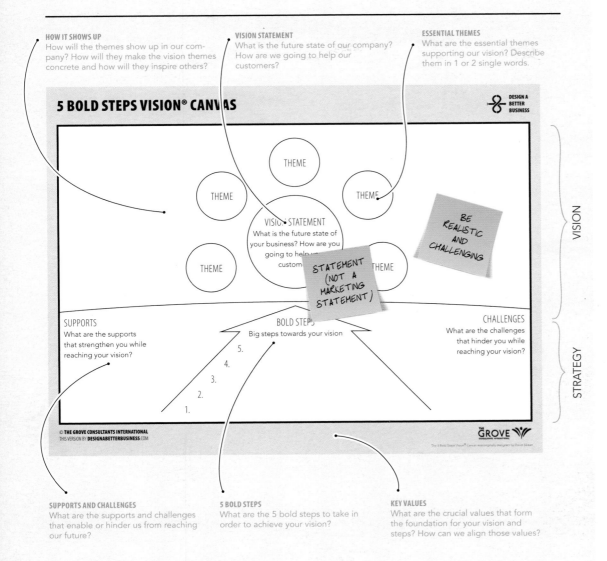

5 BOLD STEPS VISION® CANVAS

DESIGN A BETTER BUSINESS

THEME

THEME

THEME

THEME

THEME

VISION STATEMENT
What is the future state of your business? How are you going to help your custom...

BE REALISTIC AND CHALLENGING

STATEMENT (NOT A MARKETING STATEMENT)

SUPPORTS
What are the supports that strengthen you while reaching your vision?

BOLD STEPS
Big steps towards your vision
5.
4.
3.
2.
1.

CHALLENGES
What are the challenges that hinder you while reaching your vision?

VISION

STRATEGY

© THE GROVE CONSULTANTS INTERNATIONAL
THIS VERSION BY DESIGNABETTERBUSINESS.COM

THE GROVE

The 5 Bold Steps Vision® Canvas was originally designed by David Sibbet

SUPPORTS AND CHALLENGES
What are the supports and challenges that enable or hinder us from reaching our future?

5 BOLD STEPS
What are the 5 bold steps to take in order to achieve your vision?

KEY VALUES
What are the crucial values that form the foundation for your vision and steps? How can we align those values?

CHECKLIST

☐ You identified five steps to achieve your vision.

☐ Your vision statement is supported by clear themes and the realistic ways it shows up.

☐ You filtered out criteria to design your business model(s) and value proposition.

NEXT STEPS

❯ Check how this vision resonates with others.

CASE **5 BOLD STEPS VISION**® ING BANK

CONFIDENTIAL

STRATEGY DOCUMENT

PROTECTION

...KEN IN THE BANKING INDUSTRY

...FOR FINANCIAL ADVICE

5 BOLD STEPS VISION® CANVAS

ANTICIPATE

CLIENTS ONLINE 24/7

BANK IN YOUR POCKET

EMPOWER

ANY TIME ANYWHERE

SIMPLE PROCESSES

PLAIN LANGUAGE

CLEAR AND EASY

EMPOWERING PEOPLE TO STAY AHEAD IN LIFE AND BUSINESS

FAIR PRICES

CLEAR PRODUCTS

SUPPORTS

BOLD STEPS

5.

4.

3.

2.

1.

EARN PRIMARY RELATIONSHIP

TO REDEFINE THEIR VISION, ING HAD WRITTEN A CORPORATE STRATEGY DOCUMENT. VALUABLE INFORMATION, BUT HOW DO WE TRANSLATE IT INTO AN ACTIONABLE VISION?

THE TEAMS DECIDED TO CUT OUT THE HEADERS OF THE IMPORTANT PAGES AND USED THEM TO INITIALLY PLOT THE VISION THEMES AND HOW THEY SHOW UP.

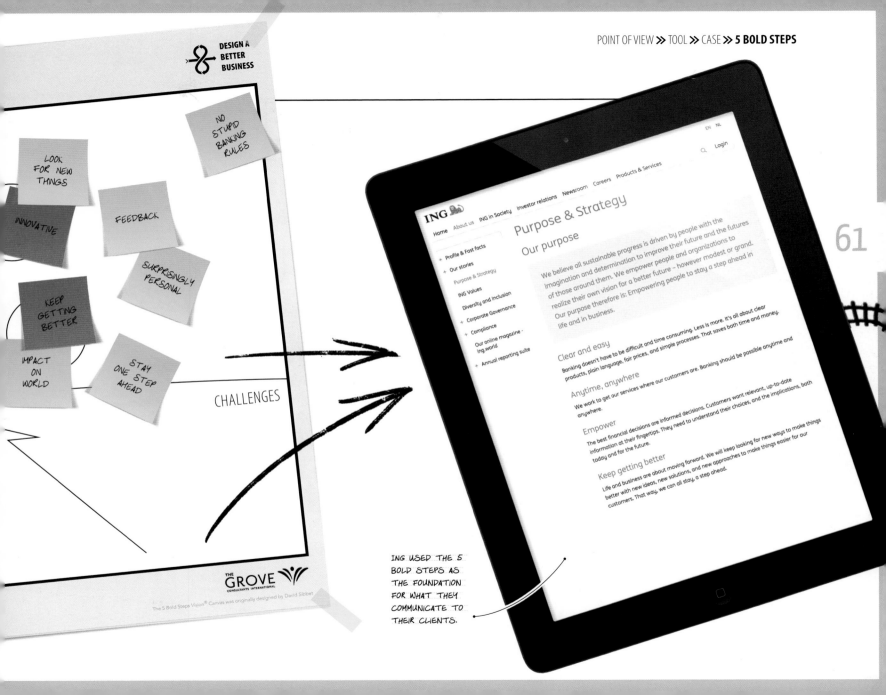

DESIGN A
BETTER
BUSINESS

NO STUPID BANKING RULES

LOOK FOR NEW THINGS

INNOVATIVE

FEEDBACK

SURPRISINGLY PERSONAL

KEEP GETTING BETTER

IMPACT ON WORLD

STAY ONE STEP AHEAD

CHALLENGES

THE GROVE
CONSULTANTS INTERNATIONAL

The 5 Bold Steps Vision® Canvas was originally designed by David Sibbet.

61

ING EN NL

Login

Home About us ING in Society Investor relations Newsroom Careers Products & Services

Purpose & Strategy

Our purpose

+ Profile & Fast facts
+ Our stories
Purpose & Strategy
ING Values
Diversity and Inclusion
+ Corporate Governance
+ Compliance
Our online magazine - ing.world
+ Annual reporting suite

We believe all sustainable progress is driven by people with the imagination and determination to improve their future and the futures of those around them. We empower people and organizations to realize their own vision for a better future – however modest or grand. Our purpose therefore is: Empowering people to stay a step ahead in life and in business.

Clear and easy
Banking doesn't have to be difficult and time consuming. Less is more. It's all about clear products, plain language, fair prices, and simple processes. That saves both time and money.

Anytime, anywhere
We work to get our services where our customers are. Banking should be possible anytime and anywhere.

Empower
The best financial decisions are informed decisions. Customers want relevant, up-to-date information at their fingertips. They need to understand their choices, and the implications, both today and for the future.

Keep getting better
Life and business are about moving forward. We will keep looking for new ways to make things better with new ideas, new solutions, and new approaches to make things easier for our customers. That way, we can all stay, a step ahead.

ING USED THE 5 BOLD STEPS AS THE FOUNDATION FOR WHAT THEY COMMUNICATE TO THEIR CLIENTS.

ALONG WITH THE FIRST DRAFT OF THE VISION, VISUAL NOTES WERE TAKEN DURING THE MEETING. THEY NOW HAVE A PROMINENT SPOT IN THE OFFICE SO EVERYONE CAN GET INSPIRED.

A VISION **ON ONE PAGE**

When our new CEO, Ralph Hamers, came on board the company was ready for a bold new strategy. Banks had emerged from the financial crisis to find themselves facing a whole new raft of fintech competitors. At the same time, seamless digital experiences from companies like Amazon and Spotify had raised the customer-expectation bar for banks as well.

After a thorough strategic review, we had a plan of 250 pages. But how could we condense that down to something that would inspire employees throughout the bank? Could we make sure everyone communicated consistently about the strategy?

We put together a team from across Strategy, Internal and External Communications, Investor Relations, and Human Resources. Using the 5 Bold Steps Vision®, we were able to co-create our "strategy on a page," linking the purpose and vision to clear strategic priorities. It provided clear direction and ensured that everyone across the bank would interpret and explain the strategy consistently. That strategy on a page still guides us today.

Dorothy Hill
VP of Strategy,
ING Bank

63

TOOL **COVER STORY VISION**

Original created by David Sibbet, The Grove Consultants International

What is the most amazing future you see for your company (and yourself)? Who has the boldest vision ever? Imagine how you will appear on magazine covers. What's the word on the street? Creating a cover story will help you get into a future state of mind.

PERSONAL

explore your vision

± 45 MIN

pressure cooker

3–5

people per group

For more information on the cover story, read: *Visual Meetings* by David Sibbet

WHAT THEY'LL WRITE ABOUT YOU

The Cover Story Vision® Canvas challenges you and your team to project yourselves in the future: how will the world respond to what you have accomplished at that time. Mind you, this tool will (probably) not provide you with a turnkey vision. But it will challenge you to think beyond the realm of the known and safe. Why else would there be a story about your company in one of the world's bestselling magazines? This canvas will provide you with plenty of material you can use when formulating your actual vision. Furthermore, because it's tactile and visual, the vision canvas will elicit tons of feedback.

MAGAZINE (OR EZINE)

To get started, huddle as a team (or, even better, multiple teams) and have a thoughtful discussion about what magazine you'd like to be featured in once you've achieved your vision. It's important to have this conversation, as the tone, voice, and readership of the particular magazine make a big difference. Whatever you decide on, you'll find this conversation fun and stimulating.

HEADLINES

Once you've decided on your magazine, move on to the headline. What are the biggest, most inspirational headlines you can think of? How are you changing the world (or at least your organization) with your idea? This article will talk about your major achievement, but will also recount the story of where you started and how you got to your a-ha moment. What's the bottom line, the facts and figures that support the headline? Capture those as well.

As in any magazine article, there's going to be some kind of interview component. What questions will be asked? How will you answer? How will your skeptics show up? What are people saying on social media?

Now comes the fun part! Draw your story. Magazines are very visual. Make your magazine cover story visual as well. Who or what's on the cover? How will this grab the reader (i.e., your team)? ∎

COVER
Make the cover really jump out. Don't limit yourself to just sticky notes. Draw or cut and paste pictures from magazines.

HEADLINES
Put down some eye-popping headlines. What would make people stop in their tracks and read the article?

BOTTOM LINE
What does it all boil down to? What has been achieved according to the article?

COVER STORY VISION® CANVAS

DESIGN A BETTER BUSINESS

MAGAZINE COVER | BIG HEADLINES | THE INTERVIEW | THE BOTTOM LINE

BIGGEST CHANGE EVER

QUOTE

CATCHY QUOTE

IS THIS FOR REAL?

@

#HASHTAGS

@

TWEETS

INSTAGRAM PICTURES

© THE GROVE CONSULTANTS INTERNATIONAL
THIS VERSION BY DESIGNABETTERBUSINESS.COM

GROVE

The Cover Story Vision® Canvas was originally designed by David Sibbet

SOCIAL MEDIA
Use social media and Instagram photos to add more flavor to your story. What would get retweeted?

QUOTES
Don't just mention the positive quotes. Ask yourself how your competition and critics will respond.

INTERVIEW
Who is telling your story in the interview? Is it someone you work with? Your customer? What is the interview about?

65

CHECKLIST

☐ You shared your cover story with your colleagues.

☐ You made your vision concrete with a engaging and visual cover.

☐ You stepped out of your (and your company's) comfort zone.

☐ You created a vision that can be realized in 5 years.

NEXT STEPS

> Make your cover story concrete by using 5 Bold Steps Vision® Canvas.

> Check how this vision resonates with others.

VISION HACKS

ASK THE CUSTOMER

Look at your vision from a fresh perspective with new insights. One way to do that is to ask some of your customers to help you with the 5 Bold Steps Vision® Canvas. What do they expect you to do? What is important to them? You'll be amazed how honored customers are when you invite them to think about your future!

VISION MOODBOARD

Collect a bunch of magazines and pass out scissors and glue to everyone on your team. What would happen if you would make a mood board about your vision? You can use the structure of the 5 Bold Steps Vision® Canvas (vision statement in the middle, themes surrounding, 5 steps + values underneath). This provides excellent conversation material and a beautiful "painting" of the first steps toward your future vision.

VISION MAGAZINE (COVER STORY)

Have your team work on a vision magazine. Collect what people think. What is their vision? What themes surface?

Design a cover that reflects your future: the big impact you will have on the world. Publish and distribute the magazine throughout your company. The best fire starter ever. (See also "Cover Story Vision®" on page 64.)

START WITH STATEMENTS AND THEMES

Another way of working with the 5 Bold Steps Vision® Canvas is starting with the vision statement already filled out, including the supporting themes. The focus of the teams can be shifted to an in-depth exploration of the themes. Each team also needs to define the 5 bold steps for themselves. See the ING example on page 60 to read more about their experience with this approach.

START FROM SCRATCH

One way of going at it is to give your teams a blank canvas and see what they come up with. Get together and discuss and sync the canvases. This is a great way to get additional insights and design a better vision.

SHARE YOUR VISION (VISUALLY)

The 5 Bold Steps Vision® Canvas is a great blueprint for a concise story on stage or as a visual representation (see the ING case on page 60).

The best way to build up your story: start with the vision statement; show how it is substantiated by the vision themes (rank them). Explain how each theme will show up. Finish by explaining what steps you need to take to get there.

TOOL **DESIGN CRITERIA**

FOCUS

define design criteria

± 45 MIN

session

3–5

people per group

Whether you're designing a new value proposition, business model, or even an entire strategy for the future, design criteria form the principles and benchmarks of the change you're after. Design criteria are not formulated from thin air. Rather, design criteria incorporate information from your business, vision, customer research, cultural and economic context, and mindset that you have formed along the way.

WHAT ARE DESIGN CRITERIA?

Don't think of these criteria as simply features of your idea. They can and should be more than that. For example, a design criteria coming from your vision might be that your business must contribute to a greener planet. Or, maybe you want your customers to feel delighted; this is another design criterion. Does your new business idea need to generate a certain amount of revenue within three years? Chalk that up to more design criteria. In short, design criteria are there to make it easy to determine if you are on the right track.

CREATING THE DESIGN CRITERIA

The design criteria you capture will likely first come from the vision you've formulated with your team. You'll find that some of the elements in that vision are so important that they are nonnegotiable. Yes, that also means that some elements are a bit more flexible (maybe not totally flexible). To find the most important elements in your vision, use the "MoSCoW" method: categorize every element under "Must," "Should," "Could," or "Won't." This will help you prioritize.

Now comes the easy part (well, maybe not easy, but doable): sort all of the nonnegotiable elements into the "Must" section of your design criteria and the rest into "Should" (if they are important) or the "Could" sections (if they would be nice to have).

Your vision makes up only part of the story when it comes to defining your design criteria. Other elements could include revenue, or your place in the market, or the impact you'll have, or the public perception of your company. Once you've come up with this list, add these to the "Could," "Should," or "Must" sections based on their respective priorities.

Once you've started this exercise, you might find that you need to adjust your vision slightly. This may prompt you to take a different direction. If that's the case, adjust the design criteria so that they match the new direction. As you continue to evolve your point of view, you may need to add or update your design criteria. ■

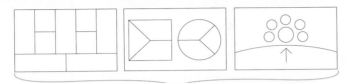

Use insights from the Business Model Canvas, VP Canvas, and Vision Canvas as input for the design criteria.

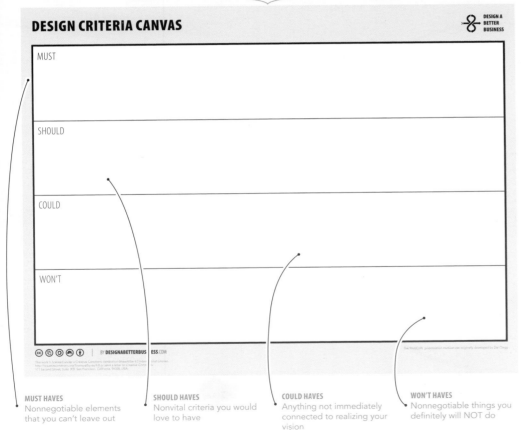

DESIGN CRITERIA CANVAS

DESIGN A BETTER BUSINESS

MUST

SHOULD

COULD

WON'T

MUST HAVES
Nonnegotiable elements that you can't leave out

SHOULD HAVES
Nonvital criteria you would love to have

COULD HAVES
Anything not immediately connected to realizing your vision

WON'T HAVES
Nonnegotiable things you definitely will NOT do

DOWNLOAD
Download the Design Criteria Canvas from www.designabetterbusiness.com

69

CHECKLIST

☐ You have sanitized the design criteria by removing unimportant criteria. Use, e.g., voting.

☐ You have spent time with your team to sharpen and quantify your criteria.

☐ You've linked up your design criteria with your vision.

NEXT STEPS

> Quantify your design criteria: make them S.M.A.R.T. (specific, measurable, achievable, relevant, time-bound).

> Revisit your design criteria. Do they still make sense?

EXAMPLE **DESIGN CRITERIA** ING BANK

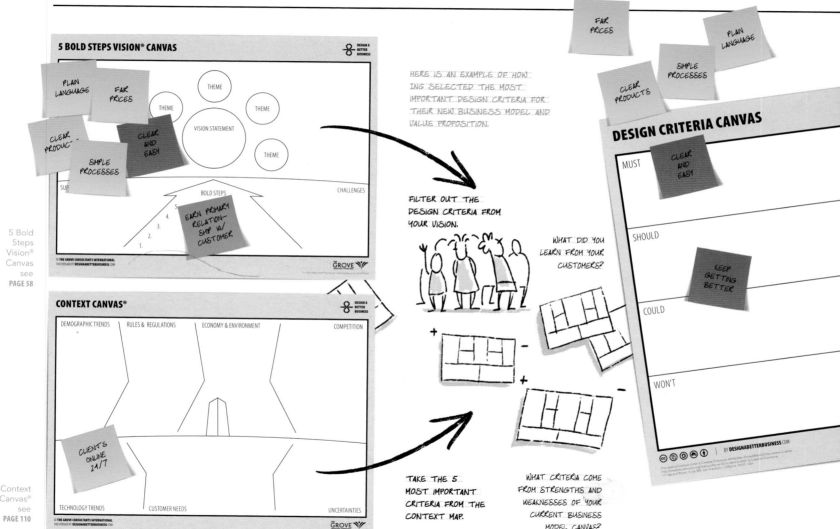

5 BOLD STEPS VISION® CANVAS

DESIGN A BETTER BUSINESS

- PLAIN LANGUAGE
- FAIR PRICES
- CLEAR PRODUCTS
- CLEAR AND EASY
- SIMPLE PROCESSES

THEME
THEME
THEME
THEME
THEME

VISION STATEMENT

SUP...   CHALLENGES

BOLD STEPS
5.
4.
3.
2.
1.

EARN PRIMARY RELATION-SHIP W/ CUSTOMER

© THE GROVE CONSULTANTS INTERNATIONAL
THIS VERSION BY DESIGNABETTERBUSINESS.COM

GROVE

5 Bold Steps Vision® Canvas see PAGE 58

HERE IS AN EXAMPLE OF HOW ING SELECTED THE MOST IMPORTANT DESIGN CRITERIA FOR THEIR NEW BUSINESS MODEL AND VALUE PROPOSITION.

FILTER OUT THE DESIGN CRITERIA FROM YOUR VISION.

WHAT DID YOU LEARN FROM YOUR CUSTOMERS?

TAKE THE 5 MOST IMPORTANT CRITERIA FROM THE CONTEXT MAP.

WHAT CRITERIA COME FROM STRENGTHS AND WEAKNESSES OF YOUR CURRENT BUSINESS MODEL CANVAS?

CONTEXT CANVAS®

DESIGN A BETTER BUSINESS

DEMOGRAPHIC TRENDS   RULES & REGULATIONS   ECONOMY & ENVIRONMENT   COMPETITION

CLIENTS ONLINE 24/7

TECHNOLOGY TRENDS   CUSTOMER NEEDS   UNCERTAINTIES

© THE GROVE CONSULTANTS INTERNATIONAL
THIS VERSION BY DESIGNABETTERBUSINESS.COM

GROVE

Context Canvas® see PAGE 110

DESIGN CRITERIA CANVAS

- FAIR PRICES
- PLAIN LANGUAGE
- SIMPLE PROCESSES
- CLEAR PRODUCTS

MUST   — CLEAR AND EASY

SHOULD

COULD — KEEP GETTING BETTER

WON'T

BY DESIGNABETTERBUSINESS.COM

WHERE WILL THE DESIGN CRITERIA SHOW UP? IN THE BUSINESS MODEL? IN THE VALUE PROPOSITION?

HOW DOES THIS TRANSLATE?

DESIGN CRITERIA WILL HELP STRUCTURE BRAINSTORM SESSIONS AND HELP YOU MAKE EDUCATED DECISIONS IN YOUR DAILY JOB.

yes   NO

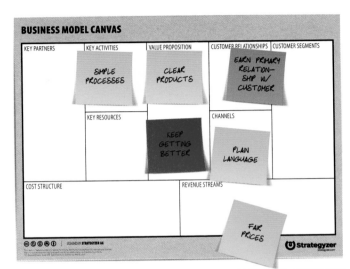

BUSINESS MODEL CANVAS

KEY PARTNERS	KEY ACTIVITIES	VALUE PROPOSITION	CUSTOMER RELATIONSHIPS	CUSTOMER SEGMENTS

SIMPLE PROCESSES

CLEAR PRODUCTS

EARN PRIMARY RELATION— SHIP W/ CUSTOMER

KEY RESOURCES

KEEP GETTING BETTER

CHANNELS

PLAIN LANGUAGE

COST STRUCTURE   REVENUE STREAMS

FAIR PRICES

Business Model Canvas see **PAGE 116**

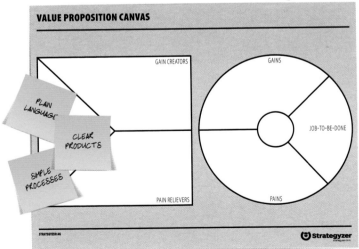

VALUE PROPOSITION CANVAS

GAIN CREATORS

GAINS

PLAIN LANGUAGE

CLEAR PRODUCTS

SIMPLE PROCESSES

JOB-TO-BE-DONE

PAIN RELIEVERS

PAINS

Value Proposition canvas see **PAGE 106**

INTRO **STORYTELLING**

As humans, we tell stories every day. We use stories to explain, explore, engage, and persuade others. During the design journey, you will have many moments when you need to tell a good story. And, just like the other fundamentals of your strategy, good stories can be designed.

IT'S HUMAN NATURE

We are all born storytellers. Some of us make a living telling stories. Others have allowed their storytelling skills to be buried by work or school. The medium does not make storytelling nor can it be replaced by slides, emails, or spreadsheets. Though these tools can be used as canvases to tell a good story, you must first design the story you want to tell.

STORY

For as much as we're all born storytellers, however, not everyone can aspire to be the next Hemingway. But there are tricks to telling great stories! Stories can be designed. And here, we are talking about a broad category of storytelling, from person-to-person chats, to cool TED-style talks, to sales pitches, and even boardroom presentations. These are all stories.

SHARED KNOWLEDGE

Stories are how we have shared knowledge and information since the dawn of humanity. Our brains are shaped by storytelling. Today, stories are still the most powerful way to transfer ideas and beliefs. We live and breathe stories. Perhaps in our daily lives this may be less obvious, but passing knowledge still is a vital skill in our survival toolbox.

ENGAGE

Neurological research shows that the same areas are activated in the brain of a listener as in the brain of the storyteller! Because stories engage emotions and other senses, the listener can "relive" the moment and really learn from it. That is something numbers on a page can never do. In their popular book *Made to Stick*, Chip and Dan Heath make this point right up front when they recall the popular urban legend (i.e., story) about "the guy" who wakes up in a bathtub filled with ice only to find out that one of his kidneys has been harvested. Remember that one? The reason this engages us is that, as the Heath brothers point out, it's simple, unexpected, concrete, credible, and emotional.

DEATH BY POWERPOINT

So, if we're such natural storytellers, why do we still bore each other to death with PowerPoint? It's because most of us have never really learned how to design stories. Even in school, we were mostly instructed in academic writing and presentation, which is often supposed to be an unemotional, objective, and efficient way of sharing information, rather than engaging.

THE STORYTELLING CANVAS

We created the Storytelling Canvas to make it easier to construct a story that people care to listen to. The PowerPoint presentations you give probably lack the emotional depth and impact you want to build in a story. However, the stories we design can be told through the medium of PowerPoint!

Like the other tools in this book, the story canvas allows you to collectively design stories that resonate: by harnessing visual, engaging, insightful, controlled, and inspiring elements. ∎

For information on presenting visual stories, read: *Resonate* by Nancy Duarte

STORY WITH A BIG **S**

Story has played a significant role in all cultures but its adoption into professional cultures has been painfully slow. That's because it's easier to give a cut-and-dried report than a well-crafted presentation that incorporates stories.

I know "story" has become a buzzword, but that's just story with a little "s." What I'm talking about is story with a big "S": the art of communicating your ideas using a persuasive narrative structure. It's a story that has a beginning, middle, and end, and uses dramatic principles of tension and contrast to move your audience to a different state of thinking, feeling, and acting.

73

Nancy Duarte
Author, Principal at Duarte, Inc.

TOOL **STORYTELLING CANVAS**

Created by Thirty-X

What you'll need to understand when designing your story is that there must be a goal. What do you want your audience to know, feel, or do afterward? Your goal needs to be quite selective: you can make only a few points in your story!

TANGIBLE

build a story

± 45 MIN

pressure cooker

3–5

people per group

YOUR AUDIENCE

In addition to knowing what you want to achieve, you need to understand who your audience is. What do they care about? Why should they listen to your story? Different audiences need different stories; one size does not fit all! You might even use the right side of the Value Proposition Canvas or a persona canvas to map the audience. Test your assumptions: while designing and telling the story, revisit your persona, and update it with what you learned.

BEFORE AND AFTER

In order to be meaningful, your story should change your audience in some way. Their beliefs, emotions, or knowledge should be transformed by the time you are finished.

How did your audience feel about your goal before they heard your story? Do they care about it now? What would you like them to think about once you're through? Trying to define it from the audience's perspective is key.

Try to come up with arguments that may change their minds, and make sure you have a list of rational, emotional, and ethical points. What is your "proof"? Do you have examples? Anecdotes? Find the ones that will resonate with your audience.

THE EMOTIONAL ROLLER COASTER

A good story is not a flat line; it has ups and downs. Now it's time to consider how you might design your own emotional roller coaster. Where is your climax moment? That is the moment you want to use to make your main point.

THREE ACTS

Like most good stories, the story canvas is divided into three parts: a beginning, a middle, and an end. The beginning is where you'll set the scene. The middle is where you'll put the meat of the story. And the end is where you'll want to leave your audience: in a new state of mind. Divide the arguments, examples, and anecdotes. And, for good measure, insert a bit of humor over the three acts. Now have a look at the emotional roller coaster again. Did you follow your idea? Or do you want to change it?

Another thing to consider while organizing the pieces of your story is to accommodate different styles of listening. Cater to the rational, organized listeners first; they want to get a clear picture of what you are talking about in order to decide whether they want to listen at all. But don't forget the others. Emotional listeners are more patient, but they do need emotion or they will get bored. Now that all this is filled in, you have the blueprint of your story. ■

SUBJECT
What is the title and subject of your story?

GOAL
What is the goal you want to achieve? Why are you telling the story?

ENERGY
How do you envision your audience's emotional roller coaster during the story? When will they have the most energy?

AUDIENCE
Who is your audience? Map them as a persona!

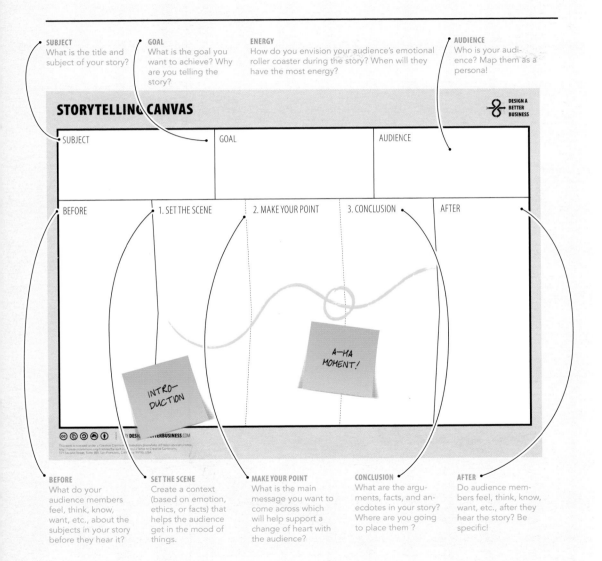

BEFORE
What do your audience members feel, think, know, want, etc., about the subjects in your story before they hear it?

SET THE SCENE
Create a context (based on emotion, ethics, or facts) that helps the audience get in the mood of things.

MAKE YOUR POINT
What is the main message you want to come across which will help support a change of heart with the audience?

CONCLUSION
What are the arguments, facts, and anecdotes in your story? Where are you going to place them ?

AFTER
Do audience members feel, think, know, want, etc., after they hear the story? Be specific!

DOWNLOAD
Download the Storytelling Canvas from www.designabetterbusiness.com

CHECKLIST

☐ You have a clear idea of what the audience thinks and feels.

☐ You have prepared clear arguments to make your point.

☐ You have one strong conclusion to end your story with.

☐ You know how to manage the energy during your story.

☐ You know the possible booby traps you may encounter and have a plan B.

NEXT STEPS

▶ Test your story.

▶ Make the visuals.

▶ Experiment with the pace and energy.

TOOL **TELLING THE VISUAL STORY** OF AUDI

A team at Audi needed to obtain buy-in within the company to move forward with an idea for the future. The car world is changing rapidly, and it was necessary to convince the company quickly. This was an important story to tell. Here's how they approached it.

STORYTELLING CANVAS

DESIGN A BETTER BUSINESS

SUBJECT — THE FUTURE OF TRANS-PORTATION

GOAL — GET THEM ONBOARD

AUDIENCE — COMPANY LEADER-SHIP

BEFORE — BUSINESS AS USUAL

1. SET THE SCENE — DRONES · PRIVATE LIFE IN- AND OUTSIDE CAR · EMERGING TECH · MORE CARS ON THE ROAD · SELF-DRIVING CARS

2. MAKE YOUR POINT — OPTIONS EXIST OUTSIDE THE CAR · FREEDOM OF CHOICE

3. CONCLUSION

AFTER — INVEST IN NEW IDEAS

STRONG BRAND

1 FILL IN THE CANVAS AS DESCRIBED ON PAGES 74–75. MAKE SURE YOU COVER ALL AREAS.

2 SIT TOGETHER WITH VISUAL ARTIST TO PLOT THE STICKY NOTES FROM THE CANVAS ON A (BIG) PIECE OF PAPER. MAKE A FIRST SKETCH: ARE ALL THE BUILDING BLOCKS THERE? IS IT THE RIGHT LOOK AND FEEL?

3 FINALIZE THE SKETCH. IT WILL BE A GREAT CONVERSATION PIECE TO SUBSTANTIATE AND SHARE YOUR STORY. AUDI OPTED FOR 1 BIG PICTURE. YOU COULD ALSO BUILD A SERIES OF IMAGES, AN ANIMATION, OR A SLIDE DECK USING THE CANVAS.

STORYTELLING HACKS

THE A-HA MOMENT

The audience's a-ha moment is something they have to create for themselves. It needs to occur as a spark in their brains. Think of it as a joke. You can set it up and make the joke, but over-explain it and nobody will laugh. Your main point should be an a-ha moment. Don't try to over-explain it.

WARNING! If you are pitching to an investor, the customers of your product are not necessarily the audience of your story. Your investor has a totally different set of needs than your customers.

USE SPEAKER NOTES

When you are telling a story in public, use speaker notes. That way, you don't have to tell the story exactly as it appears on the slides – and you'll appear more natural.

TRYOUTS

Standup comedians do multiple tryouts to make their act a success. And a tryout is not the same thing as rehearsing the story in a mirror. That is just the first step.

Find some actual people to listen to your story. See when they are engaged and when they get confused. When do you lose their interest?

USE PROPS

Just as you'll need to accommodate different listening styles, you'll also need to take into account the differing ways your audience absorbs information. Some people are more visually oriented than others. Props will help hammer home your points while providing them with something to relate to.

THE END IS REALLY THE END

When you finish the story, really finish it. Staying on stage and continuing to talk about unrelated things confuses your audience. Think about this: they will remember the last thing you say. What will that be?

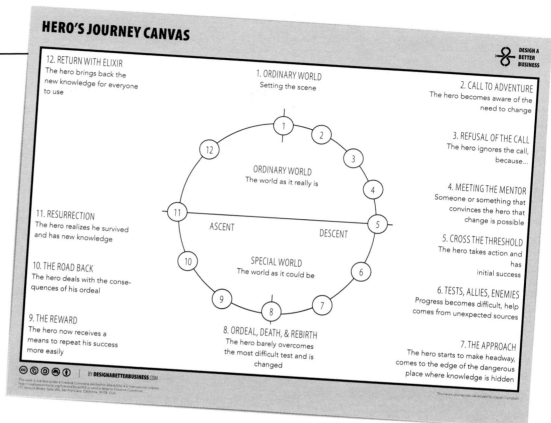

HERO'S JOURNEY CANVAS

12. RETURN WITH ELIXIR
The hero brings back the new knowledge for everyone to use

1. ORDINARY WORLD
Setting the scene

2. CALL TO ADVENTURE
The hero becomes aware of the need to change

3. REFUSAL OF THE CALL
The hero ignores the call, because...

4. MEETING THE MENTOR
Someone or something that convinces the hero that change is possible

5. CROSS THE THRESHOLD
The hero takes action and has initial success

6. TESTS, ALLIES, ENEMIES
Progress becomes difficult, help comes from unexpected sources

7. THE APPROACH
The hero starts to make headway, comes to the edge of the dangerous place where knowledge is hidden

8. ORDEAL, DEATH, & REBIRTH
The hero barely overcomes the most difficult test and is changed

9. THE REWARD
The hero now receives a means to repeat his success more easily

10. THE ROAD BACK
The hero deals with the consequences of his ordeal

11. RESURRECTION
The hero realizes he survived and has new knowledge

ORDINARY WORLD
The world as it really is

ASCENT   DESCENT

SPECIAL WORLD
The world as it could be

HAVE A PLAN B

Telling a story can be scary, and it won't always go as planned. Come up with a few "plan B" actions beforehand that you can use when a point does not come across. Use the rescue cards to plan ahead!

THINKING YOU'RE THE STAR

When you are telling the story, you're not telling it for you. You're telling it for the audience. Make sure they are the star of the story.

CULTURAL REFERENCE

If you speak to a different audience, and certainly if you tell your story in a different culture, you're in for a shock. The examples and jokes that worked so well before may not resonate at all.
Using American football metaphors in Europe doesn't work. And just try talking about cricket outside of the Commonwealth . . . Test your stories before you tell them!

HERO'S JOURNEY CANVAS

Every movie hero's fate follows a certain path: everything starts out fine, and then he encounters a great setback – usually in the middle of the movie. This historical way of telling a (hero) story is a perfect guidline to follow. Use the Hero's Journey Canvas to plot all the building blocks. ■

DOWNLOAD
Download the Hero's Journey Canvas from www.designabetterbusiness.com

For more background, read:
The Hero with a Thousand Faces by Joseph Campbell

YOU NOW HAVE...

> DRAFTED YOUR VISION
> AS **A RALLYING CRY**   P58

> YOUR FIRST SET OF
> **DESIGN CRITERIA**   P68

> DESIGNED YOUR STORY TO
> **CREATE IMPACT**   P74

NEXT STEPS

> **OBSERVE & QUESTION**   P88
> Meet (potential) customers.

> **GO OUT OF THE BUILDING**   P102
> and test your assumptions
> on vision.

> **UNDERSTAND YOUR VALUE**   P106
> How do you currently add value
> for your customers?

> **UNDERSTAND YOUR CONTEXT**   P110
> What is the context you currently
> (want to) operate in?

RECAP

BE **A REBEL.**

A VISION IS A RALLYING CRY FOR YOU AND YOUR TEAM.

A VISION **IS NOT** A VISION STATEMENT.

DESIGN CRITERIA ARE THE **BENCHMARKS OF CHANGE.**

USE STORYTELLING TO **INSPIRE AND SCALE.**

81

YEAH, WELL, THAT'S JUST YOUR OPINION, MAN.

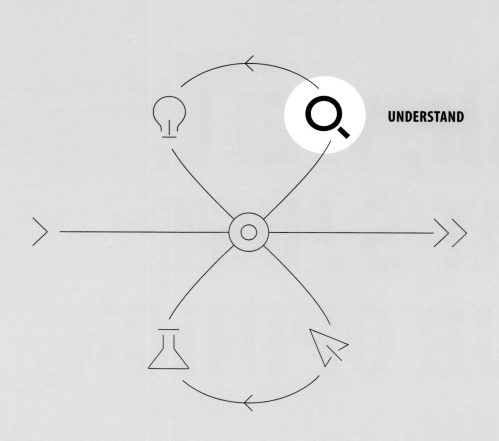

UNDERSTAND

THE DESIGN JOURNEY **UNDERSTAND**

UNDERSTAND **YOUR CUSTOMER**

UNDERSTAND **YOUR CONTEXT**

UNDERSTAND **YOUR BUSINESS**

SEEK TO **UNDERSTAND**

Whether you're designing a change for your company or a new product for someone else, the things you develop are for people, inside or outside your organization. Beyond these people exists a broader context as well as your business model. Understand these, and design for success.

WHERE ARE YOU NOW?

As a designer, you must have a complete understanding of the world in which you do business. This is true whether you're in a startup, a for-profit, or a non-profit. You must know your customer, your overarching economic context (trends, regulations, competition, etc.), and the internal mechanics of your own business. All these comprise your company's DNA.

Why is this important? The biggest and most effective business changes, strategies, and innovations come from finding the answers hidden in the noise. These may exist outside of your comfort zone. In some cases, it is for good reason. But how will you know what's out there unless you take the road less traveled and have a look for yourself?

Mastering understanding is the secret sauce of great design. Designers actively leave their comfort zones, exploring and experimenting with things that others may judge as "ineffective" or "useless." And when they spend time outside of their comfort zones, designers actually create larger and more diverse comfort zones for themselves. Their picture of the world grows richer,

and they are more likely to find new and exciting perspectives which inform their points of view.

But exploration is not just about creating new, cool innovations. Exploring your context and your business model will help illuminate your business's underlying strengths and weaknesses. For example, understanding why your customers also buy from your competitors deepens your understanding of your own business. In fact, your customers' needs almost certainly are not what you think they are! Deep exploration of your customers, context, and business will bring fresh insights. This, in turn, will give you a better sense of how you might make the future work for you.

WHAT'S YOUR EXCUSE?

It may be difficult to get out and explore. It's frightening to leave the comfort of your office building, where everyone agrees and everyone is "right". After all, the internal reports look great. This is especially true for large companies: the need to execute perfectly leads to a disproportionately strong current perspective. It becomes easier to execute when you can divide the world quickly into things that "fit" and those that don't – into "right" and "wrong." This attitude is easily and dangerously attached to reputation. People who are always right are revered; the ones who dare to be wrong are ostracized. But ask yourself: would you rather be right, or successful? The real cost of exploring usually is minimal: it often boils down to time. Nothing more. Nothing less. To a designer, a situation where everyone agrees and has the same opinion is a huge warning sign. There should be a balance between business as usual and exploring the world outside the business.

DON'T STRESS!

It's normal to feel uncertainty and stress while transitioning to this new explorative approach. Gathering conflicting and qualitative data requires a new way of thinking. It's vital to defer any analysis and judgment until after you've taken the time to simply observe. It'll be very tempting to try to immediately fit new information into the existing perspective.

Over time, you'll learn how to work with the new insights and information. You'll develop an instinct for going beyond the comfort zone, balancing comfort with being uncomfortable. You'll experience a constant flow of new information about how the world is affecting your business as well as how your customers behave, what their struggles are, what they like and don't like. The better (and more) you observe your customers, your context, and your business, the more you'll inform your own point of view, and the better your design journey will be. It's that simple. ■

UNDERSTAND YOUR CUSTOMER

Ultimately, the most important thing to understand is your customers. If you don't know what value means to them, you can't stay relevant to them. Assuming you know your customers is really dangerous. Get out of the building and find out what their needs are. You won't be sorry you did!

UNDERSTAND YOUR CONTEXT

It's also necessary to understand the field you're playing on. What are the key drivers that are influencing your business? What are the trends? What are the expected changes in economic and political climate? What are the big unknowns? Who else is playing on the field with you? Who are the competitors, and what new players exist? The world is changing. As a designer, you'll need to change with it.

UNDERSTAND YOUR BUSINESS

To make the changes you seek you must intimately understand how your business works. How do you create value? Who is your customer? This may seem like a no-brainer, but in practice it's not always clear exactly how the engine of any business actually creates, delivers, and captures value. If you can grasp and define how your business works, you can also unpack other business models, such as those of the competition. This is not so that you can blindly follow competitors: it's to understand how (and if) they solve problems in other ways.

MASTER **OBSERVATION**

Observation will influence the way you think about your customers and will help you understand them better. It will inform your point of view and help to validate or invalidate your assumptions. But, like anything, there are right ways and not-so-right ways to observe the world around you.

Think about this: you sit down to a cup of coffee or tea. How would you open your sugar packet? Okay, feel free to read on. We'll get back to the sugar packet in a moment.

Observation will influence the way you think about your customers and will help you understand them better. Observation will change the way you innovate. But, just like anything, there are right ways and not-so-right ways to observe the world around you.

As you watch your subjects (your potential customers), your goal is to discover their latent needs, desires, and ambitions – the kinds of things they may not even know they need or want. These are often things that people would not be able to tell you they want. Does the runner run just to get fit? Perhaps he is running so that he doesn't feel guilty eating pizza on the weekends. Watch him for a while and on different occasions, and you just might find out.

BE A FLY ON THE WALL

A good way to think about observation is to act like a fly on the wall, observing people in their natural habitat, finding the key moments in their lives. The decisions your customers make on a daily basis are the important ones. After all, it's their decisions that lead them not only to do what they do today, but also will affect what they choose to do tomorrow. And, just as a researcher wouldn't tell a test subject that a placebo is a just a placebo, you also shouldn't tell your subjects what you are trying to learn from them. Just watch for a while. You want people to act naturally and unconsciously, as if you're not there.

DON'T GO EMPTY-HANDED

Before you venture out to observe your customers, you'll need to do a bit of planning. First off, define the subject of your observation before you go. What people and activities or behaviors do you plan to observe? Preselect the environment or location you want to observe.

Where will your customers be at different times of the day? This, of course, is critical as people engage in different activities throughout the day. If you're keen on observing people exercising, for instance, plan to go the park, gym, track, etc., in the morning and evening. Don't forget to bring materials to record your findings as notes, pictures, sketches, and videos. It would be shame to forget about key moments. Or worse, not be able to share them with your team.

Finally, when you start exploring and observing, leave your point of view and assumptions at the door. Don't judge, just soak it in. And, the answer to the sugar packet question: you shake it before tearing it open. ■

THINK LIKE A **DESIGNER**

You can learn to think and work like a designer. It is about switching between different perspectives to find solutions. As a designer, the three most important perspectives are your own perspective, your business's perspective, and your customer's or society's perspective. When my team engages with design jobs, we need to know the customer's perspective. I want to ensure we are on the same page. Part of that perspective includes an understanding that your customers are investing time, money, and effort to make money. If we don't share this perspective there is little point to joining each other on a design journey.

Design thinking is more relevant today than it ever has been. Increasingly, it's becoming more important to design and to be agile, flexible, and adaptable. The world is changing faster and faster. As part of that change, people have more access to information – and share more than ever before. Whereas knowledge used to be the most important quality in business, today, the ability to search for and find opportunities in uncertainty has supplanted knowledge as the most important quality of business people.

DON'T GO EMPTY-HANDED
BRING MATERIALS TO RECORD, NOTE, TAPE, AND SKETCH YOUR FINDINGS. THAT WAY YOU'LL REMEMBER EVERY SMALL DETAIL MORE EASILY. AND IT MAKES IT EASIER TO SHARE THEM WITH YOUR TEAM.

87

Ad van Berlo
Chairman,
VanBerlo Group

MASTER **QUESTIONING**

Along with observation, questioning is paramount to understanding what your customers care about and why. Questioning will lead to a richer picture of your customers' lives and will inform your point of view. And as with observation, there are a few simple rules to follow to get the insights you're looking for.

QUESTION WHAT YOU SEE

Observing your customers in their natural habitats will tell you a lot about what they do, what they care about, and what decisions they make. However, observing your customers won't necessarily tell you why they make the decisions they make. In fact, observing your customers without questioning them will eventually lead to compounding assumptions.

In the previous example of the runner who longs for pizza, you would need to observe that person for a long time and over many days before you get to the core of why he runs everyday. You might even generate new assumptions based on different routes he takes. However, if you were to stop him or meet him and ask questions about his lifestyle, you would very likely begin to deduce what running (and pizza) mean to him. Added to the data you compiled while watching him run, through questioning you would create a much richer picture – one

that would certainly provide you with a deeper understanding of why he runs in the first place.

ASKING THE RIGHT QUESTIONS

It's not about the answers you get, but about asking the right questions. The right questions will always lead to interesting and telling conversations. So, how might we ask the "right" questions? When you really want to understand the current situation, avoid yes/no questions (i.e., close-ended questions) as well as product mentions: you'll have better conversations and will ultimately stand to get to the heart of what really matters.

Whenever possible, observe and question the same customers. Observe them first, and learn through their actions instead of their opinions. Then ask them questions about the choices they make and why they make them, including why they bother at all to do what they are doing. Then watch them again.

In the aforementioned example, you could ask the runner whether he prefers pepperoni or Hawaiian-style pizza. However, you could also simply watch what he orders (but if you're trying to understand why he prefers one over the other, you'll have to talk to him).

RULES OF THUMB

- People will lie to you if they think it's what you want to hear.
- Opinions are worthless. Opinions change based on context and offer no proof of what's real.
- People know what their problems are, but they don't know how to solve those problems.
- Some problems don't actually matter. To a hammer everything looks like a nail. But not every problem requires a solution.
- Watching someone do a task will show you where the problems and inefficiencies are, not where the customer thinks they are. ■

SOME BAD QUESTIONS:

(fixable by asking about their life as it is)

✕ DO YOU THINK THIS IS A GOOD IDEA?

> ONLY THE MARKET CAN TELL IF YOUR IDEA IS GOOD. THE REST IS OPINION.

✕ WOULD YOU BUY A PRODUCT WHICH DID X?

> THE ANSWER TO A QUESTION LIKE THIS IS ALMOST ALWAYS "YES."

✕ HOW MUCH WOULD YOU PAY FOR X?

> AS BAD AS THE LAST ONE AND LIKELY TO TRICK YOU BECAUSE THE NUMBER MAKES IT FEEL RIGOROUS AND TRUTHY.

SOME GOOD QUESTIONS:

✓ WHY DO YOU BOTHER?

> GREAT FOR GETTING FROM THE PERCEIVED PROBLEM TO THE REAL ONE!

✓ WHAT ARE THE IMPLICATIONS OF THAT?

> HELPS DISTINGUISH BETWEEN REAL PROBLEMS AND ANNOYING PROBLEMS.

✓ TALK ME THROUGH THE LAST TIME THAT HAPPENED.

> YOUR HIGH SCHOOL WRITING TEACHER MAY HAVE TOLD YOU THAT GOOD STORIES ARE MEANT TO "SHOW, NOT TELL."

For more background, read:
The Mom Test by Rob Fitzpatrick

EVERYBODY **LIES**

People say: Don't ask your mom whether your business is a good idea or not. Your mom will lie to you (just 'cuz she loves you). In fact: everyone you'll ask will lie (at least a little). The point is you shouldn't ask anyone this question, because it's useless. It's not their responsibility to show you the truth. It's your responsibility to find it.

Rob Fitzpatrick wrote *The Mom Test* after his own (bad) experience: "We'd spent 3 years building social advertising tech and run out of investor money. I'd been talking to customers full-time for months. And then I learned I'd been doing it all wrong!"

In his book he describes three simple rules to live by when asking the right questions:

1 Talk about the **customer's life** instead of your idea

2 Ask about **specifics** in the past instead of generalities or opinions about the future

3 Talk less and **listen more**

Rob Fitzpatrick
Founder at Founder Centric
Author, *The Mom Test*

89

THE CLEAR BLUE MOMENT

A team from a large manufacturing company for juvenile products spent time exploring their customers' journey. Their a-ha moment happened when they realized that the journey started much earlier than they had traditionally assumed. Parents begin planning purchases for products not at the moment of birth, but at the moment they find out they're pregnant – or even before that! Mapping this out on paper allowed the team to finally address this issue.

FIRST IMPRESSIONS

When they adopted Design Thinking, a team at a large hospital in the Netherlands decided to have a look (with their own eyes) at how people experienced visits to the hospital. They took a camera and walked the path of the patients. Besides finding out the parking garage was incredibly dark and hard to navigate, they noticed that the first thing patients saw when parking was a billboard for a fast food restaurant. Not at all what they had expected!

READ MY FILE, STUPID!

Doctors thought the biggest pain their patients felt was the long waiting lists at the doctor's office. When a doctor asked about this pain during a patient visit, the patient said, "That doesn't really bother me. But, next time I'm here for an appointment, please read my file beforehand. And my name is not Susan!"

GET STREET SMART

An insurance company assumed there was a huge gap in the market and formulated a great plan to position themselves in that gap. But first, they wanted to challenge this assumption. Two people were sent out on a scooter with a camera. They gathered as many responses from people on the street as they could in an hour. When the results were showed to the client, the unpolished "first reactions" of potential customers forced them to reconsider their assumptions.

SHOPPING PARADOX

A startup wanted to build an app that would help mothers have an easier and better experience when shopping for groceries. More insights were needed in order for the founders to know exactly what to build.

They first started a dialogue with potential customers about their grocery shopping habits. They compared these conversations with what they saw while observing the group shopping for groceries.

Although the mothers were very sure about their daily shopping routines, the truth turned out to be different! When asked, all of the mothers said they shop for healthy, versatile products. However, when they got the store, most of them abandoned their shopping lists and prioritized price and offers!

Are these little white lies? No matter. What's important is that if you're looking for valid insights, observing is as important as asking (the right question). Don't believe everything your customers say!

CLEANING GRANNY'S HOUSE?

Lowering the hourly rate for house cleaning was the key strategy of an elderly home care company. After visiting several grandmothers, it became clear that the value was in the attention grandmothers received, not in the clean house.

As a result, the company started giving away iPads to grandmothers instead. This enabled them to connect with their grandchildren, and it offered them services through the company's app.

THE TRUTH IS RIGHT IN FRONT OF YOU, IF YOU JUST CHOOSE TO SEE IT.

91

HOW DESIGN THINKING HELPS YOU TO UNDERSTAND YOUR CUSTOMER

CASE STUDY

CONNECT TO BETTER

WAVIN LOVES PLUMBERS

I COULDN'T BELIEVE BUILDING YET ANOTHER FACTORY WOULD HELP US IMPROVE BUSINESS RESULTS. I WANTED TO EXPLORE MORE OPTIONS EVEN IF IT MEANT GOING AGAINST THE GRAIN.

Wavin, a large manufacturer (b2b) of plastic pipes used mainly for drainage and water supply purposes, had a strong position for years in the Turkish market. In 2013 the company's market share dropped, moving it out of the top 3. Wavin's plastic pipes were perceived as commodities and competition was based only on price. The CEO asked: How can we regain our position as a well-known market leader?

Richard van Delden
Executive Director, Supply
Chain & Operations

August 2013: Wavin wanted to become the leader in the Turkish market. The local management team took on the assignment to come up with a plan. A business plan.

September 2013: Wavin wanted to build a factory near Instanbul. The current factory in Andana was far away from Turkey's most populated city, Istanbul. It was thought that a new factory in Istanbul would get Wavin back on track.

LET'S BUILD A FACTORY!

Given the CEO's challenge, the sales team crunched some numbers and came up with what they believed to be a viable solution: build a new factory. From the sales team's perspective, building a new factory to manufacture pipes closer to the growing market in Istanbul would enable the company to compete on price. To help support its point, the sales team submitted a business plan to the CFO as well as Richard. The race was on to get it done.

MORE CAPACITY? REALLY?

Richard van Delden: When I first saw the business plan for the €60M factory, I was shocked. I was handed a detailed description of how a factory built in Istanbul could produce and sell pipes at a lower price. With enough production capacity nearby, would another factory really help us to regain market share? How will

October 2013: An internal memo from the CEO starting to focus on the customer.

Talking to a plumber in the street, Richard realized that no plumber is familiar with the Wavin brand.

October 2013: Sanity check! If Wavin was to understand its customer and their job-to-be-done, could that info be used to create more options to grow their market share?

this option affect our margin? Sales was convinced they needed to be able to produce close to the main market and have stock on hand. "Our customers want products now at the lowest price possible!" I wanted to explore other options. Most of all, I wanted to understand what our customers were buying and why.

WE DON'T KNOW OUR CUSTOMER

Richard: One day while parking my car in Amsterdam I came across a construction site where I saw Wavin products. I sparked up a conversation with one of the plumbing contractors onsite, who stated: "My clients want the best quality, but they don't know Wavin." A light bulb went off in my head: "We don't know our customers!"

SANITY CHECK

Richard and the CFO Andres Capdepon made the bold decision to first understand what their customers really wanted and needed before making a decision about what to do next.

SAFARI

To learn from their customers, a team of Wavin Turkey employees, as well as Richard and Andres, visited construction sites where they could observe customers in their natural (work) habitats. The team gathered lots of great insights during their week of visits. Together they learned that there was a huge difference in the quality delivered by plumbers onsite due to misuse of equipment and materials. The team also learned that distributors loved the in-store branding. And, just as important, distributors do more than sell and distribute pipes. They also play an important social role in connecting plumbers. As the team asked more questions of the plumbers, contractors, and distributors, they uncovered hidden knowledge – which prompted even more questions.

A-HA! (NOT THE CUSTOMERS YOU THINK THEY ARE!)

After the site visits, some of the customers were invited to a local hotel in Istanbul to meet the project team and to provide feedback

Get out of the building. A special Wavin team went on safari to visit construction sites. Observe and learn what plumbers and installers are dealing with.

January 2014: Wavin realized that mechanical contractors were not their customers. They could not offer a value proposition to them. But that could mean a world of difference for plumbers.

Finally, the hard decision was made to cancel construction of the factory altogether, since it would not help them reach their goal. This meant a lot of disappointment for team members who were involved drawing up plans for the factory.

June 2014: Wavin opened their (first) academy in Turkey. Now that they have proof of concept, they know who their real customer is and how to create value (with their customer). Wavin is ready to scale the academy to other locations.

95

on various ideas generated by the team. The plumbers were really interested in everything that Wavin could do to help them do a better job and deliver higher-quality results. The team's most important discovery was that the plumbers wanted professional how-to videos, product manuals, and direct connections with Wavin experts even more than they wanted lower prices. Providing these services would make Wavin competitive and deliver better-quality results to their customers. This was a real a-ha moment for the Wavin team. They used this insight to design a new community-driven approach: they would help their customers become better plumbers by sharing knowledge (and tea) with each other. This approach turned into the (free) Wavin Academy.

SHARING KNOWLEDGE

The first prototypes of the Wavin Academy proved a success. As such, the project team decided to build the Wavin Academy on

the production site in Adana, Turkey. The center opened a few months later, in June 2014. "At the moment more than 7,000 people have visited the academy (see Facebook page)," Orhun said. "When I joined the Turkish team, I knew this was the way to better engage with our customers. We teach them, we learn from them, and we build better relationships in ways that a factory would not. In short, we've become important to our customers – and they to us – in ways that we never knew were possible."

THE MORAL OF THIS STORY IS . . .

Richard: While the factory may certainly have been one good option to grow our Turkish market share, we realized **>>**

An example of sketch notes made during the observation and the interview.

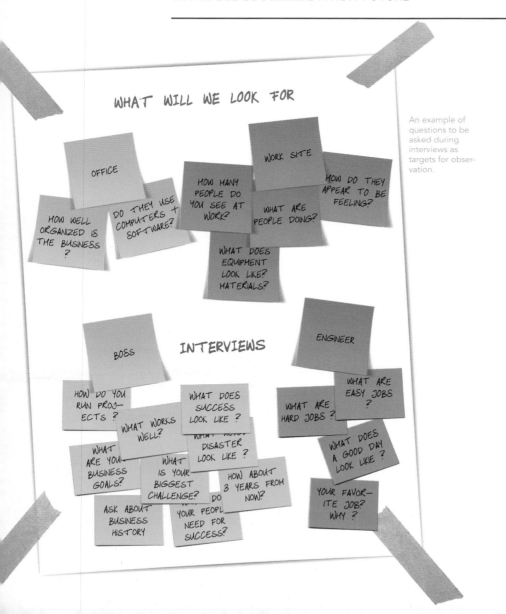

An example of questions to be asked during interviews as targets for observation.

that the business plan for the factory was based on assumptions about the market and our customers' jobs, needs, and wants. We knew that there were other options worth exploring as well. So, rather than spend time arguing about the one option on the table, we decided to first validate our assumptions and learn from our customers first hand. We got out of the building.

By doing this ourselves we learned more than we would if we had simply hired a firm to do a market study for us. In meeting our customers on their turf, we uncovered hidden context and meaning and came up with new questions based on what we learned. The answers to these questions, of course, led to further insights about our customers and the commercial plumbing market in Turkey. We also built lasting relationships with the people who install and use our products.

At the end of the day we invested a few hundred thousand dollars in the first Wavin Academy instead of the tens of millions of dollars we were prepared to pour into a factory. We now have a distribution center in Istanbul, which is closer to our customers. And, with the Wavin Academy, we have a brick-and-mortar space where we can interact with our customers and which ultimately helps to strengthen the Wavin brand in their minds. Design thinking is at the heart of our business now. ∎

The brand-new Wavin Academy in Turkey. This was such a success that it is the model for all future Wavin Academies to open worldwide.

PLUMBERS LOVED THAT WAVIN COULD HELP THEM DO A BETTER JOB.

UNDERSTAND **THE CUSTOMER**

Once upon a time there was a business. That business really understood its customers. Because of that, the products and services of the business became popular, and it started to grow. Managers came in, processes were set up, and systems were put in place. Slowly, curiosity gave way to efficiency.

For a while, the business kept going well: customers continued to buy its products, and the value proposition stayed relevant. But then, one year, sales started to take a dive. None of the managers had a clue why. It didn't make sense: the spreadsheets never predicted this would happen. According to what the managers knew, customers should still have been buying the product. Except they weren't. The company had become complacent, hopelessly out of touch with the customer.

WE'VE ALL SEEN THIS STORY

In hindsight, it's easy to say that this is not how to run a business. Yet it happens everyday. Business books and articles are littered with stories about once-famous companies that went bankrupt because they couldn't change: retail warehouses, record companies, telcos, publishing houses, etc. So, why do businesses fall victim to outmoded systems and procedures?

There is a natural tendency to codify what you know about customers, so that the knowledge can be scaled and decision making can become easier. Putting such systems in place is not a bad thing, as long as they're continuously tuned to take into account today's reality. But tuning must be done by humans, not the systems.

DARE TO ASK QUESTIONS

We put our trust in managers who specialize in something and shrink away from asking questions for fear of sounding ignorant. History, however, shows that courage and persistence in asking design-minded questions — like "why?" and "what if?" — set the foundation for discovery and innovation.

In addition to being overly deferential to experts, we also are overly concerned with looking like an expert to our customers. Asking them a question feels embarrassing and scary. What if your customers no longer trust you? Aren't you supposed to know everything already? Will they continue to buy your product?

Interestingly enough, in almost every case the opposite is true. By asking honest questions of your customers – questions that aren't focused on making the sale or showing off knowledge, but are

---

THE FUTURE IS AT ODDS WITH THE CORPORATION.

// Grant McCracken,
Cultural Anthropologist

genuinely intended to get a better understanding of who they are and what they need – your customers will feel appreciated.

EVERYBODY LIES (EVEN IF THEY DON'T MEAN TO)

Real observation is extremely important. Learning to understand body language, facial expressions, and behavior will help you paint a much clearer picture. That's also the reason why you, as the designer, must do this yourself. Be present in interviews and observe behavior yourself. Allow your own brain to make the connections and see the patterns directly. Per Fitzpatrick, "Watching someone do a task will show you where the problems and inefficiencies really are, not where the customer thinks they are."

Read more about Rob Fitzpatrick in "Master Questioning" on page 88

DEVELOP THE HABIT

For designers, observing and asking questions are daily habits of practice. When you start to notice more about the world around you, you start to pay attention to different details and quieter signals. By asking questions instead of beginning with statements, you actually become more curious. Your brain itself will adapt to this new curiosity and begin to make more interesting connections between observation, questioning, and analysis.

You'll start to see the patterns that others miss. Your intuition will develop, and you'll see things your customers need even before they do. ■

JUST **PICK UP THE PHONE !**

We were working with a home care organization. The CEO had an idea that involved a new customer segment: hospitals. She wanted to do two months of desk research. We told her not to wait, but to understand this customer segment better immediately. That is, don't rely on desk research; instead have real-life conversations.

I was standing next to her and suggested she call the CEO of a hospital that was already in her network. Feeling a bit of pressure, she picked up the phone and called him that instant. It turned out the CEO was really happy she called him and invited her to lunch.

They had a great conversation during lunch, and because of the customer insights she gained, she understood she was not focusing on the real customer need. In just one lunch, she saved months of inefficient desk research and countless hours of analysis time. Not only did she gain new insights on a better opportunity, she also deepened a valuable customer relationship.

Maaike Doyer
Strategy Designer

TOOL **CUSTOMER JOURNEY**

PERSONAL

map customer insights

± 45 MIN

session

3–5

people per group

The Customer Journey is a tool to help you get insight into, track, and discuss how a customer experiences a problem you are trying to solve. How does this problem or opportunity show up in their lives? How do they experience it? How do they interact with you?

MAPPING THE CUSTOMER EXPERIENCE

Mapping this journey will provide you with insights into how customers experience a product or service, as well as how they might be better served or even delighted. This is especially true when co-creating the journey together with your customers or when validating your assumptions with them. What are the circumstances? How do customers feel throughout? What are the moments when the experience can best be improved?

NON-LINEAR

Customer journeys are not linear. A customer can jump from one phase to another depending on many factors. They interact with some touchpoints and miss out others. It is your job, as a designer, to understand the moments when customers engage so that you can design better experiences for them in the future. This tool helps in looking at your products and services through the lens of the customers.

Of course, no customer journey is totally complete or made without assumptions. Mapping the customer journey is based on the knowledge and insights of your team. This tool simply helps you understand and explore from the customer's point of view.

BACK TO REALITY

The Customer Journey Canvas helps make things real. Through the mapping exercise you can identify where customers get stuck, where they have great experiences, and why. One outcome of using this tool with your team will be the so-called low-hanging fruit that you can deliver on immediately. Once you have co-created and assembled the customer journey maps, you can add real customer data gathered through customer safaris, interviews, and feedback. This will enable you to make informed decisions based on reality.

The customer journey is relevant for everyone. Everyone on the team, and in your company, must understand what your customers experience, how they feel, what they struggle with, and how you can improve the experience. The underlying goal: to solve our customers' problems and make them happy. ■

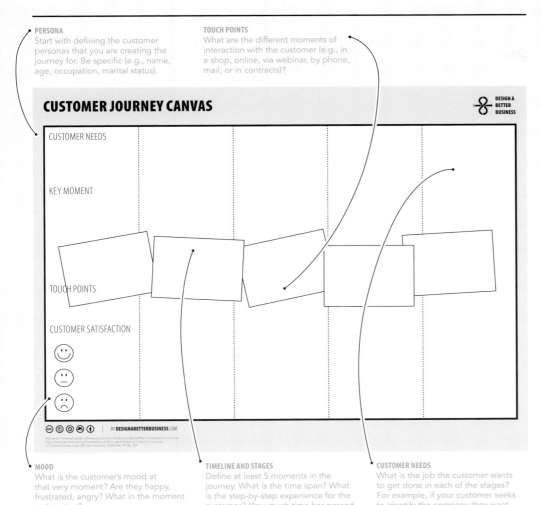

PERSONA
Start with defining the customer personas that you are creating the journey for. Be specific (e.g., name, age, occupation, marital status).

TOUCH POINTS
What are the different moments of interaction with the customer (e.g., in a shop, online, via webinar, by phone, mail, or in contracts)?

CUSTOMER JOURNEY CANVAS

CUSTOMER NEEDS

KEY MOMENT

TOUCH POINTS

CUSTOMER SATISFACTION

MOOD
What is the customer's mood at that very moment? Are they happy, frustrated, angry? What in the moment makes it so?

TIMELINE AND STAGES
Define at least 5 moments in the journey. What is the time span? What is the step-by-step experience for the customer? How much time has passed in the journey? Don't overcomplicate: test with customers (see page 86) to see what to adapt.

CUSTOMER NEEDS
What is the job the customer wants to get done in each of the stages? For example, if your customer seeks to identify the company they want to work with, we need to understand the various touch points. What are the questions customers have at each point?

101

CHECKLIST

- [ ] Is the persona specific enough?
- [ ] Is the journey is complete? Are there any moments missing?
- [ ] Ask yourself where the journey really starts and ends.
- [ ] You can't think of categories you left out.

NEXT STEP

> Validate your assumptions with a Customer Safari (see page 102).

EXAMPLE **CUSTOMER SAFARI**

The Customer Safari is the best way to meet your customers in the wild. Hold your horses – don't talk to them right away! You will learn the most while observing them in their everyday lives; interviews and questions come later. Watch out! Your customers might lie to you.

1 ADOPT THE RIGHT MINDSET

The key rule for a safari is to be prepared. Part of that preparation is filling in the Customer Journey Canvas (page 100). What are the assumptions you want to test? What are the questions you want answered? Make sure you have the right team together and that everyone has a curious mindset. Be aware that your existing mental model is coloring your perception. Doing this beforehand allows you to deviate later.

2 START WITH THE OBVIOUS

Having trouble getting started? Which customers to interview? What is a good location? Start with the obvious: interview existing customers. If you don't have any existing customers yet, go interview some customers of a competing product or service. The point is that there is no "perfect" customer to observe or interview: in the beginning everything is new.

3 DO IT YOURSELF

Sometimes finding a place to observe your customers is not enough – to get a feel for what they see and experience, it can be really worthwhile to take the tour. Just grab a notebook and a camera or phone and follow the path a customer would take. What do you see? Is there anything interesting there? To spice it up, ask customers to walk the path themselves, recording their experience, or take a customer with you.

4 WHAT TO LOOK FOR

When interviewing and observing, keep an eye out for those things that contrast strongly with your expectations. Try to find the reason why the customer gives that answer. Their thinking and feelings might give you an inroad to new perspectives or knowledge. You are trying to find both the "normal" and the "outliers" and "exceptions." Today's 1% can be tomorrow's 100%.

5 CAPTURING INFORMATION

Capture everything and take pictures and audio recordings if possible: listen now, analyze later! When you are capturing, build a rich picture. Don't edit or leave out things that don't seem to fit; analysis happens afterward. When you're constructing the picture, you can start to cluster information. Putting qualitative and quantitative information together allows your brain to see the bigger picture and come up with hunches.

6 MAKING DECISIONS

Review the captured information with the team. Use dot voting to find out what resonates as important, and decide if you need to dive deeper and do another iteration. When the rich picture doesn't change so much between iterations anymore, it is time to make decisions. Compare your rich picture with what you thought during the Customer Journey exercise. How do they differ? Do you need to revise your point of view?

103

INTRODUCTION TO **VALUE PROPOSITION**

Great business models and strategies are based on great value propositions. Great value propositions focus on customers' jobs-to-be-done. Clayton Christensen developed this (jobs-to-be-done) framework as a helpful way to look at customer motivations in business settings.

Conventional marketing techniques teach us to categorize customers by attributes – age, race, marital status, and other qualities. Ultimately, however, this creates entire categories of products that are too focused on what companies want to sell, rather than on what customers actually need.

Evaluating the circumstances that arise in customers' lives is not always easy. Customers rarely make buying decisions based on what the "average" customer in their category might do. But they often buy things because they find themselves with a problem they would like to solve. This is where Clayton Christensen's jobs-to-be-done framework as well as value propositions are most useful.

By understanding the "job" for which their customers "hire" a product or service, companies can more accurately develop and market products well tailored to what customers are already trying to do.

A way to inform your point of view and learn about the jobs-to-be-done is to observe customers in real life. By observing customer

Alex Oster-walder, Yves Pigneur, Greg Bernarda, and Alan Smith wrote the book *Value Proposition Design*, describing how to create products and services customers want.

THE VALUE PROPOSITION CANVAS HELPS YOU DESIGN AND VALIDATE CUSTOMER JOBS.

behavior, you will learn from the true problems that need to be solved. Ask yourself before you start: What is YOUR job-to-be-done? Do you want to work on existing segments or new segments? This determines the focus in working with the Value Proposition Canvas (see page 106). Understand the customer profile (right-hand side), understand the value map (left-hand side), and look into the problem-solution fit or product-market fit (the middle).

PRODUCT VS. NEED

Do you need a drill? Or do you need a hole in the wall?
Do you need a robot? Or do you need to speed up production?

Do you need to arrange a funeral? Or do you need a worthy goodbye ceremony?

Most companies are product focused. But our focus should not actually be on the product. Products are there to help customers solve problems. Once you understand your customers' problems, you can do a better job innovating.

For example, Spotify learned that people, for the most part, aren't interested in "owning" music. It's not about "owning" records or CDs. They don't even want to store music on their hard drives – this entails work on their end. When it comes down to it, people simply want to listen to music. Thus, the difference between downloading a song and streaming the same song is becoming blurry. What's not blurry is that people want access to music. "If I can get that Justin Bieber song anywhere and anytime, what is the difference?" ∎

THE HUMAN **CONTEXT**

At Intel, we try to take a truly integrated view of innovation. We bring together the best ideas and methods, synthesizing them into the best approach to solve the challenges we have as a uniquely situated technology company. We are the underlying engine that powers computing across so many different contexts, and those contexts are expanding at a blistering pace.

Because the range is so broad, we leverage the social sciences and in-person interviews to understand the human context of people's lives and how technology both informs and is informed by socio-cultural dynamics. We also use tools to help us in understanding complex systems, borrowing from fields like ecology to explore how networks of interdependent actors affect one another.

Given that our ideas at scale must become sustainable businesses, we utilize innovation tools and processes, from *Lean Startup* and *Business Model Generation*, to help us refine and improve the way we search for, discover, and test new values and new business models. At the end of the day what's important is that we have an understanding of human needs and are solving a meaningful problem.

Muki Hansteen-Izora
Senior Strategist,
Intel Labs

105

TOOL **VALUE PROPOSITION CANVAS**

FOCUS

understand your
value proposition

±45 MIN

pressure cooker

3—5

people per group

When it comes time to really understand your customers, including their jobs-to-be-done, pains, and gains, as well as your offer to them, the Value Proposition Canvas, developed by Alex Osterwalder at Strategyzer, is one of the best tools available to help you.

ALWAYS START WITH THE CUSTOMER

To get started with the Value Proposition Canvas, always start with the customer. Of course, you may have many different customer segments that you serve (or want to serve). So, as a team, your first task is to have a discussion about who the customers actually are from a high level, whereupon you can make some decisions about who you are designing for. You may need to fill out several canvases, one for each customer.

ASK ENOUGH "WHYS"

Once you've made the customer decision, as a team – using sticky notes and permanent markers – start to detail your customer's jobs-to-be-done. What social, emotional, and functional jobs does your customer do on a daily basis? They have some functional job that you know probably about. But you'll also need to uncover how they do that job, how they feel, and what social qualities come into play. For instance, a parent with the job of driving a child to school may also have functional jobs of getting them there on time, ensuring they're fed throughout the day, making sure they're not looking like an outcast (social standing may be important), providing the feeling of being loved and appreciated, etc. Ask enough "whys" and you'll get this info. Pains are usually easiest to get. What gets in the way of a person's jobs? It's gains that elude most first-time users of the

Value Proposition Canvas. Gains are NOT simply the opposite of pains. Instead, gains are the hidden ambitions people have, above and beyond pain relievers. It takes a designer's mind to uncover these. This is where asking the right questions is really important. What does your customer really aspire to do that they cannot do now? Going back to the parent-driver example, perhaps it's to look like a hero to their kids and other parents or to see their kids succeed in life. If gains sound somewhat existential to you, that's probably because great gains often are.

YOUR JOB

Finally, once you've completed the right side of the canvas, move over to the left side. First, list some solution options that come to mind. You might have some already, or you might create some during an ideation session (detailed in the next chapter). With these in place, you'll need to decide how these can be used together to address your customers' jobs, pains, and gains in unique ways that resonate with your customers.

Using this canvas a few times will help you think differently about your customers and what you offer to them. What's more, done well, your customers will think totally different about why they hired you to fulfill their needs in the first place. ■

GAIN CREATORS
What can you offer your customer to help him fulfill his gains? Be concrete (in quantity and quality).

GAINS
What would make your customer happy? What outcomes does he or she expect, and what would exceed their expectations? Think of the social benefits, functional or financial gains.

PERSONA
Who is he/she (e.g., profession, age). Is this persona buyer, user, decision maker?

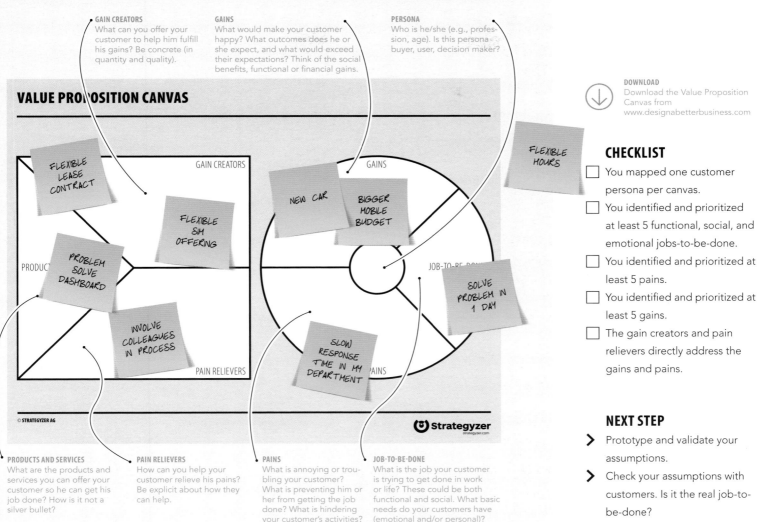

VALUE PROPOSITION CANVAS

© STRATEGYZER AG

🦉 **Strategyzer**
strategyzer.com

PRODUCTS AND SERVICES
What are the products and services you can offer your customer so he can get his job done? How is it not a silver bullet?

PAIN RELIEVERS
How can you help your customer relieve his pains? Be explicit about how they can help.

PAINS
What is annoying or troubling your customer? What is preventing him or her from getting the job done? What is hindering your customer's activities?

JOB-TO-BE-DONE
What is the job your customer is trying to get done in work or life? These could be both functional and social. What basic needs do your customers have (emotional and/or personal)?

DOWNLOAD
Download the Value Proposition Canvas from
www.designabetterbusiness.com

107

CHECKLIST

☐ You mapped one customer persona per canvas.

☐ You identified and prioritized at least 5 functional, social, and emotional jobs-to-be-done.

☐ You identified and prioritized at least 5 pains.

☐ You identified and prioritized at least 5 gains.

☐ The gain creators and pain relievers directly address the gains and pains.

NEXT STEP

> Prototype and validate your assumptions.

> Check your assumptions with customers. Is it the real job-to-be-done?

UNDERSTAND **YOUR CONTEXT**

It goes without saying that understanding the overarching context in which your company operates, such as who your competitors are and what trends you're seeing, will deliver insights about how your business must change in the future. However, most companies don't go far enough in this regard.

SIGNALS FROM THE FUTURE ARE ALL AROUND YOU

Trends and competitors will often only give you part of the picture. And, if you're only following what your competitors are doing, you risk missing something really important. You need a contextual frame that goes beyond the competitive landscape.

Understanding your context will give you a clear picture of today's trends as well as weak signals that will shape tomorrow. This kind of contextual assessment includes (at the very least) an understanding of market trends, technology trends, rules and regulations, economic climate, customer needs, competitors, and even uncertainties. It's important to not think about these signals, trends, facts, and competitors only as they are connected to your current business. To really paint the picture you'll need for the future, go wider than your business. Who are the nascent competitors, the up-and-comers too new to call competitors (yet)? What are you uncertain about that might affect your future context? Election results? Gas prices?

THE FUTURE IS ALREADY HERE. IT'S JUST NOT EVENLY DISTRIBUTED.

// Willam Gibson
Author and Essayist

THE BROADER CONTEXT

When Spotify hit the market, most people saw it as a direct challenge to the biggest competitor in the music industry at the time, Apple. Sure, this was part of the story. Apple helped to pave the way for most digital music companies. Though, if you look beyond Apple, what you'll find is that Spotify's founders also used their understanding of the broader context of the music industry to build a market-leading streaming music service. That context included cloud technology trends; customers' desire to listen to music and not necessarily own it; a changing regulatory environment (that Apple helped to create); and an economic environment that had record labels scrambling for new revenue streams.

KEEP ON SCANNING

Context is not static. It changes on a daily basis – and by the minute in some industries. Continuous understanding requires continuous scanning. As you develop clear pictures of today's context, you might also attempt to create a context for tomorrow, or five years from now, or perhaps even further out. What are the differences? What do you expect to change over time? And, as only time will tell which of your assumptions have been proven true or false, plan to update your understanding of context on a regular basis.

CURIOUS BY NATURE

VISITING THE FUTURE

Visiting the future is not as hard as you probably think it is. In fact, as stated earlier, signals from the future are all around us. Though it may sound odd, some of the places you might considering visiting when looking for signals from the future are modern art museums, hack-a-thons, and even Burning Man, the annual counter-cultural gathering held in the Nevada desert. No need to wait though. There are plenty of signals from the future right on your mobile device. Social networks and even Twitter are filled with signals you might find relevant to your context.

The key here is that your current context (and future context) is not going to be captured in a single report. Any report that sides with your strategy (or disagrees with it) will only be one point of view. And, by the time this information hits the *Harvard Business Review*, it's likely that the context has already been established. It takes a team of people to map your context. Diversity will ensure that you have captured and assessed what are likely the most salient elements affecting your business today, as well as elements that may affect your business in the future. ■

TIP! Do not confuse understanding context with market research. Market research is invaluable to confirm or deny trends in a later stage of your journey. Understanding your current context serves primarily as a way to explore and weigh possibilities.

I am a super-curious person. That's why I love my job! I am a professional trend watcher. I help companies make sense of the world around them. The keys to my job are to observe and structure information continuously. Twitter is my go-to tool. Tweeting automatically structures the information in my mind. But tweeting is not enough: to uncover trends I look for a "through line" that connects several tweets based on their context. Once I discover what I believe to be a trend, I reach out to my network to validate.

109

To do this yourself, start with a point of view. Why do you need this information? Then, collect and structure new information. Everyone in your network has information, but it's probably not organized. Explore the through lines with a framework for understanding. Look outside your industry. Find things you really have no clue about. Finally, frame the information. The frames you develop will reveal patterns and shifts or movements (e.g., from hierarchy to hub, from sending information to sharing information, etc.). This is a starting point for new ideas.

Farid Tabarki
Trend Watcher
Studio Zeitgeist

TOOL **CONTEXT CANVAS®**

Original created by David Sibbet, The Grove Consultants International

The Context Canvas® is our framework to help you understand the context. Use this template to map out the trends with your team and share different perspectives. It will help you to look for drivers outside your own company and have a conversation about the forces that (could) shape your business now and in the future.

FOCUS

understand your context

±30 MIN

pressure cookder

3—5

people per group

The Context Map was origi-nally developed by David Sibbet (The Grove). If you want to dive deeper, have a look at his book *Visual Meetings*.

THINK BEYOND YOUR COMPANY

When most teams begin to unpack the context of their product or organization, they take a myopic point of view that is rooted in the here and now. The Context Canvas® is meant to help you and your team expand your thinking beyond the boundaries of your product and organization, to have a deeper conversation about what's going on in the world and what's changing that will affect your business in the future.

WORK IN SUB-TEAMS

The best way to use this Context Canvas® is to break your team up into smaller sub-teams and to assign each team a couple of sec-tions of the canvas. You may even want to give the same team that has demographic trends the task to also cover technology trends.

Give each sub-team several minutes, maybe even up to 30 minutes, to have deep meaningful discussions about what's going on in the world for each section, adding these to sticky notes. There should be at least one sticky note per driver for each section. It must be re-iterated that what is important here is expansion beyond what were drivers of the past and your own company or product. This is about the full context of the industry you play in or the world at large that is going to drive your design criteria and options for the future.

CAPTURING THE KEY DRIVERS

Once all of the teams are finished discussing and capturing the key drivers for their sections, have a representative from each team, one at a time, add their sticky notes to a large, shared canvas (taped or drawn on the wall), discussing each driver as they put them up. This will spark further conversation with the rest of the teams about what's important and perhaps what other drivers might also be relevant.

COLLECTIVE POINT OF VIEW

With every section of the canvas totally filled out, have the entire (larger) team select the most important drivers that will influence the future of your organization, or at least your specific design journey. When you stand back from this, what you'll see is a glimpse of the future from the entire team's collective point of view, and not just one expert's opinion. ■

DEMOGRAPHIC TRENDS
Look for data on the demographics, education level, employment situation. What are the big changes in these areas? And what about policies, rules, and regulations?

ECONOMIC CLIMATE
Be specific in your descriptions, and stay away from container words and abstractions. For example, what is important to you about the economic climate?

YOUR COMPETITION
Try to find unexpected competition. Are there new entries? Competition coming from unexpected sources?

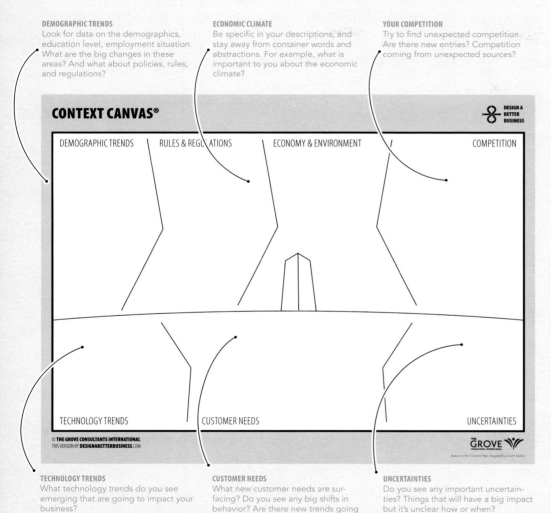

CONTEXT CANVAS®

 DESIGN A BETTER BUSINESS

| DEMOGRAPHIC TRENDS | RULES & REGULATIONS | ECONOMY & ENVIRONMENT | COMPETITION |

| TECHNOLOGY TRENDS | CUSTOMER NEEDS | UNCERTAINTIES |

© THE GROVE CONSULTANTS INTERNATIONAL
THIS VERSION BY DESIGNABETTERBUSINESS.COM

THE GROVE CONSULTANTS INTERNATIONAL

Based on the Context Map designed by David Sibbet.

TECHNOLOGY TRENDS
What technology trends do you see emerging that are going to impact your business?

CUSTOMER NEEDS
What new customer needs are surfacing? Do you see any big shifts in behavior? Are there new trends going mainstream?

UNCERTAINTIES
Do you see any important uncertainties? Things that will have a big impact but it's unclear how or when?

DOWNLOAD
Download the Context Canvas® from www.designabetterbusiness.com

CHECKLIST

☐ You have completely filled all the areas of the canvas.

☐ You have proof of what is on the canvas.

☐ You have marked the top 3 threats and opportunities.

NEXT STEP

❯ Find proof for your assumptions.

❯ Check your findings against what others think.

❯ Revisit the Context Canvas® in 3 months to update and verify.

❯ Update your Point of View.

❯ Update your Design Criteria.

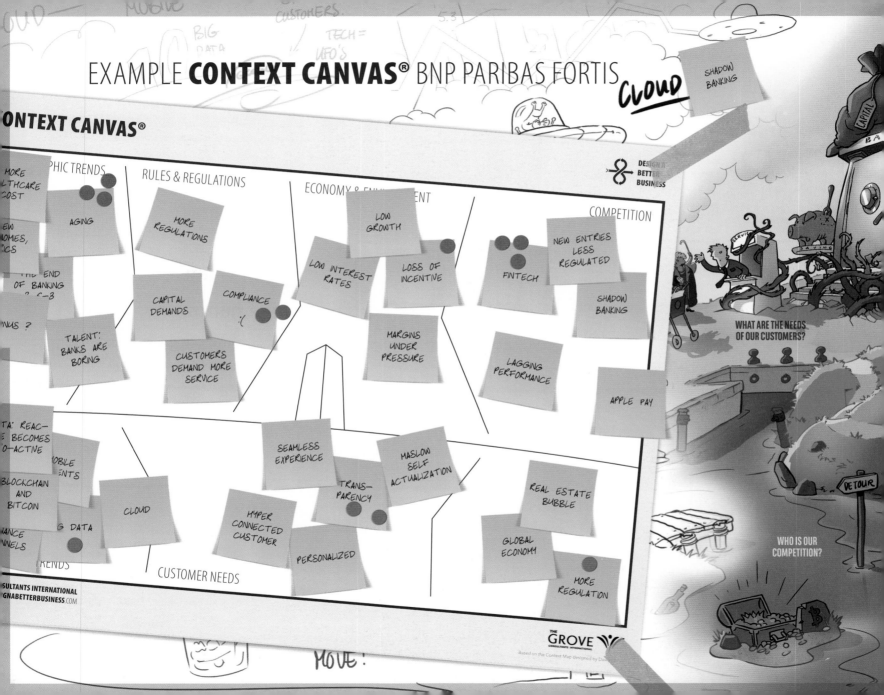

EXAMPLE **CONTEXT CANVAS**® BNP PARIBAS FORTIS Cloud

CONTEXT CANVAS®

DESIGN A BETTER BUSINESS

DEMOGRAPHIC TRENDS
- MORE HEALTHCARE COST
- NEW ECONOMIES, DEMOGRAPHICS
- THE END OF BANKING
- BONUS?
- AGING
- TALENT: BANKS ARE BORING

RULES & REGULATIONS
- MORE REGULATIONS
- CAPITAL DEMANDS
- COMPLIANCE :(
- CUSTOMERS DEMAND MORE SERVICE

ECONOMY & ENVIRONMENT
- LOW GROWTH
- LOW INTEREST RATES
- LOSS OF INCENTIVE
- MARGINS UNDER PRESSURE

COMPETITION
- NEW ENTRIES LESS REGULATED
- FINTECH
- SHADOW BANKING
- LAGGING PERFORMANCE
- APPLE PAY

UNCERTAINTIES / TRENDS
- DATA: REACTIVE BECOMES PRO-ACTIVE
- MOBILE PAYMENTS
- BLOCKCHAIN AND BITCOIN
- FINANCE CHANNELS
- BIG DATA

CUSTOMER NEEDS
- SEAMLESS EXPERIENCE
- MASLOW SELF ACTUALIZATION
- TRANS-PARENCY
- CLOUD
- HYPER CONNECTED CUSTOMER
- PERSONALIZED
- REAL ESTATE BUBBLE
- GLOBAL ECONOMY
- MORE REGULATION

SHADOW BANKING

WHAT ARE THE NEEDS OF OUR CUSTOMERS?

WHO IS OUR COMPETITION?

DETOUR

THE GROVE CONSULTANTS INTERNATIONAL
Based on the Context Map designed by David Sibbet

SHARE THE URGENCY

My job is to translate challenges of management into numbers, images, and stories that everybody understands. I try to keep this simple by using metaphors. In 2014, I saw that the bank we used to know does not exist anymore, but we still believed in our old assumptions.

Overstating, in the past bankers needed to know only three figures: 3-6-3. Give 3 percent on debit, charge 6 percent on loans, and at three o'clock you can go play golf.

To be successful in today's world, everyone in the bank needs to be aware of the context. To help them do that I needed to tell a story that sticks, going beyond numbers and graphs, and to really engage my audience and inspire them to change the bank. We co-created "The World of the Banks" with 2,000 colleagues and visualized the result with designers. In this way, the story is engaging and it can be understood in one glance, and we could easily share it with all of our colleagues.

Peter De Keyzer
Chief Economist,
BNP Paribas Fortis

113

INTRODUCTION TO **BUSINESS MODEL**

When considering the future of your business, whether it's your overall strategy or some new product and/or service, you must first take some time to really understand your business inside and out. The Business Model Canvas provides a simple way to map the way your business – or any business – creates, delivers, and captures value.

UNDERSTAND YOUR BUSINESS MODEL

Understanding just how you add value to your customers' lives is crucial. This serves as the basis for any discussion about your business.

Who are your customers and what problems do you solve for them? How do you deliver that value to them?

One of the best ways to structure this information is by using the Business Model Canvas. Since the publication of *Business Model Generation*, it's been found that the Business Model Canvas serves as a perfect platform on which to hold better, more strategic conversations built on a common understanding and with a common language.

For more background, read: *Business Model Generation* by Alexander Osterwalder and Yves Pigneur

DON'T ASSUME YOUR TEAM UNDERSTANDS YOUR COMPANY'S BUSINESS MODEL.

UNDERSTAND YOUR BUSINESS MODELS

If you work for a large organization, you might find varying value propositions and business models. Take a hospital, for example. An academic hospital consists of three separate business models at the highest level: 1) patient care; 2) education; and 3) research. Each of these business models has very different customers, value propositions, and revenue streams.

UNDERSTAND COMPETING BUSINESS MODELS

You can learn a lot from your competition. Choose some competitors and map their business models. Armed with this information, you'll have deep insight into what customers want and what they are willing to pay for. You'll have a clearer picture of just how customers' needs are met across the entire industry, not just in your company. And you'll uncover vital information about how other businesses, maybe even very successful businesses, have created their own spaces in the market.

UNDERSTAND BUSINESS MODELS IN AN INDUSTRY

Before entering into an industry with a new/startup idea, it's vital to have an understanding of the most common business models being used to exchange value with your potential customers. If, for example, you plan to play in the climate space, specifically in solar energy, you'll want to understand how leading companies, like SunEdison, do business (and add value). Jigar Shah learned by studying the industry that customers were not willing to pay for solar panels, but were looking for ways to decrease their electricity bills. He started selling energy contracts instead of solar panels. He designed what he named the Power Purchase Agreement (PPA) Business Model. This business model changed the status quo, allowing companies to purchase solar energy services under long-term, predictably priced contracts while avoiding the significant capital costs of ownership and operation of solar panels. The SunEdison business model is recognized as one of the catalysts that helped turn solar into a multibillion-dollar business worldwide.

EVALUATE YOUR BUSINESS MODEL

Any business constantly seeks to improve its understanding of the customer segments it focuses on (or wants to focus on). Following on page 117 are seven of the most popular (and useful) questions Osterwalder has compiled to assess your business model. ■

MOST COMPANIES DON'T KNOW THEIR CUSTOMERS; THEY JUST KNOW THEIR TRANSACTIONS.

SO MANY **BUSINESS MODELS**

In 2010 we wanted to design a new strategy, focused more on our patients. So where to start? We realized we had many different departments operating in the same hospital but in a different way.

They had different customers, different partners, and different value propositions. We realized we actually had a lot of different business models, so we started from the bottom up. We had to learn from each and every department in order to understand what their models looked like and how they were showing up in the hospital's business model.

115

Understanding their business model helped them to get a better insight in their own business and also in understanding the others.

(See page 117 for how Maastricht University Medical Center created their portfolio of Business Models.)

Frits van Merode
Member, Executive Board
Maastricht University Medical Center

TOOL **BUSINESS MODEL CANVAS**

Created by Alexander Osterwalder

The Business Model Canvas is a great tool to help you understand a business model in a straightforward, structured way. Using this canvas will lead to insights about the customers you serve, what value propositions are offered through what channels, and how your company makes money. You can use the Business Model Canvas to understand your own business model or that of a competitor!

FOCUS

understand your business

45–60 MIN

session

3–5

people per group

The Business Model Canvas was created by Alex Osterwalder and Yves Pigneur. For more information, read their book: *Business Model Generation*.

VALUE PROPOSITION
What are your products and services? What is the job you get done for your customer?

KEY PARTNERS
List the partners that you can't do business without (not suppliers).

KEY ACTIVITIES
What do you do every day to run your business model?

KEY RESOURCES
List the people, knowledge, means, and money you need to run your business.

COST STRUCTURE
List your top costs by looking at activities and resources.

BUSINESS MODEL CANVAS

KEY PARTNERS	KEY ACTIVITIES	VALUE PROPOSITION	CUSTOMER RELATIONSHIPS	CUSTOMER SEGMENTS
	KEY RESOURCES		CHANNELS	
COST STRUCTURE		REVENUE STREAMS		

DESIGNED BY **STRATEGYZER AG**

This work is licensed under a Creative Commons Attribution-ShareAlike 3.0 Unported License.
http://creativecommons.org/licenses/by-sa/3.0/ or send a letter to Creative Commons,
171 Second Street, Suite 300, San Francisco, California, 94105, USA

Strategyzer
strategyzer.com

CUSTOMER SEGMENTS
List the top three segments. Look for the segments that provide the most revenue.

CUSTOMER RELATIONSHIP
How does this show up and how do you maintain the relationship?

CHANNELS
How do you communicate with your customer? How do you deliver the value proposition?

REVENUE STREAMS
List your top three revenue streams. If you do things for free, add them here too.

1 Start by mapping out the business on a high level: only the most important, vital aspects of the business model.

2 Link up the building blocks: every value proposition needs a customer segment and a revenue stream!

3 Don't mix ideas for a future state with what is going on right now, and don't mix different departments!

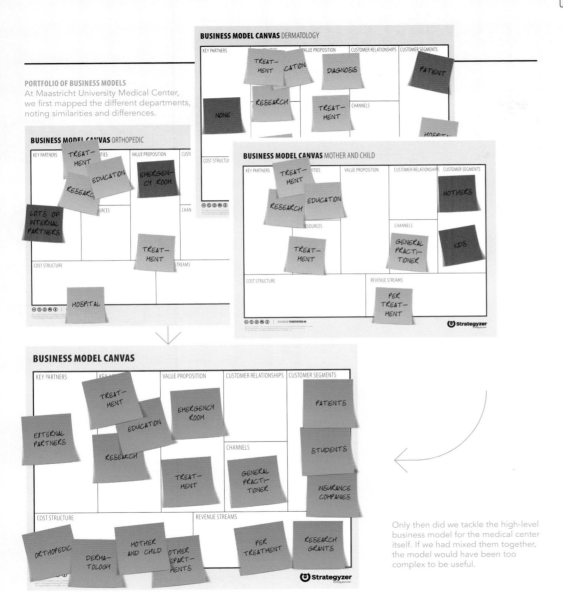

PORTFOLIO OF BUSINESS MODELS
At Maastricht University Medical Center, we first mapped the different departments, noting similarities and differences.

Only then did we tackle the high-level business model for the medical center itself. If we had mixed them together, the model would have been too complex to be useful.

CHECKLIST

Rank your business model's performance (0=bad – 10= excellent) for each question.

- ☐ How much do switching costs prevent your customers from churning?
- ☐ How scalable is your business model?
- ☐ Does your business model produce recurring revenues?
- ☐ Do you earn before you spend?
- ☐ How much of the work can be done by others?
- ☐ Does your business model provide built-in protection from competition?
- ☐ Is your business model based on a game-changing cost structure?

NEXT STEPS

> Filter out the design criteria and test your assumptions.

117

EXAMPLE **BUSINESS MODEL CANVAS** VISUAL

Sketching the Business Model Canvas can create a bigger picture and help you better engage your audience.

Details often get in the way of the main points of the Business Model Canvas: clarity, simplicity, and connectedness. "Diving into the weeds" leads to (unnecessary) discussion, which halts the creative process and the ability to see things for what they are. The solution: first do and then discuss. Focus on creating the bigger picture. This is what's really important.

When creating your business model, that of your competitor's or even when you want to compare different business models, the power is in the simplicity. Great business models are straightforward and simple. Add too many details to your business model, and your point of view will become foggy.

To simplify and clarify your point of view and the story you're telling, use sketches or pictures instead of words. Even better, puzzle your business model together using hand-drawn icons cut out from a template. For more on visual storytelling, see page 72.

Download your own set of icons at
www.designabetterbusiness.com

THIS IS AN EXAMPLE OF THE TRADITIONAL TAXI COMPANY BUSINESS MODEL. THE TAXI MODEL IS LINEAR AND LACKS A CONNECTION WITH (CURRENT) CUSTOMER NEEDS.

AS AN EXAMPLE WE HAVE COMPOSED TWO BUSINESS MODELS:
ONE FOR A TRADITIONAL TAXI COMPANY AND ONE FOR UBER.
WITH THESE IT'S EASY TO COMPARE BOTH MODELS AND
UNCOVER THEIR STRENGTHS AND WEAKNESSES.

BUSINESS MODEL CANVAS UBER

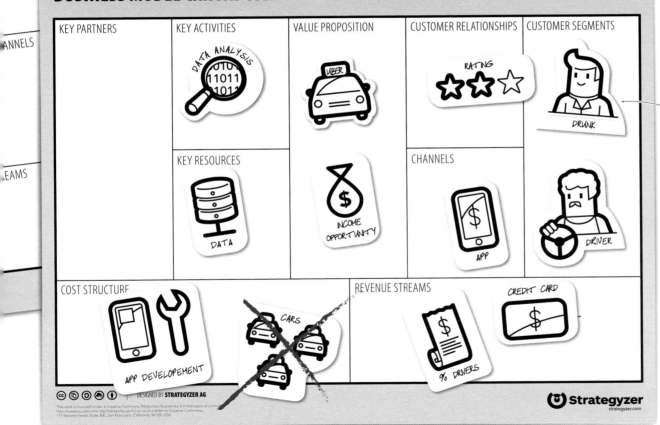

KEY PARTNERS	KEY ACTIVITIES	VALUE PROPOSITION	CUSTOMER RELATIONSHIPS	CUSTOMER SEGMENTS
	DATA ANALYSIS	UBER	RATING	DRUNK
	KEY RESOURCES	INCOME OPPORTUNITY	CHANNELS	DRIVER
	DATA		APP	

COST STRUCTURE — APP DEVELOPEMENT — CARS

REVENUE STREAMS — % DRIVERS — CREDIT CARD

DESIGNED BY **STRATEGYZER AG**

Strategyzer
strategyzer.com

119

UBER'S BUSINESS MODEL
IS A MULTISIDED PLATFORM,
CREATING VALUE BY MATCHING
TWO DIFFERENT CUSTOMER
SEGMENTS: DRIVERS—FOR—
HIRE AND PEOPLE WHO NEED
TO GO FROM A TO B. UBER'S
STRENGTHS ARE THE DATA
THE PLATFORM GENERATES
AND THE TRANSPARENCY OF
ORDERING A RIDE.

ONLINE SAFARI

In the age of the Internet it would be silly not to take an online safari. There are several tricks for getting a quick idea of what people are actually doing online. Take a look at your own user forum or that of a competitor. What are people complaining about? What conversations are they having? Use Twitter to get in touch with people that write about similar products. What kind of pictures do they post on social media? Are there any video blogs or YouTube channels that cover similar topics? How popular are they? What trends can you find there? You can get a lot of information in a very short amount time if you start following some online leads!

See page 102 for more information on the customer safari.

DO IT YOURSELF

It pays to step into your customer's shoes for a while. If you really want to understand your customers and their preferences, slip into their shoes, do what they do, and shop where they shop. We learned this trick from an expert retail food marketer. If you're interested in understanding what attracts customers, go to the stores they shop at, observe them, and start pulling things off the shelf that attract you. Compare what you bought with what you see in customers' shopping carts. You'll likely find customer segments that stick together and look for similar qualities in the things they buy. Best of all, you'll quickly learn what attracts customers to your competition.

BE THE BARISTA!

When you really want to surprise your customers and put them into a different state of mind, consider going the extra mile. Find (or build) a nice coffee cart and add to it everything you need to get people talking. Making the rounds in a place where your customers hang out is guaranteed to put a smile on their faces. You'd be surprised at what people tell their barista! What we're actually saying: be a perfect host(ess) and facilitate the interaction.

DO THE COFFEE CHALLENGE...

To help your team get over their initial uneasiness at getting out of the building, consider the coffee challenge.

We created this in a program for the Impact Hub: drink 25 cups of coffee with customers in the coming 2–3 weeks.

Every time you have a conversation, cross off a cup from the list. The person who clears the card the fastest wins! And the entire team wins every time someone comes back with a new or validating insight they learned while drinking coffee with a customer.

Be sure to set this up as an internal challenge! You will learn about a lot of coffee shops and even more insights!

121

YOU NOW HAVE . . .

> AN UNDERSTANDING OF
> HOW TO **OBSERVE AND ASK
> QUESTIONS**   P86–88

> AN UNDERSTANDING OF
> **YOUR CUSTOMER NEEDS**   P106

> AN UNDERSTANDING OF
> **YOUR CONTEXT**   P110

> AN UNDERSTANDING OF
> **YOUR BUSINESS MODELS**   P116

NEXT STEPS

> **GENERATE IDEAS**   P140
> By using some practical techniques
> that help you and your team
> become creative geniuses.

> **APPLY INNOVATION TECHNIQUES** P146
> The Innovation Matrix helps you
> filter out your best ideas.

RECAP

HOW MANY COFFEES ARE YOU WILLING TO DRINK **WITH YOUR CUSTOMERS**?

GO **BEYOND THE OBVIOUS.**

DON'T ASSUME YOUR TEAM MEMBERS UNDERSTAND YOUR BUSINESS MODEL.

IT'S NOT ABOUT THE ANSWERS. IT IS ABOUT **THE RIGHT QUESTION.**

IF YOU DON'T KNOW WHERE YOU ARE, HOW CAN YOU **KNOW WHERE YOU ARE GOING**?

123

SO, NOW YOU KNOW

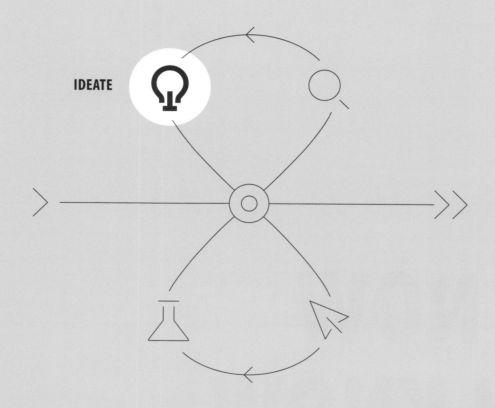

IDEATE

THE DESIGN JOURNEY **IDEATE**

LEARN TO IDEATE

EXPAND YOUR IDEAS

SELECT IDEAS TO PROTOTYPE

BECOME **A CREATIVE GENIUS**

We all have ideas. Sometimes the ideas that pop into our head keep us up at night – ideas we feel we must follow to the end; they must be executed. Surely they're the best ideas ever. But the truth is: as good as they may be, ideas are limited. Impact is only created when ideas become additive and expansive: more is better.

IDEATION

You know that idea you came up with in the shower? It's probably a great one. Yet, it's also just one of many potentially good ideas for solving a problem or addressing an unmet need. In other words, there is no one single right solution (or idea) for any problem or unmet need.

Ideation is about generating a lot of ideas quickly. Big ideas. Bold ideas. Feasible ideas. Impossible ideas. Even crappy ideas.

DO IDEAS COME FROM A MAGICAL, PARALLEL DIMENSION?

It takes a creative, optimistic mindset and the ability to use the right side of the brain to build on your – and everyone else's – shower idea without evaluation or judgment.

At the end of an ideation session, it's not uncommon to have a wall of 500+ sticky notes, each with a uniquely interesting idea. This will become the fuel for generating future options.

WHERE DO IDEAS COME FROM?

We all have random has ideas that pop into our heads at random ideas as if they're coming from some magical, parallel dimension (or the shower). Some people, however, seem to be able to come up with "good" ideas more frequently than the rest of us. Are these people creative geniuses? Do they have some sort of mental antenna that finds the best ideas?

The short answer is no. As clichéd as it may sound, we are all born with the capacity for curiosity and creativity, though perhaps we have forgotten how to harness it. The people we call "creative geniuses" have learned how to use their innate sense of curiosity to tune into ideas, trusting that all ideas are potential options worth validating. The best part about this is that you can learn to do the same thing. And with a little practice, you'll be generating the same volume of ideas as the "creative genius." Look out, geniuses!

TIP! Make sure you have plenty of fun while ideating. Fun and humor are the most important catalysts for creativity.

IDEAS ARE JUST IDEAS

What differentiates a good idea from a great one is not its context or content, but your ability to validate whether the idea is truly executable and will make a difference. Simply put, ideas are just thoughts based on assumptions. On their own, ideas have little value.

Therefore, its important to split ideation from validation. During ideation you want to cast as wide a net and generate as many ideas as you can in as little time as possible. If done well, you and your team will have innumerable opportunities to combine these initial ideas and create new ones that can be evaluated, prototyped, and validated.

PUT YOUR BRAIN(S) INTO GEAR

Maybe you find that in your daily life, you're the most creative when you're in the shower, or on a walk. That goes for most of us. When you get to work, however, perhaps you switch to execution (noncreative) mode, where you stay until you get home.

Designers must be able to shift seamlessly from a creative to an analytical and decisive mode. This is part of the design process. You'll need to do the same, so will your team. At first, it may feel awkward to add additional design and search tools, like observation, to your executional tool belt. It'll probably feel just as awkward to move away from evaluating and judging to being creative for creativity's sake. It's worth it, though. Once your team is able to work together to generate and build upon each other's ideas, you'll find that everyone gets on the same page that much earlier.

Of course, there are plenty of tools and techniques to help you and your team ideate in an expansive and systematic way. By the end of this chapter, you'll have new ways to shift into creative mode and think outside the box to generate more ideas. And you'll have new ways to evaluate your ideas before selecting (some of them) for prototyping and validation. ∎

127

MASTER **IDEATION**

1 START YOUR (CREATIVE) ENGINES

Generating lots of ideas with a team is easy if you know how to do it. It all comes down to facilitation. This entails employing the right set of tools in the right atmosphere (space) with a creative mindset focused on accomplishing this one task. It's also crucial to set a time limit for your ideation session. It would be counterproductive to generate ideas all day. Set a time bound and create within that space. And when you believe you've run out of gas, reshuffle the ideas in front of you and build off of them.

2 BUILD STEPPING-STONES

The more ideas you and your team put out there, the more chances you'll have to make interesting connections and build ideas on top of other ideas. Moreover, just like when you build a path to the future, the shape of the stepping-stones is not as important as their number and arrangement.

3 CREATE A RITUAL

It takes a bit of time even for an experienced creative to shift mental gears and get the creative juices flowing. Consider creating some kind of ideation ritual, like a fire starter (discussed later in this chapter on page 144). With practice, you'll learn how much time you need to get in the zone. Most important, plan for that time to be uninterrupted.

4 USE A TOOL

Don't think you have to conquer the idea frontier all by yourself using only brainstorming techniques. There are lots of ideation tools, like the Business Model Canvas and Creative Matrix,

TIP! HOW TO BUILD MORE STEPPING-STONES

RANDOMIZE
Use a dictionary to blindly pick random words. Once you have 10–20 words, try to make combinations. Those will lead to new associations and new ideas.

ANALOGY
Look for an analogous situation. How does your idea or problem translate to a mobile phone? Horse racing? Look at objects around you for inspiration.

COMBINE
Take your idea and combine it with another one that seems unrelated. Or, apply it to an object you see on your desk, or a person, or an activity. What does that look like?

MAKE IT EXTREME
What is the most extreme version of your idea you can come up with? Can you blow it up? What if everyone uses it? What is the opposite of your idea?

"ANIMALIZE" IT
If your idea was an animal, what would it be? What are its characteristics? Would it bite? Would you be able to domesticate it? What if it were a car? Or a person?

that can help you and your team create many valuable ideas. Using tools for ideating enables you to frame the session while simultaneously expanding on and exploring new ideas. For example, the Business Model Canvas provides a framework for digging deeper into each idea.

5 GO DEEP

It is one thing to generate, share, and expand upon lots of ideas. But you'll also need to explore some of those ideas in more depth – especially when it comes to selecting a few ideas to prototype and validate. What is the core of each idea? What and whose problems does it aim to solve? What will customers pay for and how will they find it in the first place?

You will not be able to explore every idea this deeply. But for some ideas, digging into their context and unpacking the assumptions you and your team have made when generating them is extremely valuable. ■

FREE UP SPACE FOR **DEEPER THINKING**

Developing new ideas is central to design and business, but it's easy to forget that a big part of ideation is "editing." During the ideation process, it's vital to get as many ideas as possible out of your head and onto paper, whether through words or images – or both.

Oftentimes we fear that some of our ideas might be silly or embarrassing. But that doesn't matter. Getting those first ideas out of your mind helps free up space for deeper thinking. Our first ideas may actually end up being the most appropriate, but we need to explore as many options as possible before we can assess this accurately. The more ideas we can develop, the better chance we have to select the best option. And it is crucial to allow yourself to dump an idea at the eleventh hour in favor of a better one.

Remember that ideas can come from anywhere – and that ego needs to be removed. The ideation process is most impactful when there are a number of people involved at the same time. That way we can build on the ideas of others.

Kevin Finn
Creative Director
TheSumOf

FROM 1...TO 10

As part of our Health & Wellness initiative, we were working on several prototypes for our initial concepts. We had gathered great insights from in-person and market research. What we needed, however, was a matching business model strategy.

As an electronics manufacturer, it was clear to us that we could offer a product for sale. But we were also interested in understanding how we might offer value-adds, such as online services.

As a team, we gathered in our innovation room for a couple of days to generate new ideas. We quickly mapped out our idea for this new product onto a Business Model Canvas – then used that as the basis for 300+ more ideas! We clustered these ideas into 10 different business model options that we then explored and designed.

Using this approach enabled us to quickly create new options. It also provided a framework for us to analyze our underlying assumptions. We applied a customer-centric approach to this framework in order to validate different business model alternatives.

This fresh approach to ideation revitalized our innovation efforts. We continue to use these tools as part of our process.

// Gabriel Rubinsky, Senior Manager, New Product Innovation, at Panasonic

JUST SAY NO TO DRUGS

A group from a large pharmaceutical company used the Business Model Canvas in an ideation exercise. The group was asked to identify the one thing they knew for certain about their business — selling drugs — and remove it from the canvas.

Indignantly, the CEO responded: "You obviously don't understand our business. 100% of our revenue comes from selling drugs!"

Nevertheless, we asked them to spend 30 minutes on this "ridiculous" scenario, just to see what they could come up with.

Adding this constraint made them look at their business in a whole new light! The team found that the company actually had an incredibly valuable (key) resource it had never considered as a potential source of revenue: its knowledge of cancer treatments.

DON'T MAKE LISTS WHEN IDEATING AS A TEAM, AS THIS SEEMS TO LIMIT PEOPLE'S ABILITY TO COME UP WITH MORE THAN SEVEN IDEAS. THIS MAY BE A RESULT OF THE URGE TO BE CONSISTENT OR COMPLETE. INSTEAD, MAKE AN UNORGANIZED PILE OF STICKY NOTES FIRST!

IMPROVING THE LIVES OF MILLIONS

I was running an ideation session with representatives from our clinical, technology, marketing, and sustainability functions. We sketched out a long list of ideas and then thought about how to filter them. I wanted just one criterion: it had to improve the lives of over 10 million people in the developing world. By the end of the day, we were looking at a handful of best-guess business models that had the possibility of not only achieving commercial success but of transforming lives. I remember being genuinely moved. Fast forward three years: that same guy from sustainability is exploring how to evolve these models in the market – but this time he has over 100 million people in his sights.

// Alex Davidge, Head of Business Architecture and Strategy Development, Bupa

131

MAKING IT SAFE TO SPEAK

A traditional financial services firm held a two-day offsite with its top 60 executives to discuss disruptive ideas for growth. Because the firm's culture emphasized detail orientation and risk mitigation, the participants were unaccustomed to sharing wild ideas in an open format.

To help the participants become more comfortable, the facilitator created custom "Safe to Speak" playing cards with clearly identified behaviors that supported provocative questioning and candid feedback. This encouraged participants to reward one another for modeling more open and inquiry-based behaviors.

The cards not only stimulated exciting new ideas, but the participants had more fun and got a chance to see their colleagues' creative sides.

HOW TOYOTA FINANCIAL SERVICES SPURRED CREATIVE GENIUS IN THEIR MIDST

WE DON'T WANT TO BECOME THE RECORD COMPANY OF THE CAR INDUSTRY

// GEORGE BORST, FORMER CEO, TFS

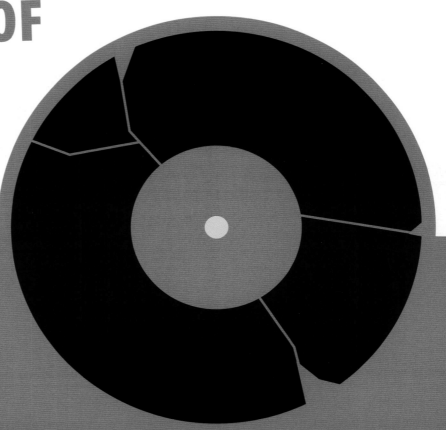

CASE STUDY TOYOTA

TOYOTA FINANCIAL SERVICES
& THE BIG IDEAS

133

In 2012, the Toyota Financial Services (TFS) group, the financial subsidiary of the Toyota Motor Corporation, was under a lot of pressure. Toyota had experienced a substantial number of automotive recalls, and the external business environment was transforming. The CEO, George Borst, knew he needed to transform his business along with the environment.

RAISING THE STAKES

To raise the stakes and create a shared sense of urgency, Borst wanted to set the bar almost impossibly high for his executive team. He was going to ask them to double the company's profits in five years without increasing spending. And, he was going to do it at an offsite, using new and unfamiliar ways to innovate.

In the past, many smart people at TFS had tried to implement a future focus. But when they tried to come up with new disruptive opportunities, they consistently were foiled by their traditional tools and practices. As one person put it, "There was a curse of knowledge, with plans on top of plans, spreadsheets on top of spreadsheets, metrics on top of metrics, and score-cards on top of scorecards. Lots of business plans everywhere, and everything had to come from a trend report." The executive team knew that traditional methods of innovation wouldn't be enough to move the company toward its future goal. To bring in new tools and techniques, TFS organized an offsite.

PREPARE FOR CHANGE

The organizers wanted to get a feel for how people within the company wanted to grow the business over the next five years. They asked employees to submit ideas via an internal web portal, focusing on across the following dimensions: increasing revenues, optimizing resources, and managing costs.

Over 60 new ideas were submitted. But when they plotted them on an Innovation Matrix, the executive team noticed two things.

First of all, every one of the ideas fell on the left-hand side of the Business Model Canvas: internal operations. However,

INSIGHT COMING UP WITH WAYS TO CUT COSTS IS EASY. **FINDING NEW IDEAS FOR VALUE CREATION IS NOT.**

none of the ideas did much to address the right-hand side of the canvas: where value is created for customers and the company.

INSIGHT THE RIGHT FIRE STARTERS REALLY **KICKSTARTED OUR PROCESS!**

Secondly, the executive team noticed that the ideas would only bring incremental changes, not substantial ones. No one was convinced that incremental changes would enable TFS to double profits in five years.

FIRE STARTERS TO THE RESCUE

The executive team needed a way to help the participants think bigger, expand beyond their initial ideas, and place more emphasis on value creation. With some outside help, the team prepared four fire starter questions to inspire the participants. These served two purposes. They helped frame the challenge around simple, straightforward questions. And they split the overarching goals (double profits in five years and focus on value creation) into more manageable parts that the participants would ideate on.

PREPARING FIRE STARTERS

1 RETHINKING INSURANCE

What if we rethought insurance? What if we restarted the business from scratch?

2 CUT OPERATIONAL EXPENSE BY 50%

How can we cut operational expenses by 50%? What are the knobs we can turn?

3 PARTNERSHIP SURPRISE

How can we surprise our partners, the dealers? Can we co-create with them?

4 LOVE BRAND

How can we become the customer's financial love brand?

They visualized the fire starters and stuck them to the walls in the workshop space to give the teams an anchor while ideating.

DESIGNING A BETTER FUTURE IS YOUR DAY JOB!

//George Borst, former CEO, TFS

DRY RUN

Prior to jumping into ideation and trying to figure out what would work for the executive team, the organizers held a pre-workshop session. A small group of key leaders from a few business units spent a day and a half creating Business Model and Value Proposition Canvases depicting the current state of TFS and its customers.

The committee learned during the pre-workshop that there was a lack of agreement about and understanding of the current business model, even within company leadership. In turn, this created a lack of unity within the executive team about the company strategy. The committee also realized that using tools and working visually would make the larger conversation much easier and more substantive.

ACTUAL OFFSITE

Once the dry runs were completed, 55 top executives and managers of Toyota Financial Services came together in Santa Monica, CA, USA, for a 2½-day strategic planning workshop. After their detailed preparation, the organizers had high hopes that the participants would walk away with a better understanding of how to design a brighter future for the company. **»**

135

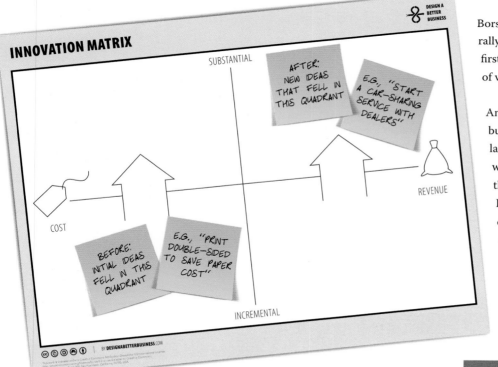

INNOVATION MATRIX

DESIGN A BETTER BUSINESS

SUBSTANTIAL

AFTER: NEW IDEAS THAT FELL IN THIS QUADRANT

E.G., "START A CAR-SHARING SERVICE WITH DEALERS"

REVENUE

COST

E.G., "PRINT DOUBLE-SIDED TO SAVE PAPER COST"

BEFORE: INITIAL IDEAS FELL IN THIS QUADRANT

INCREMENTAL

BY **DESIGNABETTERBUSINESS**.COM

Toyota Financial Services used
the Innovation Matrix to plot how ideas scored against the criteria.
The matrix helped them filter out the really promising ideas.
See page 146 on how to use it.

Borst opened the offsite and, to set the scene, he gave the rallying cry: "Double profits in 5 years' time!" since on this first day, the participants mostly would be refining their point of view.

An incredible breakthrough occurred as each team began building their business models. The group realized they lacked consensus on who the primary customers actually were: the car dealers, or the end consumers, or both. Were the dealers their customers or were the end consumers? Borst told the participants, "We can discuss, debate, and disagree – but we need to decide and do." So the team decided that the key customers TFS serves in their business model were both dealers and end consumers.

They ended day one with consensus on their current business model, something they never had made explicit before.

INSIGHT WE HAD TO START WITH A RALLYING CRY TO **CREATE A SHARED SENSE OF URGENCY.**

DAY 2
IDEATION

DAY 3 **THE
DOUBLE LOOP**

INSIGHT USE IDEATION TECHNIQUES TO
FORCE PEOPLE TO THINK OUTSIDE THE BOX.

The next day, the participants started ideating new business models, using the fire starters as a starting point.

They were instructed to make sure that the left and right sides of their new business model canvases were connected by the goals of creating, delivering, and capturing value. They made sure each of the building blocks supported the goal and was linked up to the other building blocks.

At the end of the day, each group selected their most promising idea for a new business model, based on the design criteria and their enthusiasm, and presented it onstage. The audience rated each idea as if they were the CEO, allocating funds only to those models that would result in doubling profits.

By the end of the second day, the group had come up with four very concrete models for moving the company forward.

Closing the offsite was just as important as starting it, and the team made sure next steps were laid out.

"This time, we made the ideas concrete before we left and knew how we were going to take them forward. We had no shortage of volunteers who wanted to work on it in some way. I've never had that happen before," said Chris Ballinger, the CFO.

Borst concluded the offsite by endorsing the new tools in a very real way, emphasizing that the offsite was not pie in the sky and that this work had to continue on a regular basis in order for TFS to get to where it needed to go. He went on record saying his job was to enable the executive team and managers to continue their effort begun that week.

INSIGHT WE CAN DISCUSS, DEBATE, AND DISAGREE, BUT **WE NEED TO DECIDE AND DO!**

Designing for a better future is not something to do on the side; it is your job. ∎

We visualized the fire starters and stuck them to the walls in the workshop space to give the teams an anchor while ideating.

TOYOTA

137

INTRODUCTION TO **IDEATION TOOLS**

While everyone can and should bring their shower ideas to the table, expanding and exploring ideas is much easier done with the right-sized group using the right tools. Here are some ways to ideate together.

STARTING OUT

When you're starting the ideation process, you'll need to shift your – and your team's – mindset away from evaluation. That's not always easy, especially when you have a job that involves critical thinking, making many decisions, and evaluating other people's work. But don't fret. With a bit of practice using the tools and techniques made for ideating, you'll get it in no time!

TAKE YOUR TIME

It may take you and your team some time – perhaps even 15–20 minutes – to switch into ideation mode. This is where ice breakers make a big difference. Shifting to a more playful, fun mindset will help the mental transition from execution to ideation tremendously. Like everything, the more you practice, the better you'll get at it.

One caveat: Don't spend the entire day in ideation mode. Not only will it be counterproductive, you'll quickly run out of gas and more than likely begin arguing about the ideas rather than expanding upon them.

DON'T BLOCK

Be aware of "blocking" behaviors that break the flow of creativity. Prematurely evaluating and judging ideas will block the creative flow. To overcome this, try using "yes, and . . ." rather than "yes, but . . ." statements. And make sure your team is wearing their yellow thinking hats; they can don their black hats later.

DON'T OVERTHINK

The key to ideating is not overthinking every idea or word on the sticky note in front of you. Let your brain come up with anything it wants, and take the role of recorder rather than trying to direct the flow of your thoughts. This is also something you'll get better at with practice.

USE A CANVAS

Sometimes it's hard to get the creative engines started. Sure, people come to work with their favorite shower ideas. But in ideation, you're looking to build upon and expand beyond the shower ideas. Often, the best way to do this is to use a canvas, like the Business Model Canvas or Value Proposition Canvas, to help frame the ideation session and expand from there. The

Business Model Canvas has the added benefit that it also requires people to go a bit deeper.

GO INTO SPACE

Sometimes it's necessary to force yourself and your team to take a trip to space. What if you had to start from scratch? What if you stopped doing what you do today? Asking these questions will help your team expand beyond the boundaries of your current strategy and its limitations. As you leave reality behind, start to build on others ideas to make the big idea even bigger. When you land back on earth, you'll likely find that you've learned something new that can augment your current strategy – or spark an entirely new one.

WALL OF IDEAS

The wall of ideas is a great way to record the results of your ideation session. When they fasten their sticky notes to the wall, everyone, from the introverts to the extroverts, is working together creatively and feeling a sense of achievement. As the team adds ideas to the wall, they will no doubt come up with new ones or point out ones that are funny or interesting.

COMING BACK TO EARTH

When you have been ideating with your team for a while, the arc of tension will naturally come to an end at some point. Everyone will slow down their idea generation; it will start to feel more

TIP! Don't allow the dust to settle on the results of your creative session! Immediately process the results and look for any hidden gems.

like an effort to come up with another idea. Be cognizant of this state as this is the point where the collective energy is starting to dissipate. This is a perfect moment to call for a break. When you come back, you and the team can begin evaluating ideas, which will help to increase the energy level.

THE FRUITS OF YOUR LABOR

Once the team has generated tons of ideas – perhaps several hundred (no, really) – and stuck them to the wall of ideas, it's time to start organizing them. It's important not to think of this as busywork. Organizing ideas will actually lead to new combinations and more ideas (remember the stepping-stones concept). One of the best ways to do this is to cluster similar ideas together and give them some big title or headline.

After you've clustered the ideas to your satisfaction, you'll want to filter the ones that are most promising to work on. No need to deliberate or agonize over this, either! At the end of this chapter we've shared a great tool that will help you do this quickly and in a structured way, since long discussions about which ideas are better on paper simply are a waste of time. ■

TOOL **CREATIVE MATRIX**

GENERATE

generate ideas

± 15 MIN

pressure cooker

3–5

people per group

When you're finding that everyone's ideas are falling in and around the same areas of exploration, it's time to expand the boundaries of your thinking. This is a perfect time to use a Creative Matrix.

CREATIVE MATRIX

The goal of ideation is to expand the thinking and ideas of every-one on the team, to create something that is greater than the sum of its parts. However, without context and practice, most of us have a tough time expanding beyond what we know (or came up with in the shower).

The Creative Matrix was designed with this in mind. Essentially, the Creative Matrix is a tool that will help spark new ideas at the intersections of discrete categories. This tool is all about divergent thinking. Best of all, you get to design your own Creative Matrix based on your design criteria, the market you play in, or the cus-tomers you serve (or wish to serve).

THE GRID

To design your own Creative Matrix, draw a grid on a whiteboard or poster paper with no more than five rows and five columns. Give it a topic or a central "how might we…?" question.

For each of the columns, designate a customer segment (existing or new). For each of the rows, designate a particular technology, enabling solution, or value proposition. You might also opt to

designate the end column and/or row as a wildcard category, for placing open ideas.

FILL IN THE CELLS

With your matrix in place, it's time to ideate! Using sticky notes, have each person randomly and rapidly add as many ideas as they can come up with to the cells in the matrix. Words are good. Pictures are better! The goal is to fill every single cell in the Creative Matrix with at least one idea.

To incentivize people to generate more ideas, assign a point for each sticky note. The highest total score wins.

Once every cell has been filled in and the time limit is up, it's time to review everyone's ideas. Have the team huddle around the create matrix as if it were a painting. Once everyone has had an ample chance to look at each other's work, have each person call out their favorite ideas (or top two). From there, as a team select the most promising ideas to move forward. ■

Add the different things you want to come up with, e.g., a channel, value prop, and revenue model, for each segment. Or ideate for variations of the same thing.

Try to put in the different customer segments along the top. That way you can generate ideas for each segment and accommodate their needs.

You can add as many columns as you want. However, for an effective result, we don't advise going over a total of 20 cells.

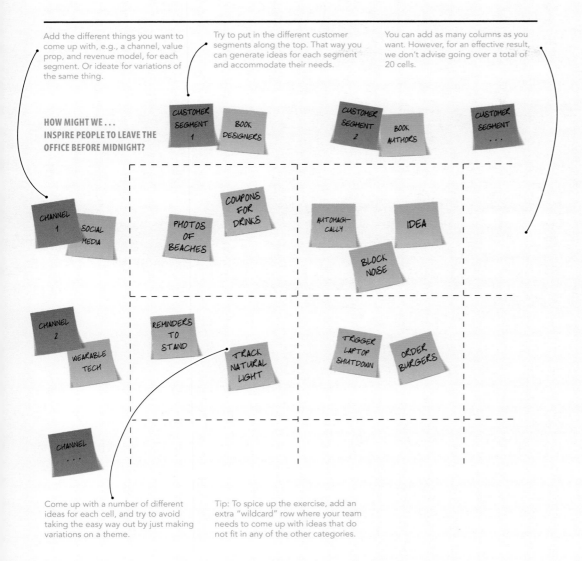

HOW MIGHT WE . . . INSPIRE PEOPLE TO LEAVE THE OFFICE BEFORE MIDNIGHT?

Come up with a number of different ideas for each cell, and try to avoid taking the easy way out by just making variations on a theme.

Tip: To spice up the exercise, add an extra "wildcard" row where your team needs to come up with ideas that do not fit in any of the other categories.

141

CHECKLIST

- [ ] All of the cells are filled with ideas that make sense.
- [ ] The ideas are concrete and well defined.
- [ ] You can't think of any categories you left out.

NEXT STEP

> Validate your new ideas.

TOOL **BUSINESS MODEL CANVAS** IDEATION

GENERATE

generate ideas

± **30** MIN

pressure cooker

3–5

people per group

The Business Model Canvas is described on page 116.

The Business Model Canvas can be a terrific ideation tool if you know how to use it as such. The tools on this page help you generate different options that you can either explore further or put on the shelf for later.

FRESHWATCHING

Need a jump-start for ideating based on your current business model? Why not use another company's business model to rev your creative engine? This is the purpose of the freshwatching ideation technique.

Freshwatching is mixing and matching business models from other companies – often totally outside your business or industry – to see what you can come up with. For instance, what if you applied Uber or Amazon's business model to your own? What if you operated like Netflix or Spotify? How would your value proposition change if it was informed by EasyJet or Apple?

It doesn't matter if the company is an online business, an offline retailer, or even a well-known one. With freshwatching, you're simply looking at your company through the lens of another.

REMOVE YOUR CORE

Examine your business model to find your company's special sauce – that one thing you are absolutely certain defines how your company creates, delivers, or captures value. For instance, if you're running a software business, this might be the proprietary software you develop and sell. It could also be an irreplaceable partner or a specific customer segment.

Now remove that sticky note. Chances are, your business model now has a big hole in it. Your task: try to fix it. No cheating: Don't sneak the removed sticky note back in! This constraint will definitely give you new ideas.

EPICENTERS

The Business Model Canvas represents a dynamic system. There is interplay – cause and effect – between each and every block; changing an element in one will affect another. This lends itself well to a technique called epicenter-based ideation.

With epicenter-based ideation, you effectively have nine different boxes, or epicenters, to play with in order to generate more ideas. One way this works is to clear your business model of eight boxes, leaving the focus on one. What would you build if you kept that one? For instance, what if you were able to bring to bear your company's resources to create an entirely new business model?

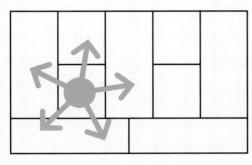

EPICENTER: RESOURCE DRIVEN
All businesses contain key resources that are the fundamental elements of the engine under the hood. In Amazon's case, this was its IT infrastructure. If you were to start over with just your key resources intact, what could you do with them that you're not doing now?

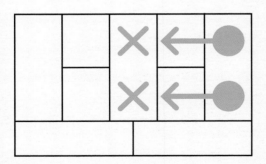

PATTERN: MULTISIDED PLATFORM
Multisided platforms are business models that serve two or more customer segments, whereby one customer segment usually uses the platform as the channel to exchange value with the other customer segment. Google makes money from advertisers via AdWords using a multisided platform.

Amazon did just that when it figured out that it could use its cloud infrastructure to generate revenue.

Other areas to focus on using this method might be your customer segments (what else could you offer them?); your value proposition (what other customer segments could you address?); revenue streams (what other ways might you sell, lease, or rent your product/service?); and even your channels (what else could you leverage your channels to do?).

FOLLOW PATTERNS

When you scan the landscape of existing business models, you'll notice many patterns exist. Business model patterns are like formulas that can be applied to a business model to address a new customer need, create a new revenue stream, etc. Some well-known examples of business model patterns use subscription revenue streams and/or have product platforms whereby one part of the product relies on the other to make money (think cheap handles, expensive razor blades, or cheap printers, expensive ink). ∎

143

CHECKLIST

- [ ] You came up with more than six new business model options.
- [ ] The options you came up with are all very different.
- [ ] You made the options concrete and specific to your business.

NEXT STEP

> Pitch them and see which ideas resonate with others.
> Select a business model that you want to turn into a Value Proposition Canvas.
> Select a business model you want to turn into a prototype.

TOOL **WALL OF IDEAS**

GENERATE

generate ideas

± **30** MIN

pressure cooker

SOLO

but all together

Asking "what if?" is a powerful way to fill a wall with great ideas. Feel free to use these trigger questions, or create your own! Ask them of your team at a fast pace, challenging each person to create lots of ideas.

WHAT IF . . .

TRIGGER QUESTIONS
Aim for 20–30 trigger questions, which will take 10–15 minutes to ask.

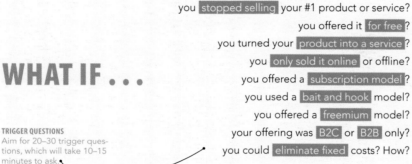

you stopped selling your #1 product or service?
you offered it for free?
you turned your product into a service?
you only sold it online or offline?
you offered a subscription model?
you used a bait and hook model?
you offered a freemium model?
your offering was B2C or B2B only?
you could eliminate fixed costs? How?

> **500** IDEAS

ASK TRIGGER QUESTIONS

The purpose of this tool is to fill up an entire wall with the ideas generated by a team in a short amount of time. This technique uses trigger questions to get the creative juices flowing.

The wall of ideas requires preparation. First, decide on a list of trigger questions that you're going to ask the team in rapid succession (one every 30 seconds or so). Use the ones above to get you started, taking out the ones that don't apply to your business. Use

your existing Business Model Canvas as fodder for creating new questions. If, for instance, you sell a product today through retailers, what would happen if you sold it directly to customers through an online channel? What would that look like? You get the picture.

As the trigger questions are asked, each person will simply write whatever comes to mind on a sticky note using a permanent marker. By the end of this exercise there should be a pile of at least as many sticky notes as there are questions in front of each participant.

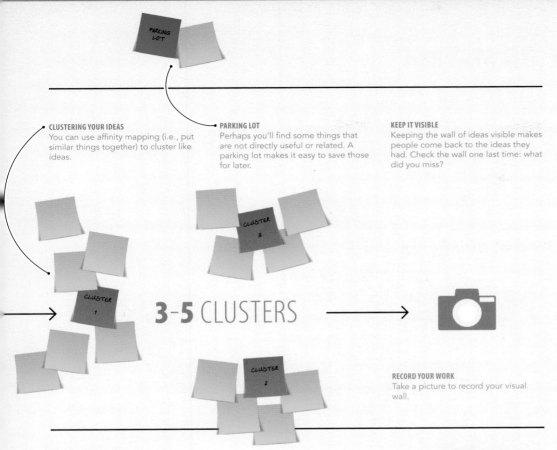

CLUSTERING YOUR IDEAS
You can use affinity mapping (i.e., put similar things together) to cluster like ideas.

PARKING LOT
Perhaps you'll find some things that are not directly useful or related. A parking lot makes it easy to save those for later.

KEEP IT VISIBLE
Keeping the wall of ideas visible makes people come back to the ideas they had. Check the wall one last time: what did you miss?

3-5 CLUSTERS

RECORD YOUR WORK
Take a picture to record your visual wall.

145

CLUSTER YOUR IDEAS

Once the questions run out, have everyone affix their sticky notes to the wall, one at a time, calling out the idea, so everyone is clear about what's been added. Don't worry about organization at first.

Next, organize the ideas into a maximum of five high-level clusters. You can define the clusters beforehand, or you can use affinity mapping and let them emerge.

When you're done clustering, record your result. Photos make it easy to do that. Send them around to the team, and don't forget to keep them informed of future progress! ■

CHECKLIST

☐ You came up with over 500 ideas (or about 25 per person).

☐ You clustered them into sensible themes.

NEXT STEPS

> Make a selection: Select the most promising ideas to continue to work on.

TOOL **INNOVATION MATRIX**

Your wall of ideas is filled with hundreds of ideas, and the time has come to make a selection. What are the really promising ideas? Use the Innovation Matrix and the ranking system on this page to filter out the best ideas.

CATEGORIZE YOUR IDEAS

We humans are fantastic at categorizing things. We spend much of our professional lives categorizing and sub-categorizing the work we do. When it comes to pairing down your wall of ideas, a 2x2 matrix is a perfect tool to harness our innate ability to categorize.

The Innovation Matrix lays out rows delineating incremental and substantial changes and columns delineating reducing cost and increasing revenues. You can certainly use your own decision criteria for the rows and columns. Whatever criteria you choose, make sure they have clear distinctions that will help you organize your ideas and select the ones to move into prototyping and validation.

GO BIG OR GO HOME

This tool is designed to separate the ideas that result in incremental, easy-to-accomplish changes from the ones that will make a big difference. For instance, an idea to reduce costs by mandating that everyone print double-sided pages is incremental and small. Sure, for a large company, this could certainly reduce operational costs. However, it is probably a change that can and should be implemented anyway. A big change will cause bigger shifts. These ideas will show up in the top quadrants of the matrix.

USING THE MATRIX

To use the Innovation Matrix, pull your ideas off the wall or canvas and, as a team, discuss where each idea belongs on the matrix. Unless you've modified the canvas to represent your own axes, the discussions you have at this point are not about feasibility or even viability. They're about the potential for change. Is it an incremental change, one that your company could take on with little work or resources? That idea should probably placed in the bottom half of the matrix. Is it an idea for generating more revenue? The right half is where that one belongs.

THINK BIGGER

As described in the Toyota Financial Services case, when you find people sticking to small, incremental ideas on the bottom half of the matrix, you'll need to find ways, such as fire starter questions or an "into space" exercise, to push the boundaries and get people thinking bigger.

INNOVATION MATRIX

DESIGN A
BETTER
BUSINESS

SUBSTANTIAL

SUBSTAN-
TIAL COST
REDUCTION

SUBSTAN-
TIAL REVENUE
INCREASE

COST

REVENUE

TIPPING
POINT
+/- 10%

INCREMENTAL
COST
REDUCTION

SMALL OR
INCREMENTAL
REVENUE
INCREASE

INCREMENTAL

BY **DESIGNABETTERBUSINESS**.COM

147

THE TOP QUADRANTS
The ones where you want
your ideas to end up in.

DON'T STOP
If you have categorized your ideas and
the top quadrants aren't quite filled in, try
another round of ideation.

LOW-HANGING FRUIT

There could be low-hanging fruit
in any one of the quadrants that
represent quick wins. When the
matrix is completely filled in,
you might even distribute these
to people who can take them
further. But the ideas on the top
make the biggest changes. ∎

CHECKLIST

☐ Most of your ideas are in the
top two quadrants.

☐ The outcome from the voting
was significant.

☐ You were able to make a clear
selection based on the design
criteria.

NEXT STEP

> Can you validate your ideas?

IDEATION HACKS

YOUR WORST NIGHTMARE

A great ideation exercise based on the Business Model Canvas is to imagine your company's worst nightmare.

What if you had to start from scratch without a legacy to stand on? What competing business could take yours completely out of the game? These are your organization's worst nightmares. And if you aren't exploring them, chances are, someone else is . . .

GAMIFIED IDEATION

Direct the participants' attention away from the quality of their ideas and onto the quantity.

Perhaps the person contributing the most ideas wins a prize.

The point is not the prize, but the fact that a bit of healthy competition can make people overcome uncertainty and fear.

THINK LIKE A STARTUP

What if you were to look at the opportunities and challenges your company addresses through the eyes of a startup founder? To use this method, start over with a new, clean business model canvas and reinvent your company.

What would you do differently? What do customers need and want, and how would you align your value propositions to match?

149

PICTURE IT

Have people draw their own or other's ideas instead of writing them down. It's fun, and forces them to be concrete rather than abstract.

If people are nervous about their drawing skills, they can use Lego Serious Play instead.

OUTDOOR IDEATION

Take the team outdoors, to a busy, noisy area in town, with lots of different stimuli. Do the ideation session in that location.

Draw the participants' attention to the myriad of signals and inputs around them as a source of inspiration. Tuning in to the noise can help your brain make even wilder leaps.

THE UNUSUAL SUSPECTS

Ideation is not the exclusive domain of the creative or R&D departments. Ask some unusual suspects to join; they will surprise you.

Break away from your usual perspectives. Don't ideate only from your current point of view. If you keep coming back to what you already have and already know, try to start with a completely different base.

YOU NOW HAVE . . .

> **4–6 NEW BUSINESS MODEL CANVASES** FILLED OUT — P142

> A WALL OF IDEAS WITH **AT LEAST 500 IDEAS** — P144

> **4–6 NEW VALUE PROPOSITION CANVASES** FILLED OUT — P106

NEXT STEPS

> **CRASH TEST YOUR IDEAS** — P156
> Using prototype

> **REVISIT YOUR POINT OF VIEW** — P46
> Did you challenge your vision enough? Do you need to readjust your point of view?

> **SELECT BUSINESS MODELS** — P68
> Based on your design criteria.

> **DESIGN VALUE PROPOSITIONS** — P106
> Based on your business model(s).

RECAP

THERE IS NO **SINGLE RIGHT SOLUTION.** IDEAS ARE STEPPING-STONES.

FUN IS THE BEST **IDEATION ELIXIR.**

IDEAS DON'T COME FROM A MAGICAL DIMENSION. **START YOUR CREATIVE ENGINES.**

USE A TOOL TO EXPAND YOUR THINKING. GO DEEPER FOR BETTER IDEAS.

SELECT IDEAS BEFORE MOVING FORWARD. YOU CAN'T TEST 500 IDEAS AT ONCE.

FREE UP SPACE FOR DEEPER THINKING.

151

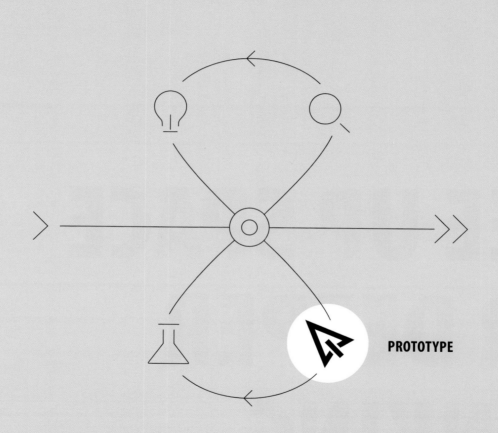

PROTOTYPE

THE DESIGN JOURNEY **PROTOTYPE**

LEARN TO **BRING IDEAS TO LIFE**

SKETCH A PROTOTYPE

MAKE A PROTOTYPE

THE **MAKER MINDSET**

It probably feels safe to spend time and energy on the aspects of your idea that you can grasp. The technical challenges are often much more visible and well-known. It's tempting to skip ahead and spend time "solving the big problems," such as developing the right algorithms. But why do that?

THE MYTH OF "BUILD IT AND THEY WILL COME"

When you're by yourself or with your team, it often feels exciting (and quite safe) to riff all day on your ideas. You've probably spent countless hours, energy, and brainpower on the "coolest" details of your idea. When you're a technical person, or part of a technical team, you probably even start heading down the road of how to solve the technical challenges of your idea before you've even explored how to test the idea itself.

We do this because the things we know and can figure out on our own, without having to step outside of our box, feel comfortable, and frankly, they are often rewarding personal puzzles to solve. Hence, we're tempted to skip ahead and spend time "solving the big problems," such as developing the right algorithms, distribution channels, or manufacturing systems.

While solving puzzles is fun and can create lots of energy on its own, when it comes to customer-facing products, there simply are no shortcuts. You must figure out how to solve the toughest challenge: will this idea resonate with customers? There is no point in solving future problems if you haven't solved today's problem first. Start at the beginning!

START SMALL

Think like an engineer or an architect. Just like the Wright brothers built kites before they ever attempted to build a human-scale plane, architects always start with models first. Of course you know why they do this: if you're designing Stonehenge, it's a lot cheaper to test it on a small scale before hiring hundreds of people to move 60-ton megaliths around.

Likewise, Leonardo da Vinci created hundreds of sketches and built scale models of his machines in his workshop, weeding out problems before he ever shelled out real money to build the real thing. Sketches not only helped da Vinci solve potential construction problems; they also helped him to explain and sell his ideas to his patrons.

The Wright brothers, the architects of Stonehenge, and Leonardo da Vinci were prototyping masters. They understood to their cores that it is foolhardy to assume that you understand your abstract idea well enough to construct it flawlessly on the first attempt. Moreover, these masters of their craft understood that other people need to get a clear grasp of an idea in order to become enthusiastic about it. The idea needs to be tangible first!

IDEAS ARE NOT REAL

After all, an idea is nothing more than an idea: something that seems great on paper based on a bunch of assumptions. Ideas are abstract and have little substance on their own. Of course, some ideas are truly great and have potential to be game changing. But that potential can only be unlocked by introducing the idea to reality. The cool part of this is that building simple prototypes early on in the design journey will make it easier to find that potential.

PROTOTYPES ARE TANGIBLE; THEY ARE ARTIFACTS

There's a well-known story about how the Dropbox founders prototyped their idea with customers. The idea seems simple today: enable people to save files anywhere and have them synced everywhere. However, when Dropbox was just getting started, there wasn't really anything like it on the market. While technically feasible, what Drew Houston, Dropbox's CEO, really wanted to know was whether customers would even be willing try his product. So, instead spending time and money putting a piece of code into the world that didn't really do his idea justice in terms of the experience and vision he was shooting for, he put

PROTOTYPING GIVES IDEAS FORM AND FUNCTION.

out a video that showed the experience. This wasn't a sales video. It was a prototype of the experience that cost him only the time to make it. Ultimately, the prototype helped Drew and his team learn enough about their customers that they launched what is today a brand name.

Prototypes, like Dropbox's video, are not meant to be a full-blown product. They're built such that they can be experienced by the customers with the real value being the lessons learned which will ultimately lead to a better idea. In this way a prototype is much richer than an idea, or even a description on paper. A prototype allows you to explore different perspectives.

Why prototypes – especially visual prototypes – work best is science: we are visual, auditory, and crave experiential. Being

155

TIP! Practice putting form to idea using the tools at your fingertips. Whether it's a pen and paper, sticky notes, or presentation software, sometimes the simplest things make the most practical prototyping tools.

able to see, touch, and manipulate something, to feel the weight of it and see it respond to an action, gives us a deeper, more visceral understanding than a description. This is what prototypes can do for us.

CRASH TEST YOUR IDEAS

Give your idea life and accelerate your learning in doing so. This is what prototyping is all about. Think of your prototype as the controlled crash-test experiment. What is the aspect of it that you want to learn more about? Is it the overall experience, the download experience, the experience of driving it around the city? No matter what your idea is, there's a prototype that can help you to test it in the real world. What's more, prototypes come in two main flavors: prototypes meant for you to get a better understanding of what will work and what may not work; and prototypes meant to test something with a customer (or user).

In both cases, you'll need to ask yourself what you're testing in the first place. What is it you really want to know? In the chapter on validation there are a ton of great tools and starting points for prototyping in case you want to test your design with customers. But even when you are doing a quick mock-up with your team to see how something will fit together, it's important to know what single aspect of the idea you want to prototype.

DESIGN YOUR PROTOTYPE TO TEST THAT ASPECT

Once you have figured out what you really want to know (and crash test), it's time to design the minimal prototype that will fit the bill. Start small, and only make it more complex when you really must. Always ask yourself: Can it be made even simpler? What can we leave out? Are all these features really necessary?

Just remember, it's never too early to start prototyping. Whether you're prototyping a single element of your idea or the whole thing, the keys to prototyping are the same: define what you want to learn, get started, and keep it simple. Drew Houston, from Dropbox, said it best, "Not launching [is] painful; not learning [is] fatal."

SCRAPPY DOESN'T EQUAL CRAPPY

Especially early on, your prototypes should not be sophisticated. In fact, they may even be downright ugly. They should be built just well enough to serve their purpose, be it testing them with customers or simply looking at them with your team to see if the prototype makes sense.

This goes back to designing the right prototype for the job. In the beginning of your journey, there's simply no need to spend resources building and testing high-fidelity aspects of your design. This is a waste of resources that you can use somewhere else. In prototyping, you want to test the basics, the fundamentals. And, it's not only okay to fake it, it's expected. Keep it low-fi and learn as much as you can. But do this fast and repeatedly.

NO NEED TO WAIT

Interestingly, experienced designers are often wary of the fallacy of pretty-looking prototypes. A beautiful prototype can look so amazing that it blinds you or others to the inherent underlying problems with the idea.

People will simply like how it looks or feels, and you won't be able to tease out what you really want to learn from the tests. Often that means that you'll be led in the wrong direction altogether. The level of detail of your prototype should be linked to the stage of your journey. Do it low-fi first, and high-fi later.

In the rest of this chapter we've given you a number of examples and tools to help you get started building your own prototypes. It's never to early to get started! No, really. ■

BE YOUR OWN **GUINEA PIG**

Don't think you can figure it all out in your head. You need to prototype your design, not just for your customers, but also for yourself.

In any design process, it is vital that the design team understand the design as intimately as possible. What are you creating? How does it work? How does it feel? If it's a digital service, how might you mock it up quickly to see it come to life on your screen (or on a piece of paper)? Perhaps you can use PowerPoint or Keynote for that. If it's a physical product, are there other things you can modify to approximate the shape and weight?

With every new stage of the journey, familiarize yourself with the design. The best way to do this is to try it yourself. As a designer, you are your own guinea pig.

Prototyping it, and interacting with it, will give you many more ideas about how you might solve problems, how your customers will react, and what your next steps will be.

If you are designing a product, it's best to use the prototype, as your customers would, first. If you're designing a process or a service, you are its first user.

MASTER **PROTOTYPING**

1 SKETCH IT FIRST

Sketching is a great way to feel your way around a prototype, approaching it quickly from different angles. You can sketch on the back of a napkin, with cardboard, code, spreadsheets, Lego pieces, welding equipment, or the salt and pepper dispensers on your lunch table.

What makes a sketch a sketch is that it is low fidelity. It's rough; it's not about the details. The details can be worked on later.

2 KEEP IT SIMPLE

What if you had no budget and no time? What can you accomplish in 30 minutes or less? Funny enough, adding constraints to yourself will increase your ability to be creative. It frees you from the urge to make it perfect, and will help you avoid kne-jerk reactions, such as outsourcing or immediately hiring developers to build a final product.

MacGyver (yes, that is now an accepted verb in the Oxford Dictionaries!) together the scrappiest prototype you can, with only

TIP! Ask yourself the following question: Do you really need to build it? Is there any way to get (most of) what you need from something that is on the shelf? Can you wire together existing products?

the materials available in your desk drawer. It will be done in no time, and it will almost certainly teach you something new.

3 YOUR MATERIALS ARE AROUND YOU

In early prototyping, you don't need fancy materials if you know what you want to test. Tinkering with office supplies, paper, and everything else at hand is usually all you need. A coffee mug becomes a customer, your phone is the store manager, and you can play out the interaction in the store. Avoid the trap where you think you need some expensive component or complex process before you can test: try to figure out how to fake it first.

4 PROTOTYPE THE PROTOTYPE

It is one thing to generate, share, and expand upon lots of ideas. But you'll also need to explore some of those ideas in more depth – especially when it comes to selecting a few ideas to prototype and validate. What is the core idea about? What problems does it aim to solve and who for? What will customers pay for and how will they find it in the first place?

You will not be able to explore every idea this deeply. But there some that will require more context in order to really understand what they are all about and what assumptions you've made (or your team has made) when generating them.

5 PRESENTATION MATTERS

The presentation is part of the prototype. Even if it is just a scribbled note, if you want someone to take it at face value and give you an honest opinion, you need to present it as if it were the real thing. The way you show it sets expectations, and setting the wrong ones means you won't learn what you want from it.

6 STAY ON THE CLOCK

Make sure you have a tight deadline: timeboxing makes you more creative and means you'll try to find the fastest possible prototype you can build. Otherwise you risk turning your prototype into a product, and starting to add unnecessary features. ■

Prototyping voting as done by Team MACCR, Innovation Studio 2015, DMBA. (Riley Moynes, Cynthia Randolph, Meghan Luce, Amodini Chhabra, and Chandrima Deuri)

PROTOTYPING **VOTING**

How do you prototype ideas to solve a big, hairy problem like voter engagement? Look for the pain!

Voting pain is found in the registration process. A group of MBA students used prototyping to test their idea.

They did it by hacking together a new registration experience and recording people receiving their prototype. Priceless!

159

FAKE IT **BEFORE YOU MAKE IT**

There are many ways to "fake it" before spending big bucks on prototyping. Which method to choose depends on the idea that you want to prototype. Availability of resources is another determining factor. Sometimes a simple prototype will do the trick. Other times you need something more elaborate. Here is an overview from easy techniques to ones that require more resources.

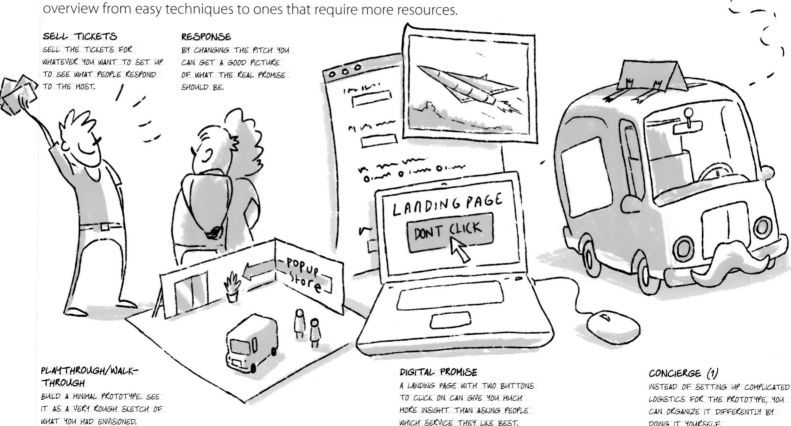

SELL TICKETS
SELL THE TICKETS FOR WHATEVER YOU WANT TO SET UP TO SEE WHAT PEOPLE RESPOND TO THE MOST.

RESPONSE
BY CHANGING THE PITCH YOU CAN GET A GOOD PICTURE OF WHAT THE REAL PROMISE SHOULD BE.

PLAYTHROUGH/WALK-THROUGH
BUILD A MINIMAL PROTOTYPE. SEE IT AS A VERY ROUGH SKETCH OF WHAT YOU HAD ENVISIONED.

DIGITAL PROMISE
A LANDING PAGE WITH TWO BUTTONS TO CLICK ON CAN GIVE YOU MUCH MORE INSIGHT THAN ASKING PEOPLE WHICH SERVICE THEY LIKE BEST.

CONCIERGE (1)
INSTEAD OF SETTING UP COMPLICATED LOGISTICS FOR THE PROTOTYPE, YOU CAN ORGANIZE IT DIFFERENTLY BY DOING IT YOURSELF.

POP-UP STORE

PLANNING ON SELLING STUFF? FOR BOTH OFFLINE AND ONLINE: A POP-UP STORE SETUP LETS YOU TEST MANY INTERACTIONS, PRODUCT PLACEMENTS, TONES OF VOICES. AND THE SPONTANUOUS NATURE MAKES IT EASY FOR PEOPLE TO INTERACT WITH.

WIZARD OF OZ

WHY BUILD A WHOLE WORLD IF AN ILLUSION IS ENOUGH? FOR THE WIZARD AT LEAST IT DID THE TRICK. HE FOOLED THEM ALL WITH SMOKE AND MIRRORS.

THIS "CON" CAN TAKE SEVERAL SHAPES. THE BASIC IDEA IS THAT FROM THE OUTSIDE IT LOOKS THE PART. THE INNER WORKINGS (OF A SERVICE, A MACHINE, AN EVENT) ARE HANDLED BY YOU OR SOMEONE ELSE.

CONCIERGE (2)

THE ADVANTAGE AGAIN IS THAT YOU ARE ALSO THE ONE OBSERVING THE RESPONSES, SEEING WHERE THINGS GO WRONG, WHAT WORKS OR IS MISSING.

3D PRINTING

A 3D PRINTER CAN BE A GREAT REPLACEMENT FOR A WHOLE PRODUCTION PROCESS. ANOTHER ADVANTAGE IS YOU WILL HAVE TO SIMPLIFY YOUR PRODUCT. A GREAT MOMENT TO CHECK YOURSELF FOR FEATURE CREEP.

161

CARD DECK

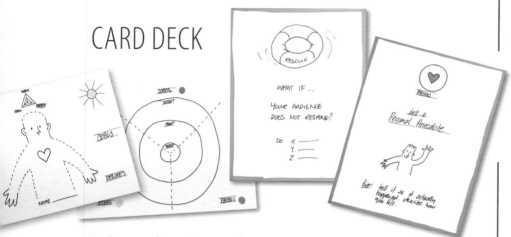

Working on a format for storytelling, we started with this prototype: a card deck to help people build and share stories in 10 steps. While prototyping we also discovered a kick-ass light version.

For more about this way of storytelling, see page 74.

PROTOTYPING A VIP QUEUE

When a large remittance bank came up with an idea to add a VIP service to their offices in Russia, so loyal customers would be helped faster, they initially wanted to do a market research questionnaire to gauge customer response. We convinced them to prototype the approach in one of their offices and to do it in person. The resulting feedback from customers validated the idea and gave them input for even bigger improvements.

PROTOTYPING THE BUSINESS JET EXPERIENCE

To find out if a new idea for a business jet service between Amsterdam and Paris was feasible, the startup's founders sat in the Thalys high-speed train for a few days and showed business people the offering, asking them if they would want to buy a ticket. Not only did the founders pick the right assumption to test, they did so with what was probably the right audience. This simple, but effective, prototype cost them only the price of the train tickets. The findings they received in return were invaluable.

PLAYMOBIL® WALK-THROUGH

While we were preparing for a big strategy event involving hundreds of executives with a large European bank, their CFO came up with the idea of prototyping the run-through of the entire event using Playmobil figures. That helped all the participants understand their roles and where they were supposed to be. This really helped to iron out some bottlenecks that were impossible to spot on paper.

BURSTING THE BUBBLE

At Impact Hub Amsterdam, we helped social startups turn their ideas into running businesses. One of the participants, with an idea for an organic shampoo dispenser for when you forgot your shampoo at the gym, had a valuable a-ha moment. In his mind, the first step toward a working business was to develop an expensive dispenser, so he could put it in local gyms.

We convinced him to take a few of his shampoo bottles and put them on a table with a nice sign at the local gym a few doors away. Instead of spending hundreds of euros and a lot of time, he got his feedback the same day.

PROTOTYPE PRICETAGS

A startup wanted to prototype the price experience of their ready-to-launch product.

They placed a mock-up in different stores with different prices to see what happens. Why should your product have the same price tag everywhere?

BRAND YOUR PROTOTYPE

In an Innovation Workshop at a large consumer goods company, teams were challenged to think and work like a startup. To make it feel more "real," the whole setup of the workshop was changed and teams got brands for their startups, printed on t-shirts. This really put the teams in the right mindset!

163

PROTOTYPING THE FUTURE

AUTODESK

PROTOTYPING THE FUTURE

Autodesk, a large software company mostly known for its founding flagship design software, AutoCAD, has been developing and selling design-related software for more than 30 years.

BEYOND COMPUTER-AIDED DESIGN

While many people may not know Autodesk by name, their software has touched most people's lives. Most human-created things on earth (designed and made in the last 30 years) – from the chair you're sitting in, to the building that it's housed in, to the car you drove in on, to the special-effects blockbuster you watched – are likely to have been created, at least in part, by Autodesk software.

As pervasive as Autodesk's software may be, the company's leadership has for the last decade been aggressively exploring what's next for the company. Beyond incremental improvements to its legacy products, Autodesk has been developing new tools to solve the design problems that its customers will face in the future.

Carl Bass, Autodesk's CEO, a hardcore "maker" himself, was not only interested in finding potential markets to expand into. He was also interested in prototyping early and often in order to get real insight into what would matter to the company – and its customer – in the future. Carl is an

An illustration of The San Francisco Ferry Building from the graphic novel *Prelude to Then.*

innovator with a high degree of risk tolerance. As such, he likes to prototype and experiment to understand what's working and what's not. This principle permeates Autodesk's culture today.

Enter Maurice Conti, head of Autodesk's Applied Research Lab and the director of strategic innovation in the company's office of the CTO.

CARL BASS: QUICKLY PROVE OR DISPROVE ASSUMPTIONS IN ORDER TO LEARN

165

THE CHALLENGE

Back in 2010, Autodesk's CTO, Jeff Kowalski, tasked Conti to "go look in our blind spots," which Conti knew, by definition, he could not be directed to find. He had to go look where the company was not, seek out new opportunities to focus >>

on, and consider things that no one had yet pondered. So began Conti's search.

A-HA

As Conti scanned the horizon for blind spots, he began looking into different areas adjacent to those Autodesk traditionally focused on. For instance, as he dug into the manufacturing industry – one of Autodesk's most important areas of focus – he saw an opportunity in advanced robotics. "We [had] nothing really going on [there]," Conti said. "No strategy, no projects, no point of view. I thought we were probably overlooking something really important for the future."

Even more interesting to Conti was the idea that robots could be used to augment human capabilities. Rather than the current debate about how increasing the use of robots will fundamentally remove humans from the equation, Conti has a different point of view. In his mind, there are many jobs that neither humans nor robots do well alone. By getting them to work together, in a sort of symbiotic relationship, you could essentially change how work is done, enabling many things to be performed more safely, efficiently, and effectively.

Conti and his team dove into the opportunity headlong. After asking lots of questions (i.e., observing), the team decided to prototype a scenario whereby humans and robots could work side by side (without the fear that robots would squash the humans). To test this, David Thomasson, a principal research engineer on Conti's team, began programming small, affordable desktop-sized robots to watch and learn from humans. "There's a robot watching a craftsman, for example, carving wood. And it's learning the types of cuts you prefer, and it can come in and repeat them, or make variations of what you do, in your style, so you can both be working on a job together."

As the team continued to prototype this idea, more questions arose along with the new insights. How can we make it easier to program industrial robots? The software that comes from the manufacturers is focused on getting the robot to do one thing thousands of times. But what if you want to do thousands of different things just once? Can we interact with the robot in real time, without needing CAD and CAM? With just gestures and natural language? Or could we just teach the robot to learn how to do things on its own with deep machine learning systems, so you don't need to tell it what to do, just what you want?

Conti's philosophy is that to understand these kinds of questions deeply, one has to actually try to answer them through prototyping. ≫

KITCHEN OF THE FUTURE
Excerpt from a graphic
novel by Autodesk
Applied Research
Lab

YOU IMAGINE AND DESIGN, AND I'LL CREATE.

SEER

DESIGN JOURNEY
Excerpt from a graphic novel by Autodesk Applied Research Lab

THE MORAL OF THE STORY IS …

Conti's team has a unique approach to R&D, which they call Risk and Determinism. Autodesk's product development teams are on the hook to deliver great high-quality software on schedule. They can't assume much risk, and the company relies on their determinism. Conti's team, by contrast, can assume a lot of risk so the product teams don't have to. His small team of about half a dozen designers and engineers prototype new ideas and concepts quickly and iteratively. They can quickly develop an understanding of the core challenges and opportunities without having to invest a lot in resources.

In Conti's mind, the absolute keys to his group's success are the following: a direct connection to management gives them the air cover needed to take the real risks necessary to develop innovative ideas. It also creates a very short feedback loop so that the lab's findings can quickly influence strategy.

Short, aggressive timelines to prototype and demonstrate value are a must. Typically the Applied Research Lab works in three-month tranches. Some concepts may take longer to develop fully, but prototyping is done quickly and iteratively.

In addition, ideas and prototypes must eventually link with the company's vision and core strategy. The team has a keen focus on making sure that their work is providing value back to the company.

Finally, prototyping does not have to be physical or cost a lot of money. In fact, storytelling can be a great way to prototype ideas early.

In this vein, Conti and his team have been developing methodologies to effectively explore deep-future concepts. They call it Strategic Futures, but the technique is sometimes called SciFi Futures, scenario planning, or world building.

By using storytelling, in the form of graphic novels, to explore futures that are relevant to the company, Autodesk can validate and execute new business models without wasting time and money trying to bring every idea to life. ■

DISTANT FUTURES

BY AUTODESK APPLIED RESEARCH LAB

Prototyping distant futures takes a lot of creativity and a strong point of view.

GETTING SCRAPPY

A lot of what goes on at Autodesk is about prototyping possible futures, often no more than 18 months out. However, when it comes to prototyping distant futures, this is where the Applied Research Lab steps in.

When you think about the distant futures of design, you may envision robots and *Minority Report* – style user interfaces. Go further, and deeper, and you'll find entire fields of study that, at first glance, seem otherworldly. Take synthetic biology, for instance. At this very moment, Auto-desk researchers and engineers are prototyping software to design biological structures at the nano scale. Like biological lockboxes that carry single molecules of cancer medicine through a person's bloodstream and only open when they encounter cancer cells. Or 3D printing yeast cells with custom-designed genomes.

The challenge in spending resources in distant futures is that it becomes difficult to describe why this research, and the subsequent prototypes, matter. This is where storytelling comes in.

STORYTELLING

For the last year, Evan Atherton, a senior research engineer on Autodesk's Applied Research team, and a small cohort of interns have been writing graphic novels to prototype stories about distant futures. This scrappy team creates lush environments far out in distant futures, sometimes 300 years ahead, to help convey the possibilities of some of the tech Autodesk is working on today. These aren't brand-heavy marketing materials. Rather, the idea behind publishing these stories is to connect with people inside and outside the company, giving them a platform by which to pose questions. And, while the results speak for themselves, the cost for this endeavor is minimal. ∎

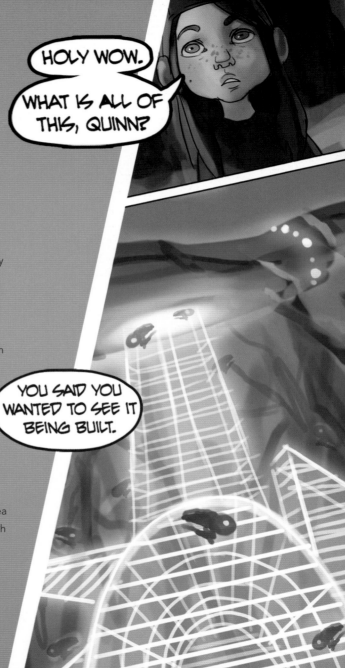

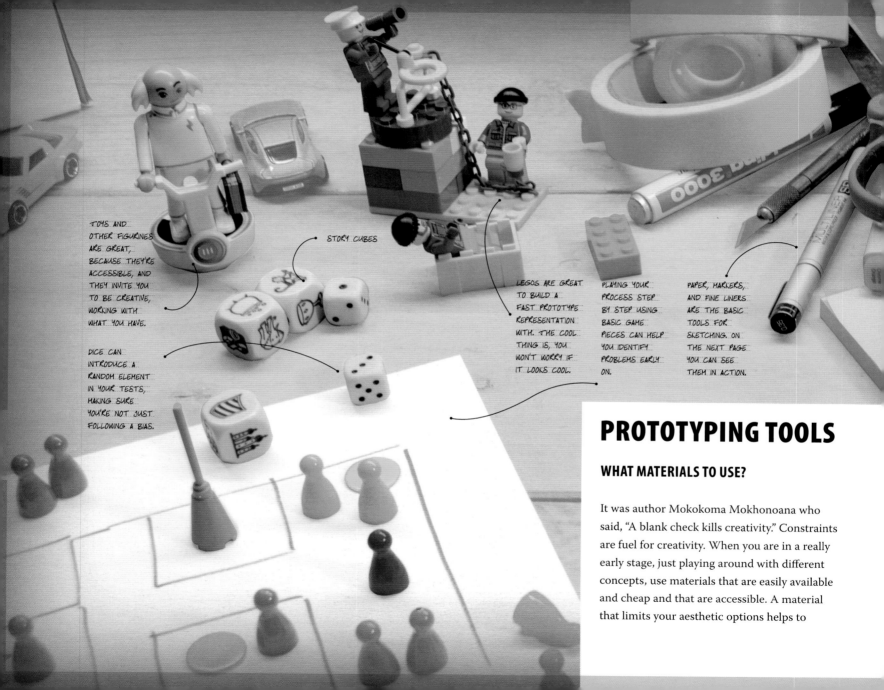

TOYS AND OTHER FIGURINES ARE GREAT, BECAUSE THEY'RE ACCESSIBLE, AND THEY INVITE YOU TO BE CREATIVE, WORKING WITH WHAT YOU HAVE.

DICE CAN INTRODUCE A RANDOM ELEMENT IN YOUR TESTS, MAKING SURE YOU'RE NOT JUST FOLLOWING A BIAS.

STORY CUBES

LEGOS ARE GREAT TO BUILD A FAST PROTOTYPE REPRESENTATION WITH. THE COOL THING IS, YOU WON'T WORRY IF IT LOOKS COOL.

PLAYING YOUR PROCESS STEP BY STEP USING BASIC GAME PIECES CAN HELP YOU IDENTIFY PROBLEMS EARLY ON.

PAPER, MARKERS, AND FINE LINERS ARE THE BASIC TOOLS FOR SKETCHING. ON THE NEXT PAGE YOU CAN SEE THEM IN ACTION.

PROTOTYPING TOOLS

WHAT MATERIALS TO USE?

It was author Mokokoma Mokhonoana who said, "A blank check kills creativity." Constraints are fuel for creativity. When you are in a really early stage, just playing around with different concepts, use materials that are easily available and cheap and that are accessible. A material that limits your aesthetic options helps to

ANY OBJECT CAN REPRESENT ANYTHING WHILE YOU'RE PROTOTYPING IN AN EARLY STAGE. LOOK AROUND YOU!

OCULUS RIFT

IN THE NEAR FUTURE VR WILL BECOME AVAILABLE FOR EVERYONE.

MAKE A TANGIBLE REPRESENTATION USING PLAY-DOH OR CLAY TO EXPLORE SHAPES.

STICKY NOTES AND COLORED PAPER, THE MAINSTAYS OF PROTOTYPING.

PAPER PROTOTYPES MAKE IT EASY TO ENGAGE THE ENTIRE TEAM EVEN WHEN THEY DON'T HAVE DEVELOPER SKILLS.

IF YOU DO HAVE ACCESS TO PEOPLE WITH THE RIGHT SKILLS, EVEN PROTOTYPING HARDWARE IS ACCESSIBLE NOWADAYS.

ARDUINO KIT

NFC CHIPS

TO GET YOUR TEAM TO PROTOTYPE, PICK 1 OR 2 MEDIA AND SET UP A TABLE LIKE THIS ONE, FILLED WITH MATERIALS.

remove fear and to avoid focusing on how it looks. That is something to tackle in a later stage. Once you're a bit further along, it still makes sense to make "throwaway" prototypes, but they will be more involved. Paper prototyping keeps your entire design team engaged, even if they don't have developer skills. ■

TOOL **SKETCHING**

TANGIBLE
sketch a prototype

± 30 MIN
session

SOLO / TEAM
share the results

A marker and a piece of paper are all you need to solve problems!

SKETCHING A PROTOTYPE

It's super effective to start your prototype by sketching it out with your team.

Let's look at this tool in practice using a fictitious example: a company wants to develop a new health-focused mode of transportation based on a bike.

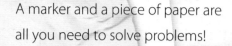

② TACKLE ONE PROBLEM AT A TIME. WHAT IS THE PROBLEM YOU WANT TO ADDRESS FIRST? BE CLEAR ON THE CONTEXT, FOR YOURSELF AND OTHERS INVOLVED. DOES EVERYONE UNDERSTAND WHAT YOU'RE PROTOTYPING?

HOW MANY WHEELS WOULD BE COOL ON OUR BICYCLE?

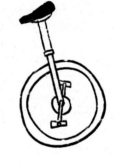

① WHAT IS THE PROBLEM YOU WANT TO SOLVE? USE THE DESIGN CRITERIA YOU HAVE PUT TOGETHER EARLIER (SEE "POINT OF VIEW" P68) TO SET THE SCOPE.

BASED ON BIKE DESIGN

HEALTHY

CALORIE BURNER

WE ALL NEED MORE EXERCISE

EASY HANDLING

LOOK GOOD!

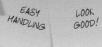

(3) DECIDE ON THE AMOUNT OF DETAILS YOU NEED TO PUT INTO THE SKETCH/PROTOTYPE. THE FEWER DETAILS, THE BETTER THE FOCUS ON THE PROBLEM AT HAND. WHEN YOU WANT TO SEE WHAT THE NUMBER OF WHEELS DOES TO THE VEHICLE, COLOR, MATERIAL, THE PLACEMENT OF THE HEADLIGHT, ETC., ISN'T IMPORTANT.

(4) WHEN YOU USE YOUR PROTOTYPE TO "CONFRONT" OTHERS WITH THE PROBLEM YOU ARE ADDRESSING, MAKE SURE YOU SET THE SCENE. YOU ARE NOT HANDING THEM A SCRAP OF PAPER, BUT PRESENTING THEM WITH A POSSIBLE GAME CHANGER! YOU WANT THEM INVOLVED AND NOT JUDGING YOUR DRAWING SKILLS. THEY NEED TO UNDERSTAND THIS TOPIC IS IMPORTANT FOR YOU AND FOR THEM!

For more on sketching, read: *The Back of the Napkin* by Dan Roam.

AS WITH ALL SKILLS, THE MORE YOU PRACTICE, THE BETTER YOU GET. BUT KNOW THIS: YOU DON'T HAVE TO BE LEONARDO DA VINCI TO SOLVE PROBLEMS!

CHECKLIST

- [ ] You created more than 20 variations that are really different.
- [ ] You are able to present the sketches.

NEXT STEP

> Gather feedback from others on the prototype.

> Use the prototype in an experiment.

DOWNLOAD
Download visual thinking examples from www.designabetterbusiness.com

SKETCHING IS PROTOTYPING

Visual thinking and sketching is about taking advantage of our innate ability to see – both with our eyes and with our mind's eye – in order to discover ideas that are otherwise invisible, develop those ideas quickly and intuitively, and then share those ideas with other people in a way they simply "get."

Welcome to a whole new way of looking at design in business. Whether you're sketching a new org chart on the whiteboard or sitting around a table drawing simple – maybe funny – pictures on sticky notes, sketching is an incredibly powerful and effective way to communicate your point of view and your ideas.

If you can draw simple shapes, such as a rectangle, triangle, circle, and line, you can visualize your ideas by sketching them.

173

Dan Roam
Author, *The Back of the Napkin*

TOOL **PAPER PROTOTYPE**

TANGIBLE

build a paper prototype

± 30 MIN

session

MAX 5

per group

Four ways to make your idea come alive with paper prototyping

1 PROTOTYPE A PROCESS

CREATE A GAME BOARD
Sketch out the process as a game board. Don't forget to include pitfalls, dead ends, energy boosters, necessary steps in the process.

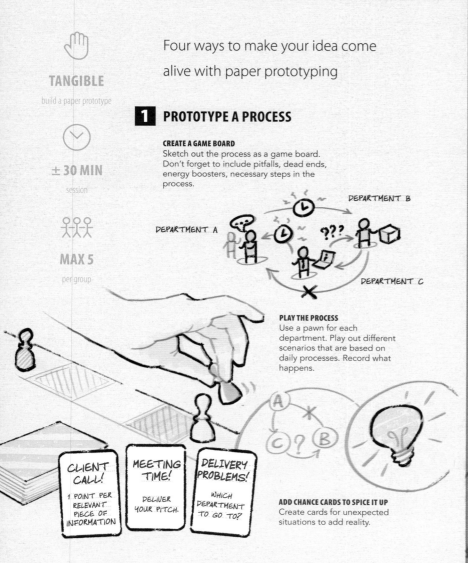

DEPARTMENT A
DEPARTMENT B
DEPARTMENT C
???

PLAY THE PROCESS
Use a pawn for each department. Play out different scenarios that are based on daily processes. Record what happens.

CLIENT CALL!
1 POINT PER RELEVANT PIECE OF INFORMATION

MEETING TIME!
DELIVER YOUR PITCH.

DELIVERY PROBLEMS!
WHICH DEPARTMENT TO GO TO?

ADD CHANCE CARDS TO SPICE IT UP
Create cards for unexpected situations to add reality.

2 PROTOTYPE A PRODUCT

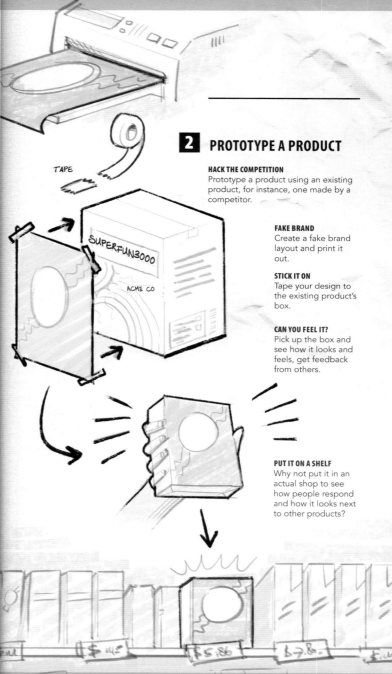

TAPE

SUPERFUN3000

ACME CO

HACK THE COMPETITION
Prototype a product using an existing product, for instance, one made by a competitor.

FAKE BRAND
Create a fake brand layout and print it out.

STICK IT ON
Tape your design to the existing product's box.

CAN YOU FEEL IT?
Pick up the box and see how it looks and feels, get feedback from others.

PUT IT ON A SHELF
Why not put it in an actual shop to see how people respond and how it looks next to other products?

3 PROTOTYPE AN APPLICATION OR WEBSITE

BEFORE YOU START TO MAKE WIRE FRAMES
Don't talk through wire frames if you first need to see if it works at all on a small screen.

BE SELECTIVE
Boil it down to what you really want to validate.

DON'T SHOW EVERYTHING
Leave out the details and stuff you don't necessarily need to test – now – when showing it to your test subjects.

ITERATE
Work on it until you feel it hits the right spot.

STICK IT ON
Stick it onto a smartphone or tablet.

SEE IF IT RESONATES
Try it out and feel it. Take it outside or to the environment where you would use the app.

ÓÓH!

?!

A-HÁ!

THAT WAS EASY TO PROTOTYPE!

FEEL IT
Does it feel too small? Too big? Too cramped? Can you reach the buttons easily?

4 INTERACTIVE PROTOTYPE

USE AN ONLINE TOOL
Need to test some more interactivity? You can use online mockup tools to make your sketches come alive!

☑ DETERMINE PRIORITIES
☑ CREATE AND REVIEW SKETCHES
☑ BUILD WIRE FRAMES
☑ PUT IN LOGICAL ORDER
☑ TEST ON 10–15 PEOPLE
☑ REVIEW FEEDBACK
☐ BUILD REAL VERSION

SEARCH FOR: "ONLINE PROTO-TYPING TOOL"

175

CHECKLIST

☐ You built something you can interact with and show to others.

☐ People respond to your prototype and give you new insights.

NEXT STEP

> Gather feedback from others on the prototype.

> Use the prototype in an experiment.

HB

PROTOTYPING HACKS

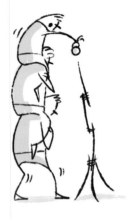

BUILD IT TOGETHER

Building a prototype together works like visually thinking out loud: more iterations, people get involved, and you create ambassadors for the idea and prototype.

Everybody will build off each other. A quick caution: groups shouldn't be bigger than five people. That is the (proven) maximum to keep the dynamics going and to keep everybody active.

CREATE WITH CUSTOMERS

If you want to go for the unexpected and out of the realm of security, let your customers tackle the problem you want to solve for you!

Make sure you agree on the design criteria and scope. One thing is certain: they will never look at the issue at hand from your company's perspective. An outside-in approach will certainly help you pinpoint your blind spots.

COMPETITOR HACK

Use the product (and the packaging) of a competitor, and rebrand it with your product name and other particulars.

This approach saves you the time mocking up your own future product.

This works perfectly if you want to prototype, e.g., branding, color, dimensions, weight, and want to learn what people think of existing products.

PLAY IT OUT

Have people draw their ideas rather than write them down. You can have them either draw their own ideas or make drawings of other people's ideas. It's fun, and forces them to be concrete rather than abstract.

An alternative is to use Lego Serious Play, when people are nervous about their drawing skills.

USE YOUR FAVORITE OFFICE TOOL

In the book *Sprint*, by Jake Knapp, John Zeratsky, and Braden Kowitz, from Google Ventures, the design team mocked up an interface for a robot using only Keynote, the popular presentation software.

Not only did the prototype look real enough to get reactions from customers, it took them only a few hours and cost them nothing, as they already owned the software.

VISUAL DRINKING

Where do most interesting and open brainstorms take place? In coffee shops and bars! Outside the corporate setting, people tend to get less inhibited by rules, agendas, second-guessing.

The ideal place to introduce visual drinking is outside of work. Make sure you always carry a marker. Use coasters, napkins, table tops, menu cards to brainstorm visually. Your next best idea may be on one of those coasters!!

177

YOU NOW HAVE . . .

> LEARNED HOW TO BRING IDEAS TO LIFE THROUGH **SKETCHING** P172

> MADE AT LEAST ONE **PAPER PROTOTYPE** P174

> EXPERIENCED WHAT IT MEANS TO **GET FEEDBACK ON A PROTOTYPE** FROM CUSTOMERS P176

NEXT STEPS

> **VALIDATE YOUR PROTOTYPE** P202
> Create and run experiments.

> **TRACK YOUR FINDINGS** P206
> See how you progressed over time.

> **ITERATE YOUR PROTOTYPE** P174
> Based on your findings, rebuild your prototype.

RECAP

PROTOTYPE ≠ SOLUTION. BE YOUR OWN GUINEA PIG AND **CRASH TEST YOUR IDEAS.**

YOU CAN'T FIGURE IT OUT IN YOUR HEAD. **PROTOTYPING MEANS SOLVING (UNKNOWN) PROBLEMS.**

ADOPT THE MAKER MINDSET. SCRAPPY DOES NOT EQUAL CRAPPY. **JUST GET STARTED!**

KEEP IT SIMPLE AND **MACGYVER IT TOGETHER.**

YOU CAN PROTOTYPE THE FUTURE WITH **STORYTELLING.**

REMEMBER, DON'T SNIFF THE GLUE.

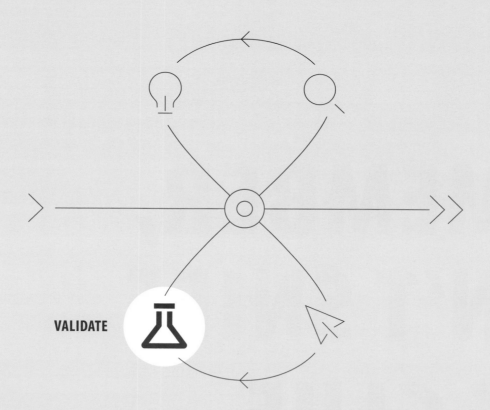

VALIDATE

THE DESIGN JOURNEY **VALIDATE**

FIND THE **RISKIEST ASSUMPTION**

RUN **EXPERIMENTS**

TRACK YOUR **PIVOTS**

KILL YOUR **DARLINGS**

We all have ideas. Sometimes the ideas that pop into our heads keep us up at night – ideas we feel we must follow to the end; they must be executed. Surely they're the best ideas ever. But the truth is, as good as your ideas are, they are only ideas. Impact is created when ideas become additive and expansive: more is better.

THE BEST IDEA IN THE WORLD

All of us, every single one of us, have the answer to solve the business problems (or address the business opportunities) we face. All day long we see other companies releasing killer apps, products, and services and executing on strategies that rocket them into the stratosphere.

THE BEST IDEAS ARE WORTHLESS UNTIL THEY ARE TESTED

You might be thinking, "Surely our idea is that good. It must be. We know our company and our products better than anyone, right?"

Except it's not. Before it has been tested in the real world, it is just an idea, based on assumptions. Like the well-known block-stacking game Jenga®, if any one of the core assumptions – the one holding up the stack – is wrong, the entire stack will fall and your idea with it. What we often fail to recognize is that our idea is just one of many possibilities. On the design and innovation journey there exists no single right solution – only many options. It's your task to use validation to find the best ones and help your idea evolve into a viable one.

NO DVD FOR YOU

In 2011, the streaming entertainment giant Netflix decided to split its streaming and DVD business into two separate businesses, with separate names and separate websites. These would be Netflix, the streaming service, and Qwikster, the DVD-by-mail service. On paper this idea probably looked great. By totally separating their subsequent business models, the company would be able to develop operational and marketing strategies specific to each. Makes sense.

Actually, to the customer, it didn't make sense at all. Netflix delivers a set of services that are all about delighting customers. The very nature of Netflix's rise to prominence was its ability to continually address its customers' specific entertainment needs. The idea and resulting decision to split the company and services in two was never validated with Netflix's customers. Subsequently, shortly after the split, Reed Hastings, Netflix's CEO, made the following announcement: "It is clear that for many of our members two websites would make things more difficult, so we are going to keep Netflix as one place to go for streaming and DVDs."

In the end, by not validating its assumptions prior to splitting the company into two separate businesses, Netflix spent a lot of time and resources executing something that drove away customers – only to reverse its decision shortly afterward.

VALIDATE YOUR ASSUMPTIONS

By validating assumptions you will learn something new everyday. And, just as often, you will find that your initial assumptions were wrong. Your experiments and tests will fail. This is actually great news. It means that you'll learn a ton about your idea early. And you'll learn how to make it better, before committing investments and taking big risks.

BE RUTHLESS

But validation also means that your idea will have to evolve. Nothing of your initial idea, even the aspects you are most in love with, your "darlings," is off limits. Belief is not enough: it's all about proof. Just like a scientist or detective, you'll need to be ruthless in your pursuit of proof, following the evidence wherever it leads. And it's essential that you learn to "kill your darlings." This is what design and innovation are all about.

So, the next time you come up with what that game-changing idea, consider validating it before you execute. Not only will you save time and resources, you'll almost certainly come up with something even better – and with the evidence to back it up. Your customers will love you for it! ∎

YOUR FIRST IDEA **SUCKS**

In over 500 startups we've seen, not a single one ended up building the idea they started out with. The ones that made it are the ones that pivoted.

"Pivot" is the hottest buzzword for startups. The term, introduced by Eric Ries, describes how startups change direction quickly based on customer insights and other technology or contextual findings that they gather from prototyping and validation.

Leveraging new findings, a startup team may decide to utilize what they've already built to test a new customer segment, try something totally different with the same customer segment, go back to an older idea and test it instead, scrap their entire line of thinking and start over, or even move on completely.

What's important is that the founders move quickly, staying grounded in their point of view and how it's been informed throughout; they need to be resilient to make these pivots. The alternative is more risky, simply jumping compulsively from one vision to another, which is likely to lead to a death spiral.

Startups that are in love with their idea and don't want to change course have a dramatically low success rate.

183

 For more background, read:
The Lean Startup by Eric Ries

MASTER **VALIDATION**

1 FAIL EARLY, FAIL OFTEN

Your first idea will very likely not survive contact with a customer. You'll need to learn and adapt, fast! How can you learn as much as you can about your customer, the problem to be solved, and the potential solution early on, when changing course is not so costly? This is what's meant by failing early.

In a sense, failing in this way is not really failing. Sure, you'll need to kiss your original idea goodbye and change direction. By doing so, you take another step on the road to success.

In validation, experiments are the tools you use to try to learn faster. Experiments allow you to "fail" in a controlled way.

2 PIVOT

When an experiment tells you that a fundamental assumption behind your idea is flawed, you'll need to change direction: you'll need to pivot.

A pivot can be relatively simple, like changing the price of a product, or it can be more complex. For instance, your findings might indicate that you need to approach a totally different

FOUR DIFFERENT PIVOTS

CUSTOMER NEED PIVOT
Feedback indicates customers don't care about the problem you solved. Find a problem your customers do care about and are willing to pay for.

CUSTOMER SEGMENT PIVOT
Your current customers don't care about your product, but feedback shows another customer segment is more receptive. Change your segment.

REVENUE MODEL PIVOT
The way you charge money doesn't seem to work. Another revenue model may work better. The "free" model doesn't generate revenue. Someone has to pay.

CONTEXT PIVOT
The market isn't ready for your value proposition. Maybe competition was there earlier than you, or rules and regulations prevent you from entering the market. Try to find another market.

customer segment, solve a different problem for your customer, or that the customers you're targeting have a completely different need.

3 PERSEVERE

Conversely, your experiment can also tell you that you are right about your assumption. In this case, you should move forward and tackle the next assumption. You should persevere and continue to move forward.

With regard to both outcomes, there is a caveat: you could also have simply done the experiment wrong. Maybe you asked the wrong people, or maybe you ran the wrong test. Before making any big decisions on pivoting or persevering, try to exclude this first.

4 DO IT AGAIN

So, when does validating your idea stop? Well, to be honest, as a designer it should never really stop. You'll keep learning new things about your customers that will tell you how to approach them even better.

And you'll keep making assumptions that turn out to be wrong. The good news is that every failed experiment will take you one step closer to a better outcome. ■

LESSONS ON **VALIDATION**

Marc has launched, sold, and closed several companies, and has gone through 22 surgeries during his lifetime; he's had to learn to walk more than four times now. Marc is literally a startup and has shared some of his lessons on validation below.

Marc: "Sometimes, when startups start out they want to build a Rolls-Royce, but I so don't care: I just want to get from A to B. The question is, will the startup understand this, or will they fall in love with their idea.

"Teams who fall in love with their product only validate what they want to validate. They jump through hoops to confirm their idea. You need to look at it as an entrepreneur and focus on the bigger picture.

"Through validation we learn. Teams who have pivoted their business model are the most likely to succeed."

Marc Wesselink
Recruiting & Alumni
Startupbootcamp

STICK TO IT

We love the Post-it notes that 3M makes, because they simply stick the best. It turns out that 3M, now famous for Post-its, actually stumbled upon the idea by accident. In 1968, a 3M scientist tried to make a new super-strong adhesive, but accidentally found a glue that was "low-tack" and reusable.

Five years later, a colleague started to use the glue to hold a piece of yellow paper in place as a bookmark. That idea gained traction within 3M and pioneered a totally new product line and customer segment.

CHEW ON THIS

The famous American chewing gum manufacturer actually didn't start out selling gum at all. At first, William Wrigley Jr. was just giving away sticks of gum as incentives with the soap he sold. Then he noticed that the gum was actually much more popular than the soap. He quickly turned around his business and started producing his own line of gum.

A CAPTIVE AUDIENCE

Today, Twitch.tv is the place where e-sports fans watch the live streams their favorite star gamers share while playing video games and performing in tournaments. E-sports fans are a very loyal audience watching millions of hours of live streams per year. Twitch.tv is a spin-off of Justin.tv, an earlier live stream, aimed at a much broader audience.

THE PIVOT.
IT USED TO BE
CALLED
"THE FUCK-UP."

// Marc Andreessen, Investor, Entrepreneur, Engineer

PAYPAL

PayPal has always focused on payments, but it has gone through many permutations. It was developed by a company called Confinity in 1999 to allow people to "beam" payments from their PDAs (handheld digital computers, such as the Palm Pilot, an early incarnation of the smartphone).

After merging with a financial services company called X.com, PayPal became the preferred online payment system for eBay sellers, which propelled its name into payment processing fame.

HEAD IN THE GAME

The popular chat app for work, Slack, currently valued at $2B, started out as something completely different: a social video game, called Glitch. When it turned out that Glitch was not going to be a popular business, the company pivoted to a new name and a new product.

The funny thing is, Stewart Butterfield, Slack's founder, made this pivot before. In 2004, he started building the game Neverending, which eventually pivoted into … the popular photo-sharing site Flickr.

187

**READ ABOUT
THE MASTER
OF THE PIVOT** >>

GOSPARC THE MASTER

THE MANY FACES OF PIVOTS

// EMANUELE FRANCIONI
CO-FOUNDER, GOSPARC

OF THE PIVOT

Any business evolves and needs to transform. If it doesn't, it will go extinct. This is what happened to Commodore, a great technical product that found great traction and interest from customers worldwide. But they forgot to figure out their next transformation.

If you ask me what and how we pivoted, I would ask you back what exactly you mean by pivot. From my point of view, a pivot is jargon in the startup world that has different meanings to different people. I do believe transformation of your business is the key to survival. You need to be open about unmet customer needs that must be fulfilled.

Our team came from Tom Tom, the in-car navigation company. We obviously had a passion for geo-positioning. Our first thought was to develop the best geo-positioning product out there. We hunkered down for almost 1.5 years and developed what we thought was the best outdoor positioning technology in the world. We just needed to find the right audience and business model.

189

CASE STUDY GOSPARC: **THE MASTER OF THE PIVOT**

1ST PIVOT = BUREAUCRACY

We identified a need for our software in the education sector in the UK. Students who get their visa to study in the UK do not always show up to the classroom. To deal with this, universities implement costly infrastructure. Whereas ours was cheaper and technically better. We found a customer need, we had a solution, and we identified more customers who wanted to pay for this. But we had to pivot. In order to sell our technology we were required to submit a tender to each of the universities, a process that would take us three years. We decided to turn away (quickly).

2ND PIVOT = NO TASTE FOR DATA

We started to look into other markets. Sports sounded interesting to us. We could offer positioning data to athletes to get insights and perform better. This was the customer need we were looking for. However, our customer base not really well developed. We were solving a problem, but we had no idea how to employ a solution. We needed to get a lot of content (data) in order for our customers to deliver relevant information back to us. To be honest, we needed to drive a lot of efforts in a market we did not care much about. If you not an expert in something, forget

it. You need to know this stuff cold. We pivoted again. Well, we half pivoted because we sold the solution to our Canadian partners.

3RD PIVOT = DIFFERENT PRIORITIES

Through our pivots, we got to a stage where we could provide licenses (for intellectual property) to interested parties whereby we could co-develop something together. With this plan we could implement a revenue-sharing business model. In this model we could keep on developing solutions and create lots of different products, commercialized by others. This meant less exploration by us. We would make money if and when our partners did.

A-HA HAPPENS, BUT YOU NEED TO KNOW YOUR CUSTOMERS. THE NEED IS THERE BUT YOU WOULD NEVER SEE IT BY NOT EXPLORING.

4

Best of all, this idea initially came to us from the same partners. It seemed that everything checked out. There was growth. We had partners wanting to sell it for us. We had their customer base. We would sell in bulk. We implemented this model with four partnerships. But there was a problem with this as well: we had zero control of sales and strategy. When your partners have other plans, they have little reason to factor you into those plans. The technology was ready, but suddenly they had different priorities. Great customer base, money in the bank, a product-market fit, and they were all market leaders. But we had to pivot again. With no control, we just had to.

4TH PIVOT = BUNCH OF SMALL PIVOTS

The current phase we're in is all about small pivots. Small and different transformations. We decided to make our own technology and do our own sales. Our first solution was just for parking: a clear problem that everybody understands. The tool we developed based on a spark of an idea is the parking charger, which can be plugged into your car and will pay for parking. This led us to another question: Is this for consumers or businesses?

CONSUMERS

The solution needs to be priced properly and consumers must like it. Their needs are different from a business. One of those needs is the coolness factor; our solution needs to be cool. We also found two other customer needs during validation: the need to 1) check out of the parking space so as not to be overcharged;

191

CASE STUDY GOSPARC: **THE MASTER OF PIVOT**

and 2) pay for parking without using coins. Our current value proposition is the following: save money. It's not really what they want. It's not really cool yet. But it does work. We've also found that some very early adopters are technology minded. They want something they can make work with other things. We could certainly chase this opportunity as well. But we'd need to support the community in a totally new way. At this stage we need to find other customers in order to scale.

BUSINESS

Businesses don't care as much about saving money. But businesses do want to expense parking for their own employees as well as manage their fleets. To test our solution with businesses, we added real-time fleet tracking. Suddenly, this became a product for business operations. We measured success by booking at least 10 paid pilots. We managed to win more of these than we lost. Even tax authorities wanted this. But again that's not enough. With proof in hand, we were happy to do a pilot. But of course, that's not what happened . . .

NOW: **WE HAVE A KILLER APP!**

We happened to have the killer app. We talked to a bunch of public transit companies during the pilots and got the same question over and over: how might we check in and out passengers?

Can a passenger tag herself onto a bus? Is this more scalable than the Dutch OV chip system, which costs 8k euros to install and another 15k per month per vehicle for maintenance? Our solution seems to satisfy customers' needs quite well.

Now we're onto something great!
. . . or so we think.

SWIPE CARD
(((

PUSH ANY KEY FOR INFO

PLUGS DIRECTLY INTO THE VEHICLES AND ALLOWS ANYONE WITH A OV CHIP CARD TO SWIPE FOR ACCESS.

THIS SYSTEM CAN BE USED IN ANY TRANSPORT VEHICLE INTERCHANGEABLY.

HEY! YOU SHOULD TRACK PETS!

What about tracking and tracing of pets or kids?

We have looked into this. We saw a first interest but in the end dog owners and parents do not care so much and do not have a strong need to buy such tooling. We would be naïve if we went that way.

HARD AND SOFT PIVOTS

I believe there are two pivots: a hard one and a soft one. A hard one makes you change your product to the core, from technology to the product. Another one from one segment to another.

Small pivots. Soft pivots. You don't really understand when you pivot those. You find yourself in a different position. You don't know how you got there but the consequence of small tweaking your business got you to where you are.

BE A **ROCK STAR**

The Business Model Canvas and lean thinking is like playing guitar. You see the chords and you need to play it over and over, until the music is internalized.

Then you should start from the beginning again. Eventually you're singing and playing at the same time. And before you know it, you've got an entire group singing with you!

193

HOW TO PIVOT YOUR WAY TO VICTORY >>

CASE ONETAB: **MATURING BUSINESS MODELS** THROUGH **PIVOTS**

If you want to open a tab in a pub in Australia (as in many other countries), you will have to hand over your credit card. And that is a hassle. Scott and Paul had an epiphany at their favorite bar Cha Cha Char (Australia): an app that would solve everything.

AFTER THREE BOTTLES OF WINE WE WERE "READY TO LAUNCH..."

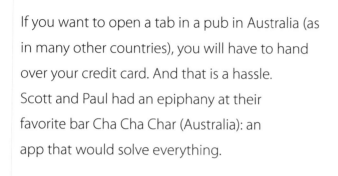

❶ HOUSE OF CARDS

Scott Cross and Paul Wyatt were convinced that settling a bill would be much easier via an app. It would solve the waiting, card loss, forgetting to sign off or even to collect your card.

❷ NOT MY PROBLEM

They had an app built based on the assumption that punters would pay for the app to have their problem solved. Scott and Paul were proven wrong. It wasn't about the app at all.

195

③ THE POURERS PROBLEM

The real problem was with the bar owner: fraud, administration, lost or forgotten credit cards, unpaid bills. They were surely willing to pay for a convenient solution that solved these pains.

④ A MATCH MADE IN HEAVEN

At OneTab they realized that more convenience for the punter and less administrative hassle for the pourer could be solved with one (multisided) platform. The latter would pay for the use as the former surely would order more!

⑤ ACCESS TO KNOWLEDGE

Using POS providers as channels made it easier for pubs to get access. An extra incentive was the rich behavior/user data that OneTab was able to record. From "app" to multisided platform: success in four pivots. ■

RUNNING **EXPERIMENTS**

If prototyping is all about bringing life to your ideas to see them, feel them, and quickly identifying your assumptions, then the focus of validation is to add rigor to the design process. Validation calls for experimentation to test your assumptions and measure the results.

WHAT DO YOU REALLY KNOW?

When you believe in your idea so much that you ignore evidence that suggests your customers really don't like it, or worse, they're totally disinterested, you're following a dangerous path, as many failed startups have illustrated. Remember, your idea is nothing more than a stack of unvalidated assumptions, assumptions that need to be picked apart and validated to see if they are true in reality. That's the only way you'll know what's true and what's not.

Before making any big decisions (and investments), it makes sense to use your other, rational side and learn as much as possible about what's going on.

EXPERIMENTS

You'll need to learn, and you'll need to learn fast. Just as small children learn to walk by falling down a lot, you will perform lots of experiments to find the truth. To validate assumptions, you'll create, run, and analyze experiments that will deliver the data you need as evidence to back up or destroy your assumptions. Using facts, evidence, and data will bring your rational mind to the equation and make it easier to prove to yourself and your team that you are on the right (or wrong) track.

THE RISKIEST ASSUMPTION GAME

So, let's start validating and experimenting. But what should we test first? Using our favorite Jenga metaphor, think of your ideas as being a tower, where all of the bricks are assumptions. When one of the assumptions on the bottom of the stack is invalidated and the brick is removed, the entire tower may fall. When you remove one from the top, not much will happen. Included in this book is a visual template to make it easy to find the riskiest assumptions with your team.

HOW DO I SET UP AN EXPERIMENT?

Once you've found your riskiest assumption, it is time to start experimenting. Over the next few pages you'll learn how to set up your experiment step by step, using the Experiment Canvas to quickly construct and run your next experiment.

FALSIFYING VS. VERIFYING

The point of your experiment is not to confirm your hypothesis; it's to try to falsify it. Only after a sufficient amount of effort, when it proves to be impossible to build an experiment that falsifies the hypothesis, can you accept it.

RUNNING **LEAN EXPERIMENTS**

Even then you're not completely off the hook. Practically speaking, if you can think of another experiment that might give a different outcome, run it. Actively look for another outcome. After all, it may cost a little to get that data, but it will save you a lot in the end!

PIVOT OR PERSEVERE

After you have done your experiment, it is time to draw some conclusions. In essence, there are three possible outcomes of your experiment. Either your experiment matches the result you predicted; it contradicts the prediction; or you're not sure.

In the case that your experiment matches the result, and you've tried your best to falsify, it's time to mark the assumption as "validated." You can "persevere" and move on to the next riskiest assumption. If you're not sure, it's time to check your experiment setup. Did you ask the right questions? Did you talk to the right test subjects? And finally, if your experiment contradicts the result, you probably need to change direction: you need a pivot.

YOUR NEXT EXPERIMENT

One thing you can be sure of: you won't get to the finish line without running quite a few experiments and experiencing a number of pivots. To make it easier to look back and see the patterns while tracking findings, we've included the *Lean Startup*'s validation board in this book. ∎

For more background, read: *Running Lean* by Ash Maurya

In 2010, I developed an approach to help startups become more successful, called the Lean Canvas. That method was based on validation: running experiments and testing assumptions. Since then, the Lean Canvas has transformed into a global movement that uses and further develops the lean approach.

While experiments are highly effective at testing guesses and assumptions, simply running experiments is not enough. The output of your experiments can only be as good as the quality of your input guesses.

It becomes more important to find the riskiest assumptions to test and to build the right experiments to get the data you need.

That is why I created the Experiment Report that you will also find in this book.

197

Ash Maurya
Founder, Lean Startup
Author, *Running Lean*

THE **RISKIEST ASSUMPTION**

We've all been there: your idea is so great that you're literally bursting at the seams wanting to launch it as soon as you can (maybe even today). Most of us feed on this excitement. But how do you know you're making the right bet with your idea? Which bets does the success of your idea hinge on? These are your riskiest assumptions; they need to be tested.

WHAT DO YOU REALLY KNOW?

Dutch people love their cheese, as evident by the long lines you'll encounter at just about any cheese shop in the Netherlands, especially the ones in central Amsterdam. With this "problem" in mind, a cool, new startup based in Amsterdam set out to address this problem with a mobile app, wherein customers could preorder sandwiches and avoid waiting in line. It seemed simple enough. After mapping out the customer journey, the team identified the riskiest assumption: customers hate standing in long lines.

With this assumption in the front of their mind, the startup team went out into the street to validate this assumption. After speaking with over 50 customers, they found that customers did not see this as a problem at all. Customers were willing to wait for freshly made sandwiches prepared by good-looking people behind the counter.

With the only cost being time spent speaking with people during a single lunch break, the team found that their riskiest assumption was false and invalidated. Whether you work for a small startup or an existing large organization, validate your riskiest assumptions as quickly and cheaply as possible so you don't waste valuable time and resources toiling away at something that likely will never work. But this is often harder than it sounds.

YOUR RISKIEST ASSUMPTION ISN'T ALWAYS EASY TO FIND

Imagine you're idea is to open a tailor-made denim jeans store on a main shopping street. Surely people love their jeans and are willing to spend money on ones that look great and are made to fit. But is this your riskiest assumption?

If you think through the customers' jobs-to-be-done, pains, and gains as well their journey, you'll find more assumptions and questions to ask: Are they willing to spend money at all? Do they have time to wait for a tailored pair of jeans to be made? Are they willing to return a couple of weeks later to pick up their jeans?

> **TIP!** Remember to ask the right questions while validating your assumptions. See *The Mom Test* on page 89.

WHEN FOUNDERS FALL IN LOVE WITH THEIR PRODUCT, THEY VALIDATE WHAT THEY WANT TO VALIDATE. NOT WHAT IS GOOD FOR THE BUSINESS.

// Marc Wesselink, Startupbootcamp

By interrogating your Business Model and Context Canvases, you'll find even more assumptions and questions to ask: What key resources can we rely on to produce something people want to buy? Can our key partners ship materials on time and for the right price? At what price would we need to sell jeans in order to make a profit?

The first key to identifying your list of riskiest assumptions is to bring a team together to unpack the idea and brainstorm together. And if you don't have people on your team who have deep experience in unpacking the business model and context, invite some industry experts from your network.

IDENTIFYING ASSUMPTIONS

As a designer, your primary focus is on the customer. It makes sense then that the first assumptions you identify will come from some customer problems you've found. But these aren't the only assumptions, nor are assumptions about customers always the riskiest assumptions. To find more assumptions, you can also use the Business Model Canvas on page 116. When you plot the customer segments and some assumed value propositions on the Business Model Canvas, you'll also need to link these to some revenue streams and channels. In all four of these boxes you'll find assumptions: (1) customers exist that want to buy (2) your product for (3) some price through (4) a specific channel. All of this exists on the right side of the Business Model Canvas. These are assumptions that you'll need to validate in order to ensure you can deliver some value in the first place.

On the left side of the canvas you'll find all of the operational assumptions as well, such as key partners and resources needed to create some value in the first place. And, of course, you cannot leave out the cost required to produce your solution.

With the team in place, use your designer tools (sticky notes, markers, and a big wall) to rank these, based on which you could not do without or which are most likely to be false. The sooner you find these, the more likely you are to be able to validate them and either move forward or pivot. ∎

199

TOOL **RISKIEST ASSUMPTION CANVAS**

FOCUS
define riskiest assumptions

± 15–30 MIN
pressure cooker

3–5
people per group

In your stack of assumptions, the riskiest one is the first gate. If when testing this assumption it continually comes back as "false," you don't get to pass go, you don't get to collect your $200. This tool will help you rank your assumptions before moving on to experimentation.

FINDING THE RISKIEST ASSUMPTION

Finding the riskiest assumption is not always easy. Discussing assumptions with your team will help to identify the ones to go after. Do this visually so it's to the point and provides you with the outcome you need!

JENGA

Jenga is a game where players in turn try to remove blocks from a wooden tower. Each block that's pulled out may make the tower collapse, but the blocks on the bottom are critical to keeping the tower upright.

Think of your idea as a big Jenga tower, where all of the bricks are assumptions. When one of the assumptions on the bottom of the stack is invalidated and the brick is removed, the entire tower may fall. When you remove one from the top, not much will happen.

We need to make sure that the base of the tower is safe. We need to start at the bottom, with what we call the riskiest assumptions. At the moment, all the other assumptions are not as important.

After all, if the riskiest assumption is incorrect, it may be totally irrelevant to think about any of the others: maybe your idea needs to change completely in the light of the new knowledge!

To find your riskiest assumption, go over your Business Model Canvas, value proposition, design criteria, and the other things you have already learned.

What are your assumptions? What are the things you're not sure about? Use this template to map them on a wall with your team as a Jenga tower. The ones that absolutely must be true for your idea to work go on the bottom of the stack. The ones that are less important or depend on other assumptions go higher up.

TRY TO FAIL

The goal is to try to make the tower fail fast! So pick the bottom-most assumption, which is the riskiest one. That's what you'll want to know more about. If it is right, you can move to the next riskiest assumption. But if it fails, your Jenga tower falls, and you'll need to go back to the drawing board to find another approach that works better.

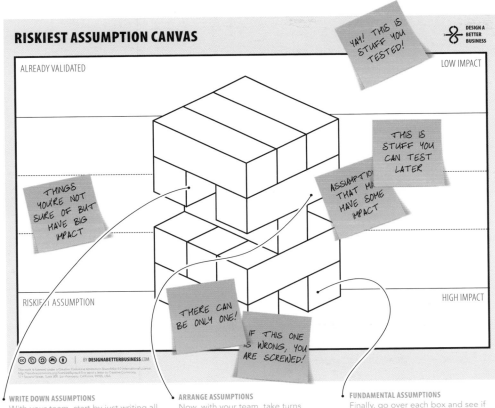

RISKIEST ASSUMPTION CANVAS

ALREADY VALIDATED

LOW IMPACT

YAY! THIS IS STUFF YOU TESTED!

THIS IS STUFF YOU CAN TEST LATER

THINGS YOU'RE NOT SURE OF BUT HAVE BIG IMPACT

ASSUMPTION THAT M... THAT HAVE SOME IMPACT

RISKIEST ASSUMPTION

HIGH IMPACT

THERE CAN BE ONLY ONE!

IF THIS ONE IS WRONG, YOU ARE SCREWED!

DESIGN A BETTER BUSINESS

BY **DESIGNABETTERBUSINESS**.COM

WRITE DOWN ASSUMPTIONS
With your team, start by just writing all your assumptions on sticky notes, but don't stick them on yet. Refer to the war room and your point of view for inspiration.

Then, put the assumptions onto the template, each team member placing them in the middle three boxes, where they think it's best. Don't discuss yet!

ARRANGE ASSUMPTIONS
Now, with your team, take turns moving sticky notes around. Try to find out which assumption is the riskiest one. When sticky notes move back and forth between boxes, put them halfway between.

FUNDAMENTAL ASSUMPTIONS
Finally, go over each box and see if there are any assumptions in there that really depend on others (move them up) or that are fundamental (move them down).

After about 15 minutes, you should have only a few left in the lowest box. Vote with your team as to which one you think is the most fundamental one.

CHECKLIST

- [ ] You clearly identified one riskiest assumption.
- [ ] You have described the riskiest assumption in a concrete way.

NEXT STEP

> Design an experiment to test the assumption using the Experiment Canvas.

201

BRING ON THE **SCIENCE**

If all of this experimentation, measurements, and metrics sounds like science, well, it is.

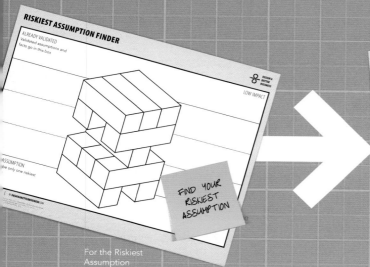

RISKIEST ASSUMPTION FINDER

ALREADY VALIDATED
Validated assumptions and facts go in this box

LOW IMPACT

ASSUMPTION
be only one riskiest

FIND YOUR RISKIEST ASSUMPTION

For the Riskiest Assumption Canvas, see page 200.

EXPERIMENT CANVAS

RISKIEST ASSUMPTION

RESULTS

FALSIFIABLE HYPOTHESIS

We believe

Will drive

Within

USE THE HYPOTHESIS FORMULA HERE!

CONCLUSION

EXPERIM

WHAT KIND OF EXPERI-MENT?

HOW MANY TEST SUB-JECTS?

☐ VALIDATED
☐ INVALIDATED
☐ INCONCLUSIVE

For the Experiment Canvas, see page 204.

ESTIMATE THE OUTCOMES OF THE EXPERIMENT. HOW MANY TIMES WILL YOU GET AN OUTCOME? WHAT WILL SUBJECTS DO?

$\sin(30) = \frac{1}{2}$

TRUE

1
RISKIEST ASSUMPTION
First, find your riskiest assumption. The one that, if it is wrong, makes the whole idea fall to pieces.

2
HYPOTHESIS
Next, create a hypothesis for your assumption. What does it really mean? How can you measure it?

3
TEST SUBJECTS
Select a representative group of test subjects for the experiment. Rule of thumb: get at least 20 to 30 people.

4
PROTOTYPE
Create the simplest possible prototype to test your hypothesis with. Get inspiration from the prototype chapter.

KEEP A LOGBOOK TO TRACK YOUR RESULTS AND THE STEPS YOU TOOK RUNNING THE EXPERIMENTS. THAT WAY YOU CAN MAKE SURE YOUR RESULT IS VALID.

THE POINT OF YOUR EXPERIMENT IS NOT TO CONFIRM YOUR HYPOTHESIS. THE POINT IS TO TRY TO FALSIFY IT. IF YOU CAN'T DO THAT, YOUR ASSUMPTION MUST BE TRUE!

AFTER A POSITIVE RESULT IT MAKES SENSE TO DOUBLE CHECK IT. DID YOU ASK THE RIGHT QUESTIONS? WERE YOU CRITICAL ENOUGH? IT WOULD BE BAD NEWS IF YOU LET YOURSELF OFF THE HOOK TOO EASILY!

EXPERIMENT CANVAS

RISKIEST ASSUMPTION

FALSIFIABLE HYPOTHESIS

We believe

Will drive

Within

EXPERIMENT SETUP

RESULTS

CONCLUSION

NOTE YOUR RESULTS HERE!

CHECK THE RESULTS AGAINST YOUR PREDICTIONS

AND DRAW YOUR CONCLUSION!

ON THE MONEY

WAY OFF

CLOSE CALL

PERSEVERE

Pick your next riskiest assumption and start to validate that.

PIVOT

Back to the drawing board! Reassess your point of view and see if you can find a different solution to validate.

REDO EXPERIMENT

We may have botched the test. Check the setup, subjects, and hypothesis. Try to replicate your result.

203

5

RUN THE EXPERIMENT

Run the experiment you designed. Don't worry if things don't go as planned. The point is to learn.

6

GET YOUR DATA

Compare your data against the predictions you made. Were they far off? Right on the money? Or is it a close call?

7

MAKE A DECISION

Based on the results you got, you can now decide to pivot, persevere, or redo the experiment.

TOOL **EXPERIMENT CANVAS**

Created by Ash Maurya

Once you've found your riskiest assumptions, you'll need a way to figure out how best to test and measure them in a quantitative way. The Experiment Canvas provides a straightforward way to break down your assumptions into measurable, observable, experiments.

TANGIBLE

experiment and create

± 15–30 MIN

pressure cooker

3–5

people per group

THE RIGHT EXPERIMENT

The purpose of the Experiment Canvas is to design the right experiment at the right time, facilitating a team to have the right conversation. With the Experiment Canvas, it is easy to design a well-defined experiment: start with identifying the current riskiest assumption, then specify a clear, falsifiable hypothesis and experiment setup. After running the experiment, check the results and plan your next steps.

CRAFTING A GOOD HYPOTHESIS

Your hypothesis is a statement you believe to be true about your riskiest assumption. Write it down before you run the experiment. It is too easy to change the conditions afterward to make the data fit, and this robs you of valuable insight.

QUANTIFY YOUR PREDICTIONS

Quantify your hypothesis. How many customers will do it? How many times? In what time frame? It's okay to use a bandwidth for this, as long as you specify it up front. The metrics you define need to be actionable (i.e., they need to directly relate to the hypothesis) and accessible (i.e., you need to be able to see the results).

Link the numbers back to the assumption you are testing. Why does having 10 positive results validate your assumption? Specify any qualitative outcomes and variables. What different answers you are expecting? How will you cluster them?

RUN THE EXPERIMENT

Armed with this hypothesis, you're ready to start your experiment. Track the data immediately and write everything down, so that later you can check if you interpreted the results correctly. ■

The Experiment Canvas template was originally created by Ash Mauriya and slightly adapted for this publication.

USE THE **HYPOTHESIS FORMULA**

We believe (specific testable action) will drive (specific measurable outcome) within (time frame)

EXPERIMENT CANVAS

 DESIGN A BETTER BUSINESS

RISKIEST ASSUMPTION

FALSIFIABLE HYPOTHESIS

USE THE FORMULA HERE!

We believe < specific,
Will drive < specific
Within < timeframe >

EXPERIMENT SETUP

HAVE A LOOK AT PROTO-TYPING!

RESULTS

CONCLUSION

☐ VALIDATED
☐ INVALIDATED
☐ INCONCLUSIVE

NEXT STEPS

RISKIEST ASSUMPTION
What is the riskiest assumption you want to validate? And why is it so important?

FALSIFIABLE HYPOTHESIS
Declare the expected outcome beforehand. Try to have a good estimate rather than fake precision!

EXPERIMENT SETUP
What is the prototype you will use to test with? What are the important variables and metrics? Is it quantitative or qualitative?

RESULTS
Enter the qualitative and/or quantitative data resulting from your experiment.

CONCLUSION
Summarize your findings. Did your result validate or invalidate the hypothesis? Or was it inconclusive?

NEXT STEPS
Do you need to pivot, persevere, or redo the experiment?

CHECKLIST
☐ You have created a hypothesis to test the riskiest assumption with.
☐ Your hypothesis fits the structure.
☐ You defined measurable outcomes.
☐ Your data is significant.

NEXT STEP
> Create a prototype to support your experiment.
> Do the experiment and collect your data.
> Pivot, persevere, or redo.

205

TOOL **VALIDATION CANVAS**

Original concept by Ash Maurya

FOCUS

check progress

± 15 MIN

session

TEAM

all together

With your experiments in place, it's time to start testing them and tracking the progress over time. Sometimes your tests will return positive, sometimes negative. Along the way you'll iterate – adding and changing as you go. This tool will help track your progress over time.

TRACK YOUR PIVOTS

Running one experiment is almost never enough to know you're right. Some startups make many pivots before they find the right product-market fit. In every case, it's absolutely essential that you know where you've been before moving on. It would be a waste of time and resources to continue to run the same exact experiment over and over again, waiting for the results to magically change. Looking back will help you understand the choices you have already made and avoid the resurfacing of invalidated assumptions later in the process.

VALIDATION PROCESS

The goal of the validation process is to learn as much as possible, as fast as possible. You'll want to spend as little time and effort as you can in this process, while you maximize the outcome. With that in mind, you'll need to run experiments iteratively. The Validation Canvas is the central nervous system of this process.

YOUR BEST GUESS

It starts with the value proposition you have at this moment. This is your current "best guess" with respect to who your customer is, what problem you solve for them, and what your solution is for that problem. No need to make this overly complicated. Start small, with the simplest solution you can test. Over time, pivots will change that best guess.

EXPERIMENT

Your current best guess is based on assumptions. Find the riskiest one: the one that, if it's wrong, completely disproves your best guess. Choose a way to test that assumption and define what the minimum criteria for success are. Plug this stuff into the experiment canvas and run the experiment.

When it comes to experimentation methods, you can choose from things like exploration, pitching, or even a concierge model. Through exploration, you'll learn more about the problem you're trying to solve for.

Pitching will help you understand how important your customer thinks the problem is. Is it a must have or a nice to have? A concierge model will help you understand whether you can deliver on the customer's expectations at first, doing it by hand. ■

The Validation Canvas was created by Ash Maurya's Lean Startup movement and adapted for this publication.

VALIDATION CANVAS

DESIGN A
BETTER
BUSINESS

	START	PIVOT 1	PIVOT 2	PIVOT 3	PIVOT 4
RISKIEST ASSUMPTION					
CUSTOMER SEGMENT					
CUSTOMER NEED					
PROTOTYPE TO VALIDATE WITH					
METHOD					
MINIMAL SUCCESS CRITERION					
RESULT: PIVOT OR PERSEVERE					

BY **DESIGNABETTERBUSINESS**.COM

Adapted from the Validation Board created by Ash Maurya

RISKIEST ASSUMPTION
What is your current riskiest assumption to test with an experiment?

CUSTOMER
Define your value proposition. Split it in parts: your customer, the customer need you are solving for that customer, and the solution you assume solves that problem.

VALIDATE
Describe the method you want to test with. What kind of experiment is it?

What are the minimal criteria for success?

RESULTS
Keep track if your experiment validated or invalidated the assumption and what your findings were. Did you pivot? Or persevere?

Over time, you can see what your progress has been.

CHECKLIST

☐ You tracked your experiment.

NEXT STEP

> Pivot, persevere, or redo.

EXAMPLE **THE JOURNEY OF Abrella**
LET IT RAIN

Three years ago, a rainy holiday in Taiwan triggered Andreas Søgaard to begin a social startup called Abrella.

DESIGN A BETTER BUSINESS

EXPERIMENT CANVAS

RISKIEST ASSUMPTION
- MORE PEOPLE WILL VISIT SHOPS ON RAINY DAYS...
- ...WHEN THEY STAY DRY WITH AN UMBRELLA

FALSIFIABLE HYPOTHESIS
- WE BELIEVE THAT BY SUPPLYING 1000 UMBRELLAS
- TO 8 SHOPS IN ÅRHUS, WE WILL SEE
- A VISIBLE INCREASE IN HAPPY SHOPPERS

EXPERIMENT SETUP
- EXPLAIN TO THEM THEY NEED TO TELL THE STORY
- WATCH WHAT HAPPENS FOR THREE MONTHS

RESULTS
- 860 UMBRELLAS LEFT
- TRUE AMBASSADORS MORE SUCCESSFUL
- 51% KNOW ABRELLA, 22% USED IT

CONCLUSION
- ✓ VALIDATED
- ☐ INVALIDATED
- ☐ INCONCLUSIVE

NEXT STEPS
- SEE IF WE CAN SCALE UP!

BY **DESIGNABETTERBUSINESS.COM**

1 ANDREAS WAS ON A WET VACATION IN RAINY TAIWAN, WHEN HE SPOTTED A STAND OF LOST UMBRELLAS. HE DECIDED TO TAKE ONE WITH HIM AND BROUGHT IT BACK TO WAIT FOR ITS OWNER WHEN THE RAIN STOPPED.

171 DAYS/YEAR IN DENMARK

2 THAT GAVE HIM AN IDEA. HIS NATIVE DENMARK IS BLESSED WITH OVER 171 RAINY DAYS EVERY YEAR. PERHAPS HE COULD MAKE THOSE DAYS A BIT BETTER FOR EVERYONE BY STARTING A SOCIAL UMBRELLA BUSINESS! HIS FIRST ASSUMPTION: SHOPKEEPERS WILL LOVE THIS IDEA. ABRELLA WAS BORN.

3 BACK IN DENMARK, HE DID HIS FIRST EXPERIMENT: HE WENT TO TALK TO SHOP OWNERS ON RAINY DAYS AND ASKED THEM HOW BUSINESS WENT. THEY TOLD HIM THEY LOST 75% OF THEIR REVENUE WHEN IT RAINED.

4 NEXT ASSUMPTION: SHOPPERS DON'T VISIT THE SHOPS BECAUSE THEY DON'T WANT TO GET WET. AN UMBRELLA MAKES THAT PROBLEM GO AWAY.

5 TO TEST THIS ASSUMPTION, ANDREAS STARTED A PILOT PROJECT. HE ALSO WANTED TO FIND OUT IF PEOPLE WOULD THROW AWAY OR STEAL THE UMBRELLAS. HE FOUND 8 SHOP OWNERS, WHO TURNED OUT TO BE ABRELLA'S BEST AMBASSADORS.

ÅRHUS SHOP

-75% REVENUE IF IT RAINS

1000

8x

6 THE PILOT WAS A SUCCESS, WITH THE BIGGEST FINDINGS THAT PEOPLE DID NOT TRASH OR STEAL MANY UMBRELLAS AND THAT SHOP OWNERS WHO WERE TELLING THE STORY RIGHT SAW MORE HAPPY RETURNING CUSTOMERS WHEN IT RAINED. FOR THOSE SHOPKEEPERS, THIS WAS A NEW WAY TO BUILD A LONGER RELATIONSHIP WITH THEIR CUSTOMERS. AMBASSADORS MATTER.

ANDREAS ASKED 200 PEOPLE ON THE STREETS OF ARHUS IF THEY KNEW ABOUT ABRELLA, AND AN ASTOUNDING 52% ANSWERED "YES" AFTER THE PILOT. PEOPLE LIKED THE STORY AND SPREAD THE WORD TO THEIR FRIENDS. AFTERTHOUGHT: INSTEAD OF ORDERING 1000 UMBRELLAS FROM CHINA AND WAITING FOR 3 MONTHS TO GET THEM, IT WOULD HAVE BEEN MUCH FASTER AND EASIER TO BUY 100 OF THEM AT IKEA . . .

9 DURING THEIR JOURNEY, THEY FIGURED OUT THAT THE PEOPLE WHO REALLY NEED AN UMBRELLA ARE MOSTLY PEOPLE FROM OUT OF TOWN. LOCALS CAN ALWAYS GO SOMEWHERE TO GET DRY, BUT VISITORS AND TOURISTS HAVE NO OPTIONS. SO THEY ARE NOW ADDING HOTELS AND OTHER ENTRY POINTS AS NEW AMBASSADORS.

1000 UMBRELLAS WERE STOCKED IN HIGHLY VISIBLE DISPENSERS. THE WATER FROM THE WET UMBRELLAS MAKES FLOWERS GROW IN THE TOP OF THE DISPENSER

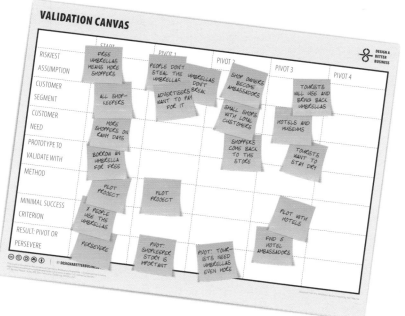

VALIDATION CANVAS

	START	PIVOT 1	PIVOT 2	PIVOT 3	PIVOT 4
RISKIEST ASSUMPTION	FREE UMBRELLAS MEANS MORE SHOPPERS	PEOPLE DON'T STEAL THE UMBRELLA / UMBRELLAS DON'T / ADVERTISERS BREAK WANT TO PAY FOR IT	SHOP OWNERS BECOME AMBASSADORS	TOURISTS WILL USE AND BRING BACK UMBRELLAS	
CUSTOMER SEGMENT	ALL SHOP-KEEPERS		SMALL SHOPS WITH LOYAL CUSTOMERS	HOTELS AND MUSEUMS	
CUSTOMER NEED	MORE SHOPPERS ON RAINY DAYS		SHOPPERS COME BACK TO THE STORE	TOURISTS WANT TO STAY DRY	
PROTOTYPE TO VALIDATE WITH METHOD	BORROW AN UMBRELLA FOR FREE				
MINIMAL SUCCESS CRITERION	PILOT PROJECT / X PEOPLE USE THE UMBRELLAS	PILOT PROJECT		PILOT WITH HOTELS	
RESULT: PIVOT OR PERSEVERE	PERSEVERE	PIVOT: SHOPKEEPER STORY IS IMPORTANT	PIVOT: TOUR-ISTS NEED UMBRELLAS EVEN MORE	FIND 5 HOTEL AMBASSADORS	

DESIGNABETTERBUSINESS

SCALING UP, THEY STARTED TO FOCUS ON OTHER PROBLEMS, SUCH AS LOGISTICS: SOME PLACES LOST LOTS OF UMBRELLAS. AT ONE POINT, THEY SUDDENLY FOUND OUT THERE WERE NO MORE UMBRELLAS LEFT IN STORAGE! IN THE END, THEY PIVOTED TO A MORE ENGAGED PART OF THEIR CUSTOMER SEGMENT: ONLY SHOPS THAT WERE TRUE AMBASSADORS. THEY STAYED IN TOUCH WITH THE AMBASSADORS BY HAND-DELIVERING UMBRELLAS BY BIKE.

7 AFTER THE PILOT, MATTIAS EDSTRØM JOINED ABRELLA AS A CO-FOUNDER AND THEY STARTED TO SCALE UP. MORE ADVERTISERS, MORE SHOPS, MORE UMBRELLAS . . . THEY WERE VOTED THE MOST INNOVATIVE STARTUP OF DENMARK IN 2015. THINGS WERE LOOKING GREAT!

8

VALIDATION HACKS

TIP! The next time you plan an experiment, go through it first with a few of your colleagues and fix any problems. After all, it would be terrible if you went out and asked thousands of people the wrong questions.

QUALITATIVE VS. QUANTITATIVE

Although the results from a quantitative test are often easier to interpret, your first step in experimentation is to find out what to test. Do a qualitative experiment for that. What are the typical things people do? Why do they think they do those things? Remember, running a qualitative test does not mean you can't gather numerical data.

Qualitative experiments are great when you want to capture richer data about what customers experience. Make sure you're testing what people actually do, rather than what they say they do. It's also important not to ask about fu-

ture behavior, as your customer probably won't be able to answer without guessing (the future is uncertain). Instead, ask about current behavior.

After doing that, it's often great to back it up with a quantitative test to see how many people actually display the same behaviors in reality. A qualitative test will provide insight as to how well your quantitative test is geared up to measure the things you want to measure.

Keep in mind that qualitative tests are difficult to use in situations where you are testing the response to a very small change. If you want to test two different colors of button online, the data you'll get from a qualitative test would be quite useless.

Another thing that people will happily tell you when you ask them is that they will (or won't) buy your product. However, that information is useless. Only a test where they actually buy it has any real value.

RUN A SMALL-SCALE TEST

Running an experiment takes time and effort. Before going out and doing a large-scale experiment, try it out first on a small scale to iron out any issues with the test itself.

On the Discovery Channel show *Mythbusters*, the hosts regularly try out their experiments on a small scale to see what the possible outcomes could be and to make sure their large-scale tests will yield reliable results.

DON'T INFLUENCE THE RESULT

When running your test, make absolutely sure nothing you do or say is secretly influencing your result. Don't "sell" your prototype to the test subjects. Let them experience it as they would without you present.

Online, this is quite easy to do using analytics, but offline it can be more difficult. Go out of your way to present the prototype in as natural a way as possible.

One way of doing this is to have a test subject record their experience using a camera or notepad that you give them beforehand.

TESTING THE COMPETITION

When you don't yet have a prototype to test, or want to get a head start, try this: get people to test a competing product or service. Find out what they say about it.

Even if you don't have any direct competitors yet, this can give you valuable insight. Some of the assumptions you have about your own idea hold true for other things as well.

There are some cool examples of appliance companies which have employed this simple experiment using a similar commercially available kitchen product, for instance, and have invalidated some of their most important assumptions. For the price of a food processor and an afternoon of their time, they figured out they had to really make a big pivot.

OFFLINE A-B TESTING

Online, A-B testing is all the rage. Show users different versions of the same advertisement or web page, and find out which one they click on the most. The data will tell you beyond doubt if the change makes sense to implement.

Offline, you can use exactly the same tactic. You don't have to show every test subject the same prototype. Mock up a brochure of your product (using Keynote or PowerPoint, for instance) and change the price, show different colors, or play with another variable, and see how this influences the result.

Make sure you only change one variable at the same time, though, or your result will be confused!

If you run a few experiments at the same time with a different value for the variable you are testing, you can save a lot of time. ■

TIP! Include a few versions that are out of your comfort zone. If you are testing a price range, include a price that is bordering on the ridiculous, too. Maybe it turns out that customers find that price less ridiculous than you thought.

211

YOU NOW HAVE . . .

> IDENTIFIED YOUR **RISKIEST ASSUMPTION** P200

> DONE AT LEAST 1 **EXPERIMENT** P204

> VALIDATED YOUR **RISKIEST ASSUMPTION** P206

NEXT STEPS

> **RUN YOUR NEXT EXPERIMENT** P200
> Tackle the next riskiest assumption

> **REVISIT YOUR POINT OF VIEW** P68
> Did you challenge your vision enough? Do you need to readjust your point of view?

> **GO BACK INTO THE LOOP** P46
> Go back into the loop

> **ARE YOUR READY?** P244
> Check your investment readiness level

RECAP

THE BEST IDEAS IN THE WORLD ARE **WORTHLESS** UNTIL **THEY ARE TESTED.**

YOUR FIRST IDEA SUCKS; YOU NEED TO **FAIL EARLY AND FAIL OFTEN.**

FAILURE IS LEARNING. **KILL YOUR DARLINGS.**

DON'T VERIFY, BUT **FALSIFY.** TRY TO MAKE YOUR IDEA FAIL.

PIVOT OR PERSEVERE. THE PIVOT USED TO BE CALLED THE FUCK-UP. THERE IS NO SINGLE PIVOT; THEY ARE ALL DIFFERENT.

THIS
IS NOT
A DRILL.

213

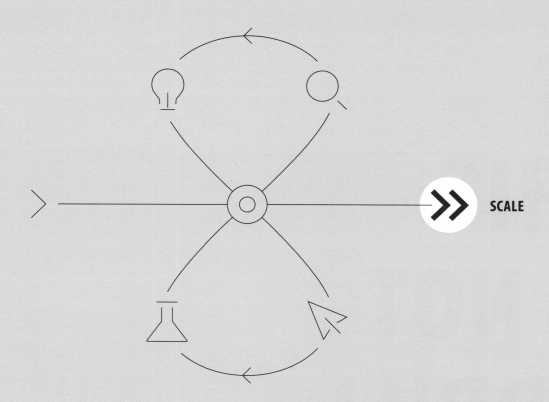

SCALE

THE DESIGN JOURNEY **SCALE**

LEARN WHEN TO **SCALE**

SEE DIFFERENT WAYS TO **SCALE**

INVESTMENT READINESS LEVEL

WHEN TO **SCALE**

Whether you embark on the design journey as a startup or an existing company, one thing is certain: it's a roller-coaster ride, and it doesn't end when you come up with an idea. It's a journey that is meant to scale both the design process and the execution of the idea.

THE END OF THE LINE

This is the last leg of the journey . . . well, this journey anyway. After going through the double loop, designing a better business, and learning from your customers, the world, and yourself, you should give yourself a hand. You did it! At least once.

Now buckle up, it's time to get back on the ride.

DISTRUST KILLS INNOVATION.

Designing one innovation is not enough. It's simply not a one-off thing. As with any profession, design takes practice. Doing it over and over will lead to mastery. Only then will the practice of designing for better business become a mindset.

RIGGING THE GAME

Rigging a game will turn the numbers in your favor; using design processes to build better businesses will improve your odds (and your organization's odds) of success. A design mindset that favors understanding, ideation, prototyping, and validation will allow you to execute and scale. Best of all, when you start to develop this mindset and see the world through your own design-colored glasses, you'll find that not only are your odds better, but you'll also be able to confidently bet on multiple games at once.

If recent history has proven anything, it's that organizations that build this drive for exploration and learning into their DNA are the ones that have the best chance to turn uncertainty into opportunity. They are the ones that successfully rig the game in their favor. And it's never too late to start.

LEARN FROM OTHERS

So, how can we scale up from one successfully designed outcome to incorporating design into our core culture? The best way to start is to learn from others' journeys, successes, and failures. In this chapter we'll explore and evaluate a number of approaches to scale design.

We'll look at a special co-working space, a successful accelerator, a large bank setting up an innovation lab of their own, and a large energy company building design capacity through acquisitions. We'll also look at a couple of large software companies using the design process to embed this mindset into their respective cultures.

> **TIP!** Think about not only scaling design, but also scaling the network of people your team will need to tap into to get better answers to their questions.

INGREDIENTS

There are four main ingredients necessary for scaling design within your own organization.

First and foremost, we've said it before and we'll say it again, don't go it alone. To scale design you'll need to build a network and find ways to tap into it. You need access to customers; talented, like-minded people; feedback; experts; and even investors. Anyone can put on a cape with a giant "D" printed on it. But without a network, you're just a guy with a stack of sticky notes and a marker who's wearing a cape to work.

Second, you'll need support for your design endeavors. As Maurice Conti from Autodesk stated, you must have a direct connection to management when embarking on the design journey. This will give you access to the resources you need, like time, space, funding, people, etc.

Third, you'll need quick access to practical knowledge. A validated methodology, like the one laid out in this book, will go a long way in helping you gain the support you need to move forward. But you also need to learn from others who already have made a lot of the mistakes implementing the methodology.

The final, most important ingredient is trust. You'll need to trust the process. And you'll need others to trust you, so that you can feel empowered to make mistakes, take risks, and fail (in small ways) in a fail-safe environment. For most existing companies, this trust is hard won. But it is so so very worth it. Why? Distrust kills innovation. And with distrust comes detailed budget scrutiny and time-clock behavior.

ARE YOU INVESTMENT READY?

We have included Steve Blank's Investment Readiness Level (IRL) as a way to gauge where your company is right now and what the next steps might be as you drive toward a successful sustainable business. ■

See the Investment Readiness Level on page 244

> **TIP!** To scale you'll need a direct line to management. This is where ambassadors really help.

THE CONTINUUM OF **SCALE**

Oracle

Eneco
Quby
P226

Startup-
bootcamp
P223

Autodesk
P164

RBS
P224

Matter
P228

PEOPLE DRIVEN

COMPANIES THAT SCALE DESIGN BY
SKILLING UP PEOPLE

OUTSIDE IN

COMPANIES THAT MAKE OUTSIDE
INVESTMENTS IN STARTUPS,
WITHOUT AFFECTING THE
LARGER COMPANY'S CORE
CULTURE OR PROCESSES

The continuum
of scale is a
2x2 matrix
that describes
how different
companies
approach the
question of how
to scale design
processes.

THE END OF THE LINE

Scaling is something that you do when
your simple idea is ready to fly into full-on
execution mode. For existing companies,
execution all too often signals the end
of the design process. For startups still
searching for their sustainable business
model, scaling is about building a bigger,
better product, perhaps one that finally
makes money.

Startups never stop following the double
loop; they continue validating and adjusting
their point of view based on evolving understanding about their customers.

DESIGNING SCALE

What we mean when we talk about scale is
more akin to the startup: scale is about tackling
a different problem, raising the stakes, and
continuing the design journey (as a culture).

PROCESS DRIVEN

COMPANIES THAT FOCUS ON BUILDING
THE CORE DESIGN PROCESSES BY WHICH
TO INFUSE SCALE AT A MACRO LEVEL.

1871
P222

DMBA
P232

Google

SEB LAB
P225

Uber

INSIDE OUT

COMPANIES IN WHICH DESIGN
PERMEATES EVERYONE ON EVERY
TEAM, THROUGHOUT THE
CULTURE OF THE COMPANY

Amazon

Walmart

Scaling is about using the same process described in this book to figure out how to scale the process to an entire organization of people, wanting and needing better ways to create opportunities from uncertainty. How meta!

There are many ways to scale design in an organization. However, although this book describes tools to design and innovate

businesses, scale is less about specific tools and more about an organizational mindset. Because each organization comes with its own cultural constructs and unique challenges, opportunities, and makeup, there is no one perfect process or tool for scaling. Rather, scaling permeates an organization's culture such that design tools flourish. ◼

Adobe
P227

ACCELERATORS.
THE NEW HUNTING GROUND FOR SCALE. **»**

219

DIFFERENT WAYS TO **SCALE**

Accelerators, incubators, and startup studios are relatively new constructs that focus on scale, and scale only. In these programs, startups use design to churn through pivots until they find scale or burn out. If you want to scale design in your organization, it's important to know how the successful ones do it.

A BIT ABOUT ACCELERATORS

If you were to do a web search for accelerator programs, you would find more than 2,000 of them across the globe. Partly because of inexpensive capital and partly because of the success of well-known accelerators, like Y Combinator, Techstars, and others, the accelerator space has seen explosive growth in the last few years. With all of the press and success accelerators have generated, big companies like Royal Bank of Scotland, Sephora, Nike, Target, Google, and the Los Angeles Dodgers have started their own accelerators.

Accelerators work for both startups and big companies, although bigger companies, with their larger network and greater resources, can use accelerators to sponsor startups, promote entrepreneurship, and nurture founders.

WHAT IS A STARTUP ACCELERATOR PROGRAM?

A startup accelerator program is an intensive business and personal development program that supports a small team of founders, who have big ambitions for growth and impact.

The support comes in a form of mentorship, affordable office spaces, and some starting capital. In a nutshell, a program consists of the following core elements:

- A highly competitive application process that is open to all
- A provision of pre-seed investment, normally for an equity share
- A focus on a limited number of small teams
- Time-limited support comprised of programmed events and intensive mentoring
- A final "Demo Day" when startups pitch their ideas to raise their first big round of funding

It used to be investment management companies that looked for the most promising, early-stage companies to invest in. The hope was that the startups would go on to raise the next rounds of funding and ultimately (and hopefully) get acquired or offer an IPO. Today, there is a new mindset and different kinds of accelerator programs, each with its own vision and ambition. ■

OVERVIEW OF ACCELERATORS

 WORKSPACE — An office location that provides desks, office space, and facilities (infrastructure) at a reduced or low rate to startups and growth businesses.

 STARTUP WEEKENDS, HACK-A-THONS, AND BOOT CAMPS — Events run for 48–72 hours and are intended to create new startup teams that are actively engaged in developing a business idea under a strict time limits.

 STARTUP ACCELERATOR — Profit-driven (theme-based) programs that accept open applications to attend classes (or "cohorts") of new companies run by small founding teams. The initial ideas are expected to be already developed by the founders.

 CORPORATE STARTUP ACCELERATOR — Not-for-profit-driven programs that accept open applications to attend classes of new companies run by small founding teams. The focus of these programs is to build the network and ecosystem, change the corporate culture, gain access to ideas and technology, and create jobs to benefit for a wider society.

 STARTUP STUDIO — A smaller, more hands-on and intimate version of an accelerator: a startup studio houses a few startups under one roof wherein the principals of the studio invest personal time and effort into each startup, trying to help them scale.

RIGHT PLACE, **RIGHT TIME.**

We were at the right place and time when we launched Startupbootcamp. We've seen many new accelerators pop up all over the world and are excited to see the interest in helping entrepreneurs with their businesses.

Running an accelerator is not rocket science but it requires a long-term vision, patience to build the ecosystem with knowledgeable funding partners, and the ability to pivot your business model. Our key findings: founding partners must fund the business model, and most models require other revenue streams, such as innovation programs and corporate innovation education.

Most startups won't exit for some time. We're in it for the long haul.

Ruud Hendriks & Patrick de Zeeuw
Founders,
Startupbootcamp

221

1871. THE CO-WORKING PLACE WITH A TWIST

1871 was founded in Chicago, IL, USA, as a not-for-profit community of designers, coders, and entrepreneurs who learn from each other, encourage each other, and share the journey up the steep startup learning curve.

> ## LET'S FACE IT: THE GARAGE IS OVERRATED. IT'S COLD IN WINTER, HOT IN SUMMER, AND LONELY ALL YEAR ROUND.
>
> // Howard Tullman, CEO, 1871

BACK TO 1871

The Great Chicago Fire (1871) dealt a major blow to the booming economy. The direct need to rebuild the city led to great innovations, cross pollination, and practical ingenuity. In 2012, a group of Chicago's technology boosters wanted to rekindle this passion. This became 1871.

What does a booming economy look like? A booming economy is as much about creating an environment that fosters entrepreneurship and innovation as it is about big companies growing bigger. 1871, an entreprenuerial hub for digital startups, housed on the 12th floor of Chicago's historic Merchandise Mart, is a place where entrepreneurs seeking a collaborative and flexible work environment can go to design and build the businesses of their dreams.

What's perhaps most interesting about 1871 is that it's designed from the ground up to help entrepreneurs network at scale.

Through this network, existing startups have readily available access to a potential customer base that can validate their ideas. And newly forming startups, or even single founders, are able to find co-founders and others to help develop their ideas further. In this way, 1871 is all about scale: scaling the network to scale the opportunities for design to flourish.

TAKEAWAYS

It's hard to build a successful business. It's even harder if you're not plugged into a community of people. 1871 helps founders build their teams and works on building resilience and perseverance.

PEOPLE ORIENTED

INSIDE-OUT

WORKSPACE

 **STARTUPBOOTCAMP.** THE ACCELERATOR

Patrick de Zeeuw visited the US and fell in love with the Techstars concept. He wanted to help as many startups as possible, but realized he couldn't do it on his own. With his friend Ruud Hendriks, they launched Startupbootcamp. This is what they learned.

PEOPLE ORIENTED

OUTSIDE-IN

STARTUP ACCELERATOR

HOW WE RECRUIT TEAMS

We've honed our application criteria over the years. You can join Startupbootcamp if you comply with the 4-M's:

MARKET	Have you defined your niche clearly?
MODEL	Are you here to make money?
MANAGEMENT	Do you have three partners to start with, including a product person in the middle, the back, and the front?
MOMENTUM	Is this the right moment?

Well, the last one is a bit slippery.

TAKEAWAYS

Running an accelerator is not about real estate; it's about adding value through network and knowledge. It's about pushing teams to go out of the building to find customer needs.

You cannot be afraid to fail. Business school or big corporate companies may have taught you to fear failure. But here, failing means learning.

Don't be afraid to say: "I don't know." That's okay. We don't know either. Be vulnerable and clear about what you don't know.

Founders' shit will always hit the fan. Some companies lose themselves in internal battles. Make sure you mediate right away: fix internal issues before they become big problems.

DIVERSITY IS HARD TO "ORGANIZE," BUT IT MAKES FOR HIGH-ENERGY TEAMS.

// Patrick de Zeeuw, Co-Founder Startupbootcamp

223

RBS. CORPORATE STARTUP ACCELERATOR

NatWest, RBS, and Ulster Bank are three banks with eyes focused on the future. Their accelerator hubs offer free workspace and the opportunity to unite with fellow entrepreneurs, specially trained bank staff, and experienced businesses.

> ## WE HELP THEIR BUSINESS TO GET GOING.
> // Ross McEwan, CEO, RBS

ACCELERATOR HUBS

NatWest, RBS, and Ulster Bank, in partnership with Entrepreneurial Spark, run free business accelerator hubs across the UK, targeting applicants from all sectors and offering free workspace and the opportunity to unite with fellow entrepreneurs, specially trained bank staff, and experienced business mentors.

At the end of the program each will hosts a "graduation" event bringing together entrepreneurs and business advisors. This gives accelerator graduates the opportunity to pitch to potential investors.

Alison Rose, chief executive of commercial and private banking at RBS: "We are determined to support entrepreneurs across the UK and the positive impact they have on the economy. That is why we are creating entrepreneurial ecosystems across the country that give startups the best chance of success and the free hubs remove concerns on things like office facilities, letting them concentrate on their business."

TAKEAWAYS

Gordon Merrylees, Head of Entrepreneurship for NatWest, RBS, and Ulster Bank: "We will support 7,000 entrepreneurs for free over a five-year period. With our partners Entrepreneurial Spark we teach them new mindsets, behaviors, business models, and how to pitch. We work with them as a bank providing expertise, knowledge, and access to networks and markets that help build strong entrepreneurial communities and cultures. And, just as important, our staff gets involved, not just to help but to learn themselves too. We now have our own Entrepreneurial Development Academy where colleagues can develop and learn about entrepreneurialism. It means they can have better conversations with customers and better understand and support the challenges businesses face."

PROCESS ORIENTED

OUTSIDE-IN

CORPORATE ACCELERATOR

SEB INNOVATION LAB. THE IN-HOUSE INCUBATOR

Mart Maasik, Head of Innovation at SEB LAB, describes the LAB as a great place to collaborate and contribute with "nonprofessional" (business) developers and diversified teams. We started to experiment with external partners' students.

PEOPLE ORIENTED

INSIDE-OUT

CORPORATE ACCELERATOR

OUR AMBITION

Our ambition is simple: we want to enable and inspire our people and make innovation happen. It's first and foremost about people. We want to have a critical mass of "lighthouses" who have experienced and are inspired by delivering solutions as part of the LAB. Sometimes we call the LAB a base camp where people come for personal development and to systematically future-proof the organization.

TAKEAWAYS

We have learned a lot since launching the LAB. Many of these things show up as new skills that people learn as part of their experience. Firstly, it's about learning to understand the customers and see their experiences as part of a larger journey. They also hone their ability to connect the dots. If the service in question has to be redesigned or simplified, it's better to see the whole system than to put on an engineer's hat and dive right into the tech. If we are targeting a new service concept, it's critical to learn how to set a vision balanced with the ability to collect proof points that support the vision and help with the overall story. Finally, leading a team is a big learning curve for most people. On diversified teams it helps to be a multiskilled leader.

We've also learned that people really like to experiment if they're given a safe environment. We also find that customer interviews are hard for most people at the beginning, but the insights and stories that they bring back with them are really powerful: learning speeds up as validation increases.

FOR PEOPLE WHO ARE USED TO FOCUSING ON EXECUTION ALL DAY, THE INNOVATION PROCESS CAN SEEM FUZZY.

// Mart Maasik
Head of Innovation at SEB LAB

QUBY & ENECO. GETTING IT TOGETHER

Quby

When Ivo de la Rive Box joined Quby in 2005 to help the startup scale, he had no idea what he was in for. After five years and several pivots, Eneco's Tako in 't Veld convinced them to join forces and launch a successful thermostat system.

WE STAYED UNDER THE RADAR

In order not to stifle the startup as they came on board, Tako shielded them from the full force of corporate scrutiny and bureaucracy. Only later, when the team was successfully integrated into the organization and the pilots were successful, did the board need to have full insight for the next, high-stakes phase.

TAKEAWAYS

If you bring on board a startup with a different culture and different work styles, don't expect the members to flawlessly integrate with an existing corporate setting.

Also, you don't want that to happen. They shouldn't adapt to you, but you should adapt to them! Become a member of their team, bring a case of beer to their Friday happy hour, and understand what it is that makes them such different players.

As the startup gets more traction, have other members in the organization jump on the moving train, but do it in a durable way. The corporate world's culture of rapidly shifting teams and allegiances and interchangeable job descriptions is alien to a small startup.

At Eneco, the energy and enthusiasm of the initial Quby members has now spread far and wide, and the people in the organization are proud of their new product. The startup infusion has helped shift the company's mindset, as well. Instead of being an energy company in a commodity market, Eneco now sees itself as a data-driven and service-based company providing a top-quality product that supports energy sales and savings.

PEOPLE ORIENTED

OUTSIDE-IN

BUY A STARTUP

Adobe® **ADOBE.** THE INNOVATION HIVE

When Ann Rich, a Senior Manager for Adobe's Accelerated Design & Innovation team, first joined Adobe, she recognized that the design process being used in Adobe's HIVE was good for finding solutions to big challenges, and it needed to scale.

PROCESS ORIENTED

INSIDE-OUT

CORPORATE PROGRAM

SOLVING PROBLEMS AT SCALE

Adobe, a software company with over 14,000 employees, is not unlike many other large organizations. With a global workforce and many products that serve different markets, from consumers to creative professionals to marketers, it's a challenge to collaborate and solve problems at scale.

PILOT PHASE

In 2014, CTO Chief of Staff Joy Durling and Kim Mains, Director of Planning & Business Operations, came up with a new vision for accelerating innovation and tackling Adobe's biggest challenges. In partnership with 8Works, a consulting firm, they launched a prototype and transformed an existing space at Adobe's headquarters into what is now known as The HIVE. Durling and Mains wanted to test whether Adobe was ready for design-led thinking at scale and to use design to accelerate solution development for (big) business challenges.

More than 400 people solved big problems together using the HIVE methodology, specifically designed to enable collaboration. HIVE was a proven success. Now it was time to scale. In 2015, Ann Rich, an innovation and design strategist, was hired to oversee scaling HIVE principles throughout the entire organization.

TAKEAWAYS

One of the key takeaways from this journey was that highly facilitated engagement can make it difficult to relate experiences to everyday work. To scale, HIVE must move beyond sessions to capability development. The best feedback Ann has received was from an Adobe employee in Bangalore: "When can you teach us how to do this?" ∎

THIS IS WAY BIGGER THAN THE PHYSICAL SPACE.

// Ann Rich, Senior Manager
Accelerated Design & Innovation

Matter. THE DESIGN-DRIVEN ACCELERATOR

Corey Ford, Managing Partner at Matter: "Matter is a design-driven accelerator program that supports entrepreneurs who want to change media for good. It is about venture acceleration, about getting where you want to go faster. It's intense, but it pays off."

VENTURE ACCELERATION

Matter is about venture acceleration. It's about getting where you're headed faster. It's not about getting a workspace. It's about helping portfolio companies reach product/market fit better and faster than they would through their existing operations, funding, and their advisor networks.

Matter's five-month accelerator program starts with a one-week boot camp, followed by four one-month design sprints. It's really intense, but it pays off.

DESIGN THINKING DRIVES EVERYTHING

Design thinking applies throughout the lifecycle of a company. Our program lies at the intersection of design thinking, entrepreneurship, and the future of media. The first piece is absolutely critical. Because design thinking is fundamentally driven from a human-centered point of view, its lessons don't apply only as you push toward a first beta, they also apply to sales strategy, fundraising, geographic expansion, and hiring practices.

The teams who come through our program leave with a skill set that keeps them moving faster for years after they launch out of our program.

WHAT MAKES MATTER DIFFERENT?

At Matter, we've created a very intentional culture of experimentation. We're focused on creating an experience for these entrepreneurs and our partners trapped in old-school media organizations to help them reach their absolute highest potential. We do so much more than provide space and funding for our entrepreneurs. It's not just about getting the highest financial return.

MINDSETS DRIVE OUR WORK

There are clear and visible messages about unique mindsets we live by. Behind each mindset, such as "Be Bold and Disruptive" and "Tell Stories," we articulate clear behaviors and prompts for action. The signs act as reminders of how we want to show up to our investors, our strategic partners, our entrepreneurs, our

HOW DO WE CREATE A DESIRABLE, VIABLE, FEASIBLE IDEA IN A 20-WEEK PROCESS?

mentors, and the broader community. They are the "signal generators" of the culture that we want. You have to carry the culture in everything you do.

IT IS ALL ABOUT FEEDBACK

Regular and disciplined feedback cycles are core to our process. Every month our entrepreneurs have to deliver an elevator pitch and demo a product to a panel of diverse experts and an extended group of trusted mentors in what we call a Design Review. It's a safe space to get constructive critique from different angles and fresh perspectives. It's focused on uncovering the unknowns about the business. Each design review runs through a gauntlet of nine questions that are hung up on the wall for everyone to see. For example: "Does your excitement outweigh your hesitation?" We ask the entire audience to respond to them, including the other entrepreneurs in the cohort. This makes them better givers and receivers of feedback, too.

My hypothesis is that the entrepreneurship journey is lonely. Most people wait way too long before getting feedback. By the time they do get feedback, it's too late and the feedback comes across as too harsh. Feedback is everything here.

ONE-PAGE VISUAL BUSINESS PLAN

The one-page business plan allows us to understand our business through very intuitive and clear questions. It's the driver of the viability question.

ENTREPRENEURS THAT CAN KILL THEIR PUPPIES ARE THE BEST IN THE WORLD

There's lots of business stuff tied up in the plan. It unpacks business-speak into "how might we" questions. It helps us cut through the jargon of business.

For example, if you asked my entrepreneurs if they know what "sustainable competitive advantage" is: 90% of them will say they've heard it before, but they don't really know what it means.

THE THINGS WE LOOK FOR

We look for teams that are able to let go of their original ideas and plans. Our team GoPop, which was acquired by BuzzFeed and is now running their mobile prototyping efforts, is a great example of that. The majority of teams cling to something that is not working way too long and they run out of time.

And then there are some teams that recognize the light bulb moment. They can kill things that were once dear to them and do it confidently without knowing what comes next. They have stories of people who have done this before them and that gives them the strength to do it, the confidence of going down into the abyss. **》》**

229

EMPATHY AND THE HUMAN FACTOR

The beauty of taking a design approach is that everything starts with the human factor. You base your entire discovery process on a real need about real people. If you try to build a business that's not grounded on that, you're building the business on sand.

When you start with understanding the people who will use and purchase your potential offering, it's a lot easier to build and test the right prototypes that can maximize desirability, feasibility, and viability. Without this essential empathy, lean startups often find themselves optimizing toward the best version of what they decided to create without having ever figured out if it's what they should create. In essence, the lean startup is a great way to get to a local maxima, but not necessarily to a global one.

IT'S ABOUT SPEED, NOT STAGE

When we evaluate companies for our accelerator, we judge whether they're right for us based on the skill set and track record of the team and our excitement about their products and services.

More than anything, though, we want to see that they possess the mindsets and the drive to navigate the fog of entrepreneurship: they're mission-aligned, highly collaborative, user-centered, prototype-driven, and ready to walk through the desert to change media for good.

They take advantage of the rare opportunity to benefit from the contribution of everyone in the ecosystem – mentors, media partners, investors, and each other. They view feedback as a gift. And they want to reach the next stage of their growth much faster than they could at their current pace. ■

Dedicate time to interact with mentors and other organziations that provide feedback.

For all that's been said about scaling design within organizations, future leaders are graduating today having mastered design tools and skills, while taking on the designer's mindset. They're not just coming from art programs either.

Around the world, MBA programs, the stalwarts of business management pedagogy, are embracing design thinking. In some cases, such as the one described on the next few pages, design has been completely and totally merged with business.

As the world changes and requires different skills and a new mindset, MBA programs are evolving with it to ensure leaders graduating from these programs have the skills and mindset to match. Whether you like it or not, the future leaders of your company are designers. Design is coming. Are you ready?

FUTURE LEADERS ARE DESIGNERS  231

MASTERING BUSINESS ADMINISTRAT

Nathan Shedroff is the Founding Chair of the MBA in Design Strategy program at the California College of the Arts. Shedroff envisioned a totally different type of graduate business program that would expose emerging leaders to the mindsets, disciplines, and practices that would allow them to imagine and design better futures that were not only profitable, but sustainable and meaningful as well.

"Designers learn that you don't have to wait for someone else to make changes. In the context of sustainability and resource scarcity, we need 6 billion more people that think like this to make positive change. Let's introduce the design process to education, in kindergarten and on up. Somewhere between kindergarten and 12th grade, we tell them that they can't do this anymore."

// Nathan Shedroff, Associate Professor and Program Chair, Design MBA Programs; designmba.cca.edu

Are we teaching business leaders the right skills for today's dynamic, unpredictable, and yes, exciting environment?

ASK YOURSELF WHAT THE QUESTION IS AND NOT THE ANSWER

If you earned a master's in Business Administration more than five years ago, you would have studied the prescribed disciplines of marketing, economics, finance, operations, organizational behavior, and leadership through lectures, textbooks, case studies, and group assignments. You would have learned that marketing revolved around four P's, competition comprised five forces, and strategy boiled down to one of three choices: market leader, fast follower, or low-cost provider. A leader was someone who could communicate the big picture, and managers had operational skills to oversee projects and people. A lot has changed since then. Today, constant change is fueling new disruptors and disruptions, leaving old strategies in the dust.

DRIVING FOR INNOVATION

Competition is no longer based on who can grab the biggest share of (fixed) customer needs but on who can respond to real customer needs in entirely new ways, in real time, as they constantly change. With a click, customers can find any service or product they desire. And if they don't like what's offered, their global megaphone can instantly inflict damage with a few nasty tweets.

Driving for innovation is the rule today, not the exception. Viable business models now come

in a variety of flavors, and enduring success is far more complicated than outlined in the case studies used in traditional MBA courses.

So what do future business leaders need to know and experience to lead successfully in to-day's dynamic, unpredictable, and yes, exciting environment?

INTUITIVE SKILLS

Ten years ago, author Daniel Pink challenged us to think of the "MFA, or Master's in Fine Arts, as the new MBA." In his seminal book, *A Whole New Mind: Why Right Brainers Will Rule the Future*, Pink predicted the world would get more automated, outsourced, and abundant in its offerings. He argued that more educational and organizational attention should be placed on high-touch, high-concept skills such as empathy, story, play, and meaning. In short, he urged disciplined training to support the development of our creative and intuitive skills and our process-driven, quantitative skills.

WHEN WAS THE LAST TIME YOU FELT COMFORTABLE WITH "NOT KNOWING" ALL THE ANSWERS?

Pink's vision predates most of the things we couldn't do without today, like smartphones and Uber. He was right in his predictions, just wrong about how soon they would occur.

AMBIGUITY

The DMBA believes it's time to incorporate Pink's MFA as the new standard for MBA programs. We can start by changing the title of these programs. Long gone are the days of "Mastering Business Administration" (what are we administering anymore?). Today, the model

EVERYTHING IS AN

ASSUMPTION UNTIL

PROVEN OTHERWISE

// Emily Robin
DMBA graduate 2016

// Shribalkrishna Patil
DMBA graduate 2016

LONG GONE ARE THE DAYS OF "MASTERING BUSINESS ADMINISTRATION."

we must teach is more appropriately titled "Mastering Business Ambiguity."

For the last six years, Lisa Kay Solomon has been part of the groundbreaking MBA in Design Strategy, focused on integrating creative and analytical problem-solving skills that help create, capture, and scale value in sustainable and impact-driven ways. As one of 13 progressive graduate programs at the California College of the Arts, the "DMBA" curriculum is informed by the integrated pedagogy of the well-regarded 109-year-old art and design school and the entrepreneurial spirit of the Bay Area.

ADAPTIVE PROBLEMS

At the DMBA, each of the four semesters includes a studio-based course that weaves together theory, best practices, dynamic tools, and hands-on engagement with real clients or emerging world issues. Classes are designed to help students think beyond profits to consider the social, community, and environmental impacts of their work. In "Innovation Studio," students have tackled complex, adaptive prob-

lems such as the Future of Money, the Future of Work, and the Future of Voter Engagement. These challenges start on the first day of their graduate school experience, as a primer of the divergent and convergent processes they'll experience and practice throughout the program.

TEAM BUILDERS

Like any business challenge, this approach calls for courage and a willingness to take on problems that don't have single, simple solutions. Students discover their way to possible solutions, applying the same tools and skills found in this book. They learn generative skills such as visual and design thinking, perspective-taking, and empathetic, open-ended questioning. They learn to facilitate collaborative and productive teams of diverse perspectives across nearly every kind of communication channel. They have the opportunity to work directly with a wide range of industry experts and leaders who frequently come to our classes not just to lecture, but also to learn with the students as co-creators, mentors, and network builders. **»**

WHO IN YOUR ORGANIZATION CAN HELP YOU SCALE DESIGN?

// Sebastian Ibler
DMBA graduate
2016

BECAUSE...

235

WORKING ON THE TEAM IS AS IMPORTANT AS WORKING AS A TEAM.

// Jennifer Muhler

IDEAS IN ACTION

In each semester, DMBA students have opportunities to create original solutions to unfolding issues. They use dynamic frameworks and tools to interrogate existing business models – and invent new ones. They have to be ruthlessly curious investigators and methodical researchers, while also honing their own intuition and strategic judgment. They have to find new and compelling ways to translate their insights into hypothesis-driven experiments to move ideas into action. They learn to share their ideas through compelling stories and experiential presentations that highlight emotional needs, not just the financial upside of an idea. Students grow comfortable with uncertainty and ambiguity. They take risks and move outside of their comfort zones to build new competencies, even if it means early failure.

THESE ARE OUR NEW LEADERS

Most important, DMBA students learn a mindset of possibility, optimism, and abundance – they become confident that their role as leaders is not to deliver a single, proven "right" solution, but to create the space, conditions, and team to bring to life something fundamentally new. They carry with them a new language, new tools, new skills, and the ability to continuously and repeatedly harness opportunities from change. If you want to make change in the future, this is the mindset you must have. ∎

// Design
MBA
Bookshelf

DMBA ALUMNI
MASTERING AMBIGUITY IN THE REAL WORLD

WHAT'S A WICKED PROBLEM YOU'RE PASSIONATE ABOUT SOLVING?

ADAM DOLE, DMBA GRADUATE 2010
DESIGNING ACCESSIBLE HEALTHCARE SYSTEMS

SUE POLLOCK, DMBA GRADUATE 2013
DESIGNING A SUSTAINABLE PLANET

MOHAMMED BILAL, DMBA GRADUATE 2014
DESIGNING CROSS-CULTURAL COMMUNITIES

Shortly after completing the inaugural DMBA class, Adam was named a Presidential Innovation Fellow, working at the White House in partnership with the US Department of Health and Human Services to accelerate private sector partnerships and accelerate the growth of personalized healthcare in the United States.

As Project Director for the Conservation Program Development at The Nature Conservancy, Sue uses design to help its diverse staff of scientists, conservationists, advocates, funders, and nonprofit agencies work together toward common goals. "Our work is inherently about wicked problems. Convening stakeholders and building trust are the keys to getting the work done."

Mohammed Bilal is a captivating storyteller, producer, and TV personality. As the Executive Director of the African American Art and Culture Complex, Bilal oversees a dynamic institute that focuses on empowering the community through Afro-centric artistic and cultural expression, mediums, education, and programming and inspiring children and youth to serve as change agents.

THE CORPORATE

BREAK THROUGH THE

Justin Lokitz
Strategy Designer

If I were to impart one tip to the companies I used to work for, as well as to my former self, it would be this: start designing today. Start designing for customers. Start designing business models and value propositions. Start designing strategies for the future. Just start. Though I didn't always think this way.

THE BEGINNING

Before enrolling in California College of Art's (CCA) MBA in Design Strategy (DMBA) program, I had worked for very large B2B software companies, like Oracle, Hexagon, and Autodesk, for almost 15 years. During my time with those companies I held a wide array of roles, from sales engineer, to software engineer, to product manager and strategist. These product-focused (vs. customer-focused) companies tended to talk about things like market requirements documents (MRDs), product requirements documents (PRDs), and

LIFE
PARADIGM

product roadmaps. Specifically, at Autodesk, where I was the senior product manager, most things worked on one-year product cycles, which were often based on five-year roadmaps.

However, as Autodesk made big, transformative moves to the cloud, it was becoming apparent that the company would need to shift to incremental improvements over a continuous release cycle. Personally, as well, I had become frustrated by what seemed to be an endless, and often futile, guessing game. I knew there were better ways to develop software.

At about the time I began to consider getting my MBA, design practices like lean and agile development were becoming popular. Even at Autodesk, groups like mine began to switch over to agile development methodologies. As I continued to drive my multiyear roadmaps forward, I read a lot about design thinking as a way to build better products. And, of course,

I also knew that I didn't just want to build products – I wanted to build products that mattered.

TRANSFORMING INTO A DESIGN THINKER

Most people pursue a business degree to increase their job opportunities. I was no different. Being an intrapreneur, I certainly wanted to make a name for myself at Autodesk. But as an entrepreneur, I was also intrigued by the world of possibilities outside Autodesk, especially as the tech scene in San Francisco and Silicon Valley exploded.

In looking for MBA programs that had some entrepreneurial focus, I came across the DMBA program at CCA. What caught my attention was the promise that DMBA students would actually practice design thinking with a lens on the strategic implications therein, rather than just learn the theory behind these popular terms. **>>**

239

I SAW BIG-COMPANY CHALLENGES AND OPPORTUNITIES IN MY PROFESSIONAL LIFE THAT WERE MORE OR LESS HIDDEN TO MOST EVERYONE ELSE

In just two years, each student group would develop business models and strategies for/with at least six real-world clients and projects in a (relatively) safe (to fail) environment. I was hooked.

At Autodesk, I had to keep one big software ship afloat. As such, I generally was not afforded the opportunity to work on a bunch of different projects at the same time – and I certainly could not afford to fail at many of them. So, I enrolled in the DMBA program.

A-HA MOMENT

My personal journey through the DMBA was a bit different than most of my classmates. For one, I was older than 99% of my cohort – most of them were in their mid-20s; I was in my (very) late 30s. I also was far removed from my younger,

more creative self. Having worked for giant, product-focused companies for a long time, what little design skills I had left had been buried deep in my subconscious. However, the age gap between me and my classmates wasn't what surprised me the most. Rather, I was most surprised at how many extraordinarily talented and creative designers had enrolled in the DMBA. Needless to say, in a program that focuses on design, I was a bit intimidated. But I knew that what I brought to the table was of equal value: experience.

After some initial breaking-down-of-walls via well-placed a-ha moments, I was able to rebuild my approach to business and life in a brand-new way. In fact, by the second month of the program, my mindset had so changed that I saw big-company challenges and opportunities in my professional life that were more or less hidden to most everyone else in my company, save designers.

PARADIGM SHIFT

So, how did this happen? How does a design lens allow one to see things that others don't? As aforementioned, the DMBA program at CCA is developed around the core idea that anything and everything can (and should) be designed. Sure, we all know that a product, website, and/or service can be designed. But innovations, businesses, and even futures can be designed using the same tools, skills, and techniques. Design processes provide essential frameworks that focus on customer needs as well as prototyping and validating assumptions before building products. And when you start to see real-world examples of this way of thinking, like Airbnb, Uber, Amazon, Procter & Gamble, and many other organizations with groundbreaking, paradigm-shifting (deliberately designed) business models, you simply can't un-see or unlearn it. For me, this happened in month two, in a course called "Innovation Studio" taught by Lisa Kay Solomon.

As I replaced my own business knowledge with new tools, skills, and a mindset, I realized that my own experiences (life and professional) had only added to my ability to apply the practice of design-thinking in real time. Back at Autodesk, I wore new design-colored glasses, which helped me zero in on new human-centered innovations with my teams. I worked with my design colleagues to constantly test our assumptions using simple prototypes and lots and lots of questioning. I also scrapped every presentation I had ever given and designed a new visual language that I used to facilitate (what I now call) strategic conversations (without a lot of "blah blah blah"). With every new day, I added a new tool to my tool belt.

The innovations we developed (using customer-centric design thinking principles) for the products I was managing at the time were also paradigm shifting. In fact, some of those technical innovations have patents pending – which is a nice side benefit of customer-centered design. ∎

I SEE **DEAD** ~~PEOPLE~~ **MINDSETS**

In 2015, I left Autodesk to open an office for Business Models Inc., in San Francisco. Over the last year, I've worked with a wide range of clients, from large auto manufacturers to nonprofits to big data companies, and I see just how much help they need.

Since my own design paradigm has shifted so fundamentally, my work often involves helping other people to shift their mindsets (and processes). They move from focusing on two product stages – idea to execute – to adopting a design-centric, customer-first mindset. Together we find needs, co-create ideas, validate assumptions, and execute in a continuous fashion.

Trust the design tools and process. Sure, projects won't always succeed. But with the right (designer) mindset and focus (on the customer) you'll know how to iterate in the future. My number one tip to clients: start designing today. Start designing for customers. Start designing business models and value propositions. Start designing strategies for the future.

JUST START!

INTRODUCTION TO **INVESTMENT READINESS LEVEL**

Whether you're an investor, running an incubator, or a startup entrepreneur or a manager at a large company, you'll want to understand the metrics that distinguish a successful project, product, or company from an unsuccessful one early on in the process.

GUT FEELING ISN'T ENOUGH

For a long time, investors and corporate managers wanting to judge whether or not a fledging project or startup was a sound bet had to rely on a gut feeling. This required a strong constitution. Most often, the only metrics at their disposal were qualitative ones, like product demos, slide decks, and the project team. Some people's instincts are certainly better than others. But as Steve Blank states, "There was no objective way available to help judge."

THE INVESTMENT READINESS LEVEL

Today, most every project, product, and company is built atop a tower of data. What if we could use that data to qualify and quantify the progression and success of a project, product, or company? In fact, we can.

The Investment Readiness Level (IRL), developed by Steve Blank, enables anyone to compare projects, products, and companies – in a simple, straightforward way – to others across the company or investment portfolio.

MONEYBALL

Throughout this book we've explained that designing better businesses is about assembling the right team, gaining the right skills and mindset, and applying the right tools and processes at the right time. At face value, these qualities seem to be entirely intangible; how can they be measured by any metric besides the ultimate success or failure of your venture?

Interestingly enough, this belief was held by American baseball managers until 2002. As depicted in the award-winning film *Moneyball*, which is based on Michael Lewis's 2003 nonfiction book of the same name, the Oakland A's manager, Billy Beane, took advantage of analytical metrics of player performance to field a team that competed successfully against competitors with much deeper pockets.

Using statistical analysis of both hitting and on-base percentages, Beane proved that data provided a better way to determine offensive success than the qualities most other teams looked (and paid) for, like speed and contact (with the ball). As a result, the team was able to save tens of millions of dollars by signing baseball players from an open market – totally unheard of at the time. Sounds familiar, doesn't it? Oh, and the A's went from having a mostly losing record to making the playoffs in 2002 and 2003.

DO IT YOURSELF

To achieve results from scaling design, you'll need the right combination of people, skills, tools, mindset, and process. Using the Investment Readiness Level will provide you with the ability to play moneyball in order to gauge how your project, product, or company is doing by applying metrics to its achievements.

On the next page, we'll show you how you can use the Investment Readiness Level to evaluate your design project in an easy, metrics-driven way. ■

For more background, read: *The Startup Owners Manual* by Steve Blank

IT'S TIME TO PLAY **MONEYBALL!**

Many investment decisions are made on the basis of snap judgements, such as "awesome presentation," "the demo blew us away," or "great team!" – 20th-century relics of the lack of real data available for startups and the lack of comparative data across a cohort and portfolio. Those days are over.

We now have the tools, technology, and data to take incubators and accelerators to the next level. Startups can prove their competence by showing investors evidence that there's a repeatable and scalable business model. We can offer investors the metrics to do that with the Investment Readiness Level.

It's time for investors to play moneyball.

Steve Blank
Serial Entrepreneur, Author, Lecturer

243

TOOL **INVESTMENT READINESS LEVEL**

The Investment Readiness Level was created by Steve Blank

With the Investment Readiness Level, you now have a way to quantify the progress of a product, project, or company help you make investment decisions, whether you're a team leader, manager, or investor.

FOCUS

define the level

± 15 MIN

session

TEAM

people per group

Check out steveblank.com and Steve Blank's blog posts for more background information on the Investment Readiness Level.

CATEGORIZE YOUR IDEAS

Where is the project, product, or company in its lifecycle? Like all of the tools in this book, the IRL is designed to allow for a rich, strategic conversation, in this case, using a common set of metrics – related to the business model of the project, product, or company in question – as the basis for the conversation.

WHAT IS MY NEXT STEP?

The IRL is also a prescriptive tool. Regardless of where your project, product, or company is in the design process, the next milestone is immediately clear.

Many project leads, product managers, and entrepreneurs only care about launching the next product or giving a great presentation or demo. When employing the design process, however, they should be focused on maximizing learning.

How many interviews, iterations, pivots, restarts, experiments, and minimal viable products did they go through? What did they learn from that? And how did that influence their decisions? What is the evidence backing up their next step?

Whether they're giving project updates or presentations to investors using the IRL, the focus should be on how they gathered evidence and how it impacted their understanding of the underlying business models.

LESSONS LEARNED

> The Investment Readiness Level provides a "how are we doing" set of metrics.

> It also creates a common language and metrics that investors, corporate innovation groups, and entrepreneurs can share.

> It's flexible enough to be modified for industry-specific business models.

> It's part of a much larger suite of tools for those who manage corporate innovation, accelerators, and incubators.

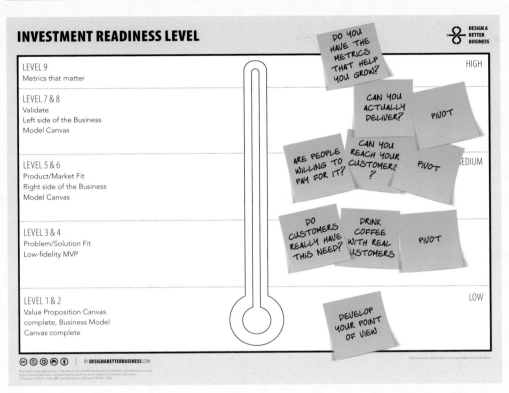

LEVEL 1 & 2
Define what you want to start or change, fill in the Business Model Canvas, and clarify your assumptions.

LEVEL 3 & 4
Get out of the building and understand your customer. Get quotes that illustrate findings and insights.

LEVEL 5 & 6
Find your product market fit, understand customer flow, channels, and how to attract and keep customers.

LEVEL 7 & 8
Understand the left side of your business model. How will you handle key parts like resources and costs?

LEVEL 9
Scale your business and the changes you've made focusing on the metrics that matter.

TIPS
What is your learning journey? Make the IRL company and industry specific. Look at the numbers game: the number of hypotheses and number of interviews.

CHECKLIST

- [ ] You've defined your Investment Readiness Level.
- [ ] You continue to come back and refine your Investment Readiness Level.

NEXT STEP

> Think what you need to do to reach the next level.

> Find an investor.

245

EXAMPLE **INVESTMENT READINESS LEVEL**

SO, YOU HAVE AN IDEA . . .

When you're starting out with nothing but an idea, you can use the Investment Readiness Level to track your progress. Or, if you already have an established startup, use it to figure out what to do next. Prepare yourself for a bumpy ride!

LEVEL 1 & 2: MAKE YOUR ASSUMPTIONS CLEAR

Start with your point of view. Fill out your Business Model Canvas and Value Proposition Canvas. Define your vision and your design criteria. All of these will be full of assumptions. Try to figure out which are the riskiest assumptions using the Riskiest Assumption Finder (page 200). Make your assumptions clear!

LEVEL 3 & 4: FIND THE PROBLEM-SOLUTION FIT

Check if the problem exists by interviewing potential customers. Try to really understand their needs.

Prototype a minimum viable product, one with just enough features (a rough representation) to gather validated findings (wow yourself with customer insights).

WHAT DO CUSTOMERS WANT AND NEED? WHAT ARE THEY WILLING TO PAY FOR IT?

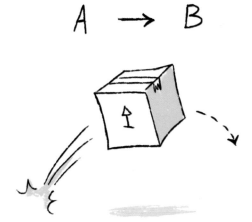

A → B

IT'S ALL A NUMBERS GAME! BUT IT'S THE RIGHT NUMBERS THAT COUNT.

LEVEL 5 & 6: VALIDATE THE RIGHT SIDE

Validate the right side of your Business Model Canvas. Validate the product market fit via a minimum viable product. Validate your value proposition, customer segment, channel, and relationship with experiments, constantly testing your next riskiest assumption.

LEVEL 7 & 8: VALIDATE THE LEFT SIDE

Finally, it's time to develop a high-fidelity minimum viable product which is quite close to the final product. We now need to validate the left side of the Business Model Canvas: can you actually realize, operationalize, and deliver the value you promise?

Validate key resources, key activities, and costs, and do partner due diligence to make sure you're working with the right partners.

LEVEL 9: METRICS THAT MATTER

Define the relevant metrics for your startup and your industry to be successful or investment ready. The right metrics are the ones that show you if you are on the right track, as opposed to "vanity metrics" that give a false sense of security. Find the metrics that correlate the strongest with the growth of your business and help you scale! ∎

247

YOU NOW HAVE...

> **YOUR INVESTMENT READINESS LEVEL** DEFINED P244

> A CLEAR PICTURE OF YOUR **NEXT STEP** P246

NEXT STEPS

> **GO BACK INTO THE LOOP** P46
> Work on the next investment readiness level

> **SHARE YOUR JOURNEY**
> Tell us about your journey online

RECAP

DISTRUST KILLS **INNOVATION.**

ACCELERATORS ARE THE NEW **HUNTING GROUND FOR SCALE.**

FUTURE LEADERS ARE DESIGNERS.

JUST START!

A CORPORATE SEES RISKS WHERE **A STARTUP SEES OPPORTUNITIES.**

FOR PEOPLE IN EXECUTION, **THE INNOVATION PROCESS SEEMS FUZZY.**

GO BIG OR
GO HOME.

NEW FUTURES.
NEW COMPANIES.
NEW PEOPLE.

"The world is changing so quickly that by the time new college students graduate, much of what they have learned is far less relevant and in many cases obsolete. This means knowledge and experience are no longer the primary commodity. Instead, what is far more valuable is to have the ability to learn and to apply those learnings into new and unique scenarios."

// Jacob Morgan, *The Future of Work*

Who would have imagined that despite the growth of digital medium by which to communicate, collaborate, connect, and track information, coupling simple tools, like sticky notes and markers, with the skills and mindset of a designer, would enable us to harness uncertainty in order to design better businesses for tomorrow?

Never before has there existed a business environment whereby companies scramble just to keep up with the change around them. And the speed of change is only accelerating. As large companies continue to execute known business models from their past, startups and other design-oriented companies are challenging the status quo. As they do, entire industries are emerging while others are being torn apart.

BEYOND THE DEGREE

For the last couple of centuries, special degrees and business acumen have been the foundations by which large organizations have grown and created new market categories. However, as the Internet continues to provide open and instant access to knowledge – plus a global forum by which to connect – formal qualifications have become less and less important. Even today, there are many that challenge the very notion of obtaining business knowledge through education. In a world where anyone can learn to design, develop, market, and sell a product simply by watching YouTube videos, formal degrees and pedigree are becoming less important. In fact, the tide is already turning:

today people with practical design skills are often more sought after than those who possess only business theories.

What's more, as the world continues to become more connected, people will solve problems and address human ambitions in entirely new ways. And they will do so through collaboration and design. Change will no longer come from the lone genius or the knowledge and experience of the individual, but from the wisdom of the crowd. After all, it's not about working harder. It's about working smarter.

THINK AND WORK LIKE A DESIGNER

The new, smarter way of working is that of a designer. Companies that embrace design will learn that growth doesn't come from pushing back against change or continually reducing costs to increase the margin. Rather, by empowering people to take a human-centered point of view with a strong focus on the customer, smaller teams of people will be able to accomplish so much more.

These companies will uncover huge opportunities in the face of uncertainty. Multitalented teams of designers – the unusual suspects – will create new products and services that improve people's lives and the bottom line, as well as the planet. The people (designers) creating these changes will value personal interaction more than the desks in the office. They will value quick, cyclical iterations – understanding, ideating, prototyping, validating, and scaling – to monolithic, linear strategies.

251

IT ALL STARTS WITH YOU.

IT ALL STARTS WITH YOU

The change in your company, your product, service, and mindset
starts with you. True change requires that you take the role of the
rebel and step outside your comfort zone. You can start small
or you can start big. But whatever you do, you must embody the
change you want to see in your organization. Only then can change
truly happen. ■

Keep searching, learning, and informing your point of view using your new tools, skills, and mindset. Share your stories about change with us:

www.designabetterbusiness.com

THE MAKING OF
A BOOK IN 100 DAYS

Hidden in our "dungeon" for three months in Amsterdam, the making of this book was a journey in and of itself. We want to share with you the messy process we went through: following our own double loop and killing many darlings. Looking back, we clearly see that the double loop shows up in our own design journey as well – as it should!

DAY 01

JANUARY 1, 2016: DAY 1 (OF 100 . . .)

To map our vision, we had a small team session with the 5 Steps® Vision Canvas (page 58)

ENTREPRENEUR

WHY BUY?

I WANT TO HAVE A SUCCESSFUL BUSINESS

I WANT TO SOLVE MY PROBLEM

EXAMPLE THAT I CAN RELATE TO

THE RIGHT TOOL

DIAGNOS-TICS

BUSINESS MODEL CANVAS

KEY PARTNERS

KEY ACTIVITIES

5 BOLD STEPS VISION® CANVAS

NO SILVER BULLET

THOUGHT PROVOKING

VISUAL STRATEGY FOR BUSINESS

PROVEN + USEFUL

SETTING UP FOR SUCCESS

EASY TO USE

SUPPORTS

BOLD STEPS

5. "100" PIVOTS

4.

"100" PIVOTS

3.

2.

DESIGN CRITERIA —

M	S	C	W
MUST	SHOULD	COULD	WON'T
BE THOUGHT PROVOKING	BE LINKED TO EXISTING THEORY	HAVE ADDITIONAL ONLINE CONTENT	BE A "SILVER BULLET"
PROVEN EXAMPLE DRIVEN	BE USEFUL AS TEXT-BOOK		BE COMPLETE
HUMAN / PERSONAL EXPERIENCE	APPEAL TO EARLY ADAPTERS		THEORETICAL APPROACH
BE PRACTICAL / TOOLS-SKILL... PERSONAL P.O.V.	STARTING POINT FOR MORE		
APPEAL 2 MASS AUDIENCE			

DESIGN FIRST

As this book is about design, we wanted to make that a major part of the end result. We used an unorthodox approach to do this and started to work design-first. Every spread in the book started as a blank page with the whole team using sticky notes defining the content and ideas for the looks.

We worked visually, and had all of the spreads on a big wall in our office, so the team could see the flow and put sticky notes with remarks and ideas on there. From these sketched spreads we'd make prototype designs in Indesign. Only then was actual text written, tailored as much as possible to the space on the page. And we would select among these prototypes, either judging them ourselves or having others give feedback first.

VISUAL DRINKING!

255

"IT'S NOT ANOTHER SILVER BULLET"

DESIGN AND CONTENT GO HAND IN HAND

DAY 10
Plotting chapters
with sticky notes
on the wall

DAY 15
Initial design
(font set, color scheme,
mood board)

DAY 28
48% finished:
proofreading
session

In design thinking wrong is right

FIRST IMPRESSION
We prototyped over 30 different cover designs and pasted them into bookshop photographs to compare them against other titles. The yellow one turned out to be the most visible. We also put dummy books in real stores to see people's reactions!

ISLANDS
To explain the design journey, we started with the metaphor of islands. People seemed to like it, so we started to make detailed designs.

Yet when we had made a dummy of the book with the island stucture, the proofreaders felt it was too gimmicky. It was too complex to tell the story with that metaphor.

DECISION-MAKING TOOL

DAY 29
Proofread session:
major overhaul navigation book needed.

HOW TO DESIGN BETTER BUSINESS

UNDERSTAND

DESIGN

HELP! THE ISLAND STRUCTURE IS TOO GIMMICKY!

START
We already tried that coast

That will never work

Cape Not Invented Here

Complacency

Comfort Zone Plate

Darlings

GOAL

Ivory Tower

Brainstorm Range

In the woods

Yellow Hat

Crazy Combinations

Pet Project

Single Solution

Random Roll

Openness

Zero G

OPTION ISLANDS

Playing Favorites

Next Best Thing

IDEATE

Idea Wall

EMOTIONAL CURRENTS

Who should read this book?

ARE YOU...

Breakthrough Reef

KILL YOUR DARLINGS

We wanted to make a book that was easily navigable and had a clear structure, and we spent a lot of attention on getting that right, or so we thought. Three times our proofreaders told us that they were completely lost in the book. And three times we had to restructure the book and change the navigation. Each time we learned more and could improve the product. We had to throw away good stuff to get there.

GOODBYE ISLANDS

HELLO DOUBLE LOOP

KILL THE ISLANDS :(

KILL YOUR DARLINGS

GETTING BACK ON TRACK

BACK TO THE DRAWING BOARD: DOUBLE LOOP

DAY 30

Dealing with uncertainty

DAY 33

Back to 0% finished
Restart design using the (new) double loop.

DAY 45

15% finished
Finishing up Understand chapter (again).

DAY 57

25% finished
Finishing up Prepare chapter.

5 BOLD STEPS VISION

OBSERVING
PROOFREADERS
LIVE AND ON
GOOGLE
HANGOUT

WE TURNED
OUT TO BE
ATYPICAL
READERS

TOCS CHECK
END CHAPTER CHECK
PAGE NRS
REFERENCES / BOOKS
BIOS & FACES
ACKNOWLD.
COVER
WRAP UP PAGE / END CH.
MAKING OF
COMMERCIAL PAGE

STILL
NOT DONE

UNDERSTAND

ARE ALL
RELEASE
FORMS SIGNED?

NEED
MORE
COPY!

PAGE
NUMBERS

UNDERSTAND **YOUR CUS**
UNDERSTAND **YOUR CONTE**
UNDERSTAND **YOUR BUSINESS**

SEEK TO UNDERSTAND
STER OBSERVATION
TER QUESTIONING
OVES PLUMBERS

TOOL   CUSTOMER JOURNEY
TOOL   VALUE PROPOSITION CANVAS
TOOL   CONTEXT CANVAS
TOOL   BUSINESS MODEL CANVAS

DAY 67

43% finished
Finishing up Point
of View chapter.

DAY 70

72% finished
Finishing up all
(planned) illustrations.

DAY 77

82% finished
Finishing up Validate, Intro,
and Prototype chapters.

DAY 82

6 dummies printed
for next proofreading
session.

SCALE
The last stretch is much more about details
and hard work, dominated by checklists,
consistency, and finalizing texts and visuals,
making everything pixel perfect.

CHECK!

IT'S NOT A LINEAR PROCESS

Designing anything, including a book, is not a
linear process. Not only in terms of iterations,
pivots, and finding the right direction, but also in
terms of planning and progress.

The progress is exponential: the first chapter took
a whole month. The second chapter went twice as
fast, and in the home stretch we rebuilt the entire
book in a week. In the beginning, we used a lot of
time to decide and explore. In the end, the blueprint
was totally clear. Knowing that, we could plan the
design process to finish exactly on time!

FINAL CHECK
FOR
"LOREM
IPSUM"

INCLUDING
PERSONAL INSIGHTS
AND EXPERIENCES OF
30 DESIGNERS
AND THOUGHT LEADERS

NEW TOOLS, SKILLS, AND MINDSET
FOR STRATEGY AND INNOVATION

DESIGN A

›BETTER

BUSINESS

Written by Patrick van der Pijl, Justin Lokitz, and Lisa Kay Solomon
Designed by Erik van der Pluijm & Maarten van Lieshout

**DAY
83**

94% finished
Finishing up Ideate
chapter.

**DAY
92**

96% finished
Finishing up
Scale chapter.

**DAY
93**

98% finished
Consolidating/deleting
redundant pages.

**DAY
98**

98.5% finished
Cleaning up page
references.

**DAY
100**

99.9% finished
Finishing up final
chapter.

PUBLISHED!

APPENDIX

VISUAL INDEX OF TOOLS

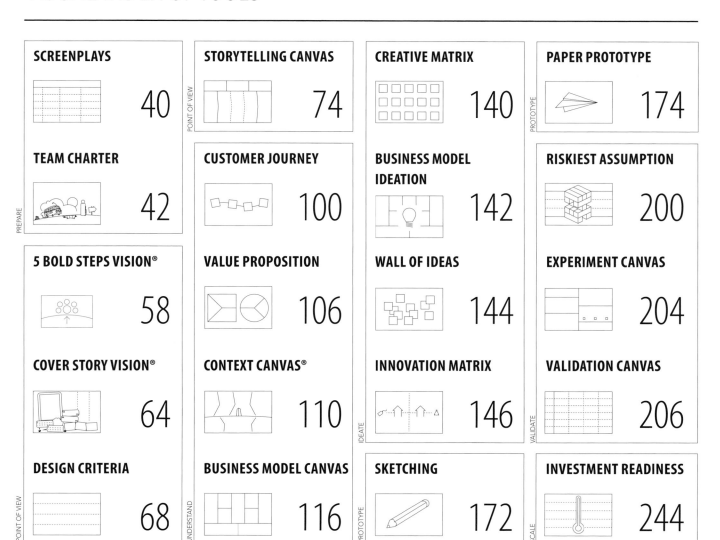

REFERENCES AND INSPIRATIONS

A MORE BEAUTIFUL QUESTION

Warren Berger (2012)

A WHOLE NEW MIND

Daniel Pink, 2006

BUSINESS MODEL GENERATION

Alex Osterwalder and Yves Pigneur, 2008

DESIGNING FOR GROWTH

Jeanne Liedtka and Tim Ogilvie (2011)

FOUR STEPS TO THE EPIPHANY

Steve Blank, 2013, Wiley

GAMESTORMING

Dave Gray, Sunni Brown and James Macanufo (2010)

JAB, JAB, JAB, RIGHT HOOK

Gary Vaynerchuk, 2013

LEAN ANALYTICS

Alistair Croll and Benjamin Yoskovitz, 2013

MAKING IDEAS HAPPEN

Scott Belsky, 2012

MOMENTS OF IMPACT

Lisa Kay Solomon and Chris Ertel (2014)

RESONATE

Nancy Duarte, 2010

RISE OF THE DEO

Maria Guidice and Christopher Ireland (2014)

SCALING UP

Verne Harnish, 2014

THE BACK OF THE NAPKIN

Dan Roam, 2013

THE HARD THING ABOUT HARD THINGS

Ben Horowitz, 2014

THE HERO WITH A THOUSAND FACES

Joseph Campbell, 1949

THE INNOVATOR'S DILEMMA

Clayton Christensen, 2011

THE LEAN STARTUP

Eric Ries, 2011

THE MOM TEST

Rob Fitzpatrick, 2013

TRACTION

Gino Wickman, 2012

VALUE PROPOSITION DESIGN

Alex Osterwalder and Yves Pigneur, 2014

VISUAL MEETINGS

David Sibbet, 2010

UNCERTAINTY

Jonathan Fields, 2012

ZERO TO ONE

Peter Thiel and Blake Masters, 2014

KEY CONTRIBUTORS

Joeri Lefévre (Illustration)

Marije Sluis (Marketing & Sales)

Moniek Tiel Groenestege (Legal & Production)

Roland Wijnen (Testing and Tool Content)

CASE STUDIES

Aart J. Roos

Ad van Berlo

Adam Dole

Alex Osterwalder

Andreas Søgaard

Ash Maurya

Dan Roam

David Sibbet

Dorothy Hill

Emmanuel Buttin

Emanuele Francioni

Farid Tabarki

Frits van Merode

George Borst

Kevin Finn

Maaike Doyer

Marc Wesselink

Markus Auerbach

Mattias Edström

Mohammed Bilal

Muki Hansteen-Izora

Nancy Duarte

Nathan Shedroff

Patrick de Zeeuw

Paul Wyatt

Peter De Keyzer

Rens de Jong

Richard van Delden

Rob Fitzpatrick

Ruud Hendriks

Scott Cross

Steve Blank

Sue Pollock

CONTRIBUTORS

Baran Korkut

Ben Hamley

Diane Shen

Doug Morwood

Duncan Ross

Eefje Jonker

Eline Reeser

Leslie Wainwright

Maaike Doyer

Marc McLaughlin

Martine de Ridder

Matthew Kelly

Michael Eales

Steve Lin

Suhit Anantula

Tarek Fahmy

Vicky Seeley

PROOFREADERS

Alexander Davidge

Andra Larin

Ann Rich

Arno Nienhuis

Bart de Lege

Bernard-Franck Guidoni-Tarissi

Bernardo Calderon

Boukje Vastbinder

Coen Tijhof

Colin Johnson

Daniel Schallmo

David Sibbet

Debbie Brackeen

Emmanuel Dejonckheere

Erik Prins

Ernst Houdkamp

Evan Atherton

Franzi Sessler

Freek Talsma

Geerard Beets

Gijs Mensing

Guy van Wijmeersch

Henk Nagelhoud

JP van Seventer

Jan & Renske van der Pluijm

Jappie Wietsema

Jim Louisse

Johan Star

Julian Thomas

Kevin Finn

Mandy Chooi

Marjan Visser

Matthieu Valk

Maurice Conti

Muki Hansteen-Izora

Nathan Shedroff

Lucien Wiegers

Patricia Olshan

Paul Reijnierse

Paul van der Werff

Petra Willems

Petra Wullings

Quint Zieltjens

Remo Knops

Rene Vendrig

Richard van Delden

Rik Bakker

Robert de Bruijn

Sander Nieuwenhuizen

Tako in 't Veld

Vincent Kloeth

Willem Mastenbroek

Yannick Kpodar

PATRICK VAN DER PIJL

Patrick is CEO of Business Models Inc. and producer of the worldwide bestseller *Business Model Generation*. He is passionate to help entrepreneurs, leaders, rebels, and corporate companies to innovate their business model and design a future strategy.

🐦 @patrickpijl in ppijl

JUSTIN LOKITZ

Justin is an experienced strategy designer and Managing Director of the Business Models Inc. San Francisco office. He leverages his experience across a wide range of industry sectors to help companies design innovative, sustainable business models and strategies for the future.

🐦 @jmlokitz in jmlokitz

LISA KAY SOLOMON

A passionate design strategist and executive educator, Lisa creates immersive leadership experiences at the MBA in Design Strategy at the California College of Arts and Singularity University. She is the coauthor of the bestseller *Moments of Impact*.

🐦 @lisakaysolomon in lisakaysolomon

MAARTEN VAN LIESHOUT

Maarten is partner at Thirty-X. He has applied visual thinking at an early stage for a Dutch idea factory, turning ideas into visual and tangible experiences. He always brings a new perspective to the table – and always stimulates others to get involved in the action.

@maartenvl mvlieshout

ERIK VAN DER PLUIJM

Erik is founder and creative director at Thirty-X. He loves making complex things simple and finding the hidden structure of things. He mixes design, code, and strategy, using his experience from art and design, artificial intelligence, computer games, and the startup scene.

@eeevdp erikvdpluijm

JONAS LOUISSE

Jonas, a visual thinker at heart, started as an entrepreneur and designer straight after receiving his MSc in Neuropsychology. He loves to use his design and psychology skills to get his head around complex stuff and to get people on the same page.

@jonaslouisse jonaslouisse